COMMANDERS IN CHIEF

MODERN WAR STUDIES

Theodore A. Wilson
General Editor

Raymond A. Callahan
J. Garry Clifford
Jacob W. Kipp
Jay Luvaas
Allan R. Millett
Series Editors

COMMANDERS IN CHIEF
Presidential Leadership in Modern Wars

Edited by
JOSEPH G. DAWSON III

Foreword by Raymond G. O'Connor

UNIVERSITY PRESS OF KANSAS

© 1993 by the University Press of Kansas
All rights reserved

Published by the University Press of Kansas (Lawrence, Kansas 66049), which was
organized by the Kansas Board of Regents and is operated and funded by Emporia
State University, Fort Hays State University, Kansas State University, Pittsburg
State University, the University of Kansas, and Wichita State University

Library of Congress Cataloging-in-Publication Data

Commanders in chief : presidential leadership in modern wars / edited
by Joseph G. Dawson, III.
   p. cm. — (Modern war studies)
  Revised papers read before a symposium of the Military Studies
Institute of Texas A & M University, April 19–20, 1990.
  Includes index.
  ISBN 0-7006-0578-9 (alk. paper) — ISBN
0-7006-0579-7 (pbk. : alk. paper)
  1. United States—History, Military—20th century. 2. Presidents—
United States—History—20th century. I. Dawson, Joseph G., 1945- .
II. Series.
E745.C65 1993
973.9′092′2—dc20   92-30601

British Library Cataloguing in Publication Data is available.

Printed in the United States of America
10 9 8 7 6 5 4 3 2 1

The paper used in this publication meets the minimum requirements of the
American National Standard for Permanence of Paper for Printed Library Materials
Z39.48-1984.

To

Stephanie Dawson Abell
and
Nelson D. Abell III

and

Susan Stokes Rolston
and
B. Steele Rolston

CONTENTS

FOREWORD

The multiple dimensions of the president's role as commander in chief during war are amply demonstrated in this book. He has been given, and has taken, the responsibility and authority for waging war, maintaining support on the home front, and making peace. But his ability to conduct a successful military and domestic policy depends on a number of factors, some of which he can control, some of which he can influence, and some of which he can do nothing about.

One significant factor is the concept of the office held by the incumbent. Some executives have believed that their powers were confined only to those prescribed in the U.S. Constitution and the laws enacted by Congress. Others have held that they could exercise any power not specifically prohibited or denied to the executive. Another factor influencing the behavior of the president is precedent—what others have done under the same or similar circumstances. He can choose to emulate the strong, assertive leaders who dominated crises by displaying leadership and determination, or he can allow events to govern his actions. Inhibited or provoked by Congress, or by what he conceives to be public opinion, the chief executive can be either the mover or the moved. Essentially, the president can do whatever he can get away with.

The president, by his conduct of foreign policy, often has determined whether the nation would go to war. Once at war, his authority as commander in chief of the armed forces has enabled him to control the grand strategy of the campaigns. Some presidents have interfered more than others with the military aspects of war, with greater or lesser degrees of success. Because wars are not waged for their own sake, the ultimate purpose of the conflict is—or should be—foremost in the president's thinking, and the way that a war is fought can determine whether that purpose is accomplished.

The question of whether the president can order forces into combat against another nation without the consent of Congress has never been conclusively resolved, and precedent can be invoked to support either side of the debate. The first armed conflict with a foreign power occurred when Congress, on May 28, 1798, authorized President John Adams to employ the navy to capture armed French vessels preying on American shipping along the Atlantic coast. On July 9, Congress approved the capture anywhere of French armed vessels by American warships or by privateers, which the president was authorized to commission.[1]

The next occasion for hostilities with a foreign nation involved the Barbary States. President Thomas Jefferson, in his annual message on December 8, 1801, emphasized the outstanding troubles with Tripoli and the inability of the United States to exploit its naval superiority. "The legislature," Jefferson said, "will doubtless consider whether, by authorizing measures of offense also, they will place our forces on an equal footing with that of the adversaries."[2] Six days later Representative Samuel Smith, brother of the secretary of the navy, offered a resolution to empower the president "by law, further and more effectually to protect the commerce of the United States against the Barbary Powers." Following considerable debate in Congress, the Act for the Protection of the Commerce and Seamen of the United States against the Tripolitan Cruisers became effective on February 6, 1802. The president now could use force to protect commerce, commission privateers, and allow the taking of prizes.[3] Both Adams and Jefferson ceased hostilities when they believed their objectives had been achieved.

Although these precedents were not followed by all subsequent chief executives, presidents have taken the initiative in declaring war aims, in articulating the purpose of a conflict, and in directing the negotiations for terminating hostilities. The ambiguous term "victory" has been applied, often indiscriminately, both to the military phase of the war and to the peace treaty. Assuming that victory means the cessation of armed conflict under conditions conforming to some of the stated objectives of one of the combatants, the first of America's declared wars was not a victory.

The treaty that concluded the War of 1812 achieved none of the declared or hidden objectives of the conflict. In the diplomatic negotiations for peace, which began relatively early during the course of hostilities, the claims of each adversary gradually moved from an insistence on extreme concessions to a virtual withdrawal of all demands and a settlement on the basis of the *status quo ante bellum*. The course of the war largely dictated the treaty, which reflected the fact that neither side had prevailed militarily.

The term "limited war" became popular during the United Nations "peace-keeping" operation in Korea. As has been noted, however, both Adams and Jefferson waged a limited war, and in 1846, President James K. Polk planned what might be called a classic limited war, with the military means circumscribed and the aims clearly stated by the president. When the invasion and occupation of northern Mexico did not bring the concessions he wanted, Polk was compelled to escalate the military campaign. The Mexican refusal to yield exposed one of the fallacies of the theory of limited war, namely, that the cost must be commensurate with the gain. The amount of force necessary to achieve a particular goal is affected by the behavior of the antagonist, who may believe that the stakes warrant a greater or even an unlimited effort on his part.

For some three decades after the Civil War the peacetime U.S. Army continued its efforts to subdue the Indians, while the navy entered the age of steam, steel, and rifled guns. Then what Dennis Brogan has called "the most comic military enterprise of modern times" provided the United States with an empire and helped it secure acceptance as a world power.[4] President William McKinley merely asked Congress for permission to bring an end to a conflict in Cuba and received a mandate to give the island its freedom. As so often happens, the course of battle modified the objectives, for when the Spanish government requested terms for an armistice, the president added territorial demands and an ambiguous clause concerning the future of the Philippines. When Spain balked over the latter, it was given, as McKinley put it, "a virtual ultimatum," which it hastened to accept.[5] A signed protocol ended hostilities, and the final treaty was drawn up by commissioners of both nations in Paris. There was no surrender of all enemy forces or even a real threat to the enemy homeland. Although the Spanish believed that the United States "ought to have made more moderate use of its victory,"[6] the war ended and peace was restored in a manner more consistent with what had been the American tradition before 1865.

The American experience in World War I compounded the confusion over the meaning of victory. The idealistic motives in which President Woodrow Wilson clothed American intervention and his various proposals for peace terms baffled his constituents and his allies. Not since the American Revolution had the government dealt with "associated powers" in terminating hostilities or making the peace. Although the Central Powers were denied a place at the conference table, an armistice ended the fighting and their armed forces were not required to surrender.

During the interlude between world wars the phrase "America always wins the war and loses the peace" became a cliché. Also, the move for disarmament became popular as a means of reducing expenditures and removing a possible cause of war. Successive conferences of major powers from 1921 to 1936 led to significant reductions in naval armaments, although land forces were not affected.

Before World War II all of the conflicts between the United States and foreign nations were limited in that they did not conclude with the total military destruction or surrender of the enemy forces. Success was achieved and hostilities were terminated when the adversary indicated a willingness to accede to American demands. The great departure from this practice allegedly occurred when President Franklin Roosevelt categorically declared on January 24, 1943, that the only basis for an end to hostilities would be "the unconditional surrender by Germany, Japan and Italy."[7]

This policy, begun and pursued assiduously by Roosevelt, was continued by his successor. Italian representatives were compelled to sign a document acknowledging unconditional surrender, although they protested that it violated the original negotiating terms. Germany's capitulation was complete, and President Harry S. Truman maintained that he had received "the unconditional surrender of Japan" despite the terms of the Potsdam Declaration and the actual surrender document, which demanded the unconditional surrender only of the Japanese armed forces.

This global conflict furnished both a rationale and a setting for wars of national liberation, in which victory was conceived as the attainment of sovereignty, not merely winning battles or exchanging one set of masters for another. The position of the American government under these circumstances was somewhat ambiguous, for even though it had adopted an avowed anticolonial policy, it was not anxious to see the establishment of new nations dominated by communism.

The first engagement of American troops in resistance to communist aggression occurred when the North Korean army invaded the Republic of Korea in June 1950. Bearing many of the characteristics of a civil war, the conflict was hailed by Kim Il Sung, premier of North Korea, as "a just war for the unification and independence of the motherland and for freedom and democracy."[8] Truman, under the aegis of two United Nations Security Council resolutions, committed American forces to resist the invasion, and General Douglas MacArthur was appointed to command the UN contingents. After initial reverses, a series of military successes induced the UN, under American prodding, to change the goal of the fighting from merely resisting aggression to uniting Korea by force of arms. The introduction of Chinese communist troops led to a military stalemate, a return to the original objective, and an armistice that roughly restored the status quo ante.

In spite of MacArthur's subsequent criticism and his admonition that "there is no substitute for victory," the armistice in Korea amounted to a victory for the UN and an admission of defeat by the communists in their attempt to unify the country by force. Furthermore, the president's refusal to ask Congress for a declaration of war allowed him to define the terms for settlement without concern over a possible rejection by the Senate. There seemed to be little objection to President Dwight Eisenhower's termination of the conflict without an unconditional surrender by the enemy.

The Vietnam War found the United States involved in a conflict that had neither UN authorization nor a clear mandate from Congress. Each president was on his own in deciding the extent and degree of involvement, subject only to congressional budget restraints. Again, as in Korea, the justification for fighting was to resist communist aggression and to contain the threat to the American defense perimeter. Both ideals and self-interest were at stake, and credibility in meeting U.S. commitments was an issue. A succession of presidents, from Eisenhower through Kennedy, Johnson, Nixon, and Ford, escalated and deescalated the military commitment in an attempt to prevent the unification of Vietnam by the North Vietnamese government. Each president relied on his military advisers to tell him what was necessary to bring the war to a satisfactory conclusion, and on occasion, the president complied with their recommendations. In every case the military force applied proved inadequate to achieve the political goals.

The Vietnam War did not end in a stalemate, nor a negotiated settlement that preserved the status quo ante. The end amounted to an abdication of the commitment that had been made by a number of American presidents. Whatever the considerations that precipitated the American withdrawal, two results of the Vietnam experience can be singled out. First, it demonstrated that the United States was not omnipotent, that it could not impose its will indiscriminately. This shortcoming had been revealed previously, as in Korea. But the illusion of infallibility had persisted. A second result of the Vietnam experience was that it stimulated a closer scrutiny of what the United States stood for. Attention was focused on the grandiose phrases, the noble superlatives, and on what some contended to be the gap between accomplishing at home what Americans were trying to achieve abroad. This introspection also brought an awareness that conditions in other countries might be different from those that prevailed in the United States, that solutions to their problems could lie outside the American framework. The result of the Vietnam War shattered the innocence and naiveté with which many Americans and their leaders had viewed world affairs.[9]

In 1991 the United States again became involved in a military action abroad. The war in the Persian Gulf against Iraq began as a response to aggression, as an effort in collective security—an ideal promoted by President Wilson in his espousal of the League of Nations and by Presidents Roosevelt and Truman in sponsoring the

UN. President George Bush secured the authorization of the UN Security Council to employ armed force to evict Iraq from Kuwait. The president did not, initially, seek the approval of Congress for his military commitment, contending that it was not necessary, although he sought and obtained it later. The president's announced war aims went beyond those specified in the Security Council resolutions and embraced the destruction of Iraq's military capability, the removal of President Saddam Hussein from control of the government, and the punishment of Iraqi war criminals. This effort to thwart aggression was supported by a number of other nations, which provided military, logistic, and financial support for the operation. The course and outcome of this conflict depended not only on the president but on the allies and the UN, as well as on Congress and on what was perceived to be public opinion. This conflict demonstrates the truisms that war usually begins when one side attempts to alter an existing situation and that the consequences of war extend far beyond the battlefield. Every president has had to cope with these variables.

In the American experience of war with other nations, the president has been the crucial figure in the complex equation of the road to war, its prosecution, and its conclusion. No chief executive has evaded this responsibility, although some presidents have discharged it with greater enthusiasm, ability, or success than others. In the view of many people around the globe, the modern American president has become the leader of not only the United States but, in a larger sense, the world.

ACKNOWLEDGMENTS

Many persons assisted me in a variety of ways in the completion of this book.

Some years ago, in a conversation as we walked across campus, Roger Beaumont and I discussed the matter of holding a symposium on the president as commander in chief. That discussion led to a symposium in April 1990, sponsored by the Military Studies Institute at Texas A&M University. Then and later Professor Beaumont always has provided encouragement to the institute and sustained its activities.

The Military Studies Institute at Texas A&M University encourages interdisciplinary research into military and defense issues. I am particularly grateful for the encouragement, patience, and camaraderie of Professor R. J. Q. Adams, chair of the MSI Advisory Council. Thanks, too, to the other members of the council, including James Burk, Alex Mintz, James Bradford, John Robertson, and Larry D. Hill, head of the Department of History. MSI has benefited from the interest and support of Professor Frank E. Vandiver, director of the Mosher Institute for Defense Studies, and his associate, Dr. Art Blair.

As they have so often in the past, Professor George C. Rable and Dr. Thomas E. Schott have provided assistance and reminded me to keep a sense of humor. And, as before, I relied on the help of Mark Leutbecker for selecting photographs.

Most helpful on a daily basis has been Laura Ampol Hall, MSI's senior secretary, who entered the manuscript into the word processor and kept up with changes and revisions along the way.

INTRODUCTION

JOSEPH G. DAWSON III

Numerous foreign and domestic crises have arisen to challenge American presidents, and among the most difficult have been the modern international wars. This book addresses the president's authority as commander in chief and surveys the extraordinary actions of six presidents who bore heavy wartime responsibilities in the Spanish-American War, World War I, World War II, the Korean War, and the Vietnam War.

America's modern wartime presidents are among the more controversial leaders who have held that powerful office, and journalists and historians have engaged in partisan defense or criticism of these presidents and their policies. It is only natural this should be the case, for little in the American political system creates such disagreement as the causes of the nation's wars, the questions of how those wars are fought, and the judgments on presidential failure or success as commander in chief.[1]

Before William McKinley's years in office (1897–1901), the United States had sometimes been caught up in European rivalries or imperial competition—and it fought a long and bloody Civil War—but McKinley was the first president to commit large numbers of American ships and soldiers overseas. During the Spanish-American War, the Boxer Rebellion, and the Philippine insurrection, McKinley ordered the deployment of large and powerful navy and army contingents away from American shores. He also directed that U.S. military forces fight in Cuba, Puerto Rico, the Philippines, and China as well as land on Guam, Wake Island, and the Hawaiian Islands. The war with Spain, the decision to annex the Hawaiian Islands, and involvement in China marked a transition in U.S. policy. The United States acquired imperial possessions and achieved a new status as a world power, and McKinley's use of military power in the Philippines and China also signaled the willingness of a president to dispatch more than token or modest forces outside the Americas. Therefore, McKinley is the first of the modern commanders in chief discussed in this volume.

William McKinley and other American presidents were politicians first and commanders in chief second. Louis Smith noted that after the United States goes to war "the objective is warfare rather than welfare,"[2] but politics and the general welfare can never leave the president's mind. Of all American presidents only one—Richard M. Nixon in 1968—was initially elected when the nation was fighting a major war. Although the Constitution lists the duties of "Commander in Chief of the Army and Navy of the United States" first among presidential powers, giving orders to U.S. military forces has only been one of several executive responsibilities and not always the one most important to voters. Economic issues often have been paramount; social problems sometimes have assumed high priority. Whether they are diplomatic, social, economic, or military, presidential policies all play a part in bids for election or reelection. Everything a president does or fails to do has political consequences. Choices made on domestic matters have created intense partisan disagreement, but the heightened pressures of wartime decisions leave an indelible stamp on a president's administration. Such decisions also serve as precedent for other chief executives.

American presidents took significant actions as commanders in chief before McKinley's term, and it is worth noting selected events before 1898. For example, George Washington initiated a war against Indian tribes in the Old Northwest in the 1790s. Treating the conflict as an internal matter to be handled by the executive branch, Washington saw no need to ask Congress for a declaration of war against the Indian nations, although campaigning against those tribes might have drawn in the British, who supplied arms to the Indians and occupied forts on U.S. territory.[3] Later, President John Adams prosecuted an undeclared naval war against France, the so-called Quasi-War (1798–1800). Adams sought and gained approval from Congress for establishing the Department of the Navy, separate from the War Department, and funding to construct several new warships. On the other hand, Adams declined to ask Congress to declare war on France. The president directed the sea war until 1800, when he stopped the fighting and sought reelection, only to lose to Thomas Jefferson. Before winning the presidency, Jefferson had criticized the Federalist military program and Adams's war against France. As president, Jefferson also deployed modest naval forces on his own orders, without a declaration of war by Congress, to counteract the depredations of the Barbary pirates in North African waters (1803–1805). Despite these belligerent episodes, neither Adams nor Jefferson gave evidence of expertise or skill in military matters.[4]

The United States endured years of diplomatic and economic discomfort during the Napoleonic Wars, but relations between the United States and Britain degenerated to the point at which, in April 1812, President James Madison called on Congress to declare war over two key issues: Britain's impressment of American sailors and violations of neutral shipping rights on the high seas. The United States claimed a victory of sorts in the War of 1812—though not a military victory. By 1815 the United States had reasserted national sovereignty, ruined the previously durable alliance between the British and the Northwest Indian tribes, and pronounced that Americans would not tolerate Britain's policy of impressing U.S. citizens to serve in the Royal Navy. In the war itself, several U.S. Army and volunteer units fought badly, a number of senior officers demonstrated their incompetence, and the War Department failed to provide necessary logistical support for some field operations. Madison's choices for secretary of war were distinctly unfortunate, and his lack of understanding of military matters in general raised questions about presidential wartime leadership.[5]

In contrast to Madison's ineptitude, President James K. Polk acted decisively as commander in chief during the war with Mexico (1846–1848). Mexican leaders plainly stated that they were not interested in selling a large portion of their nation and became distraught when the United States annexed the Republic of Texas in 1845. Both nations quickly began to build up military forces along a disputed border near the Rio Grande. In a message reviewing the Mexican-American disputes over the years, President Polk prepared to ask for a declaration of war based on the crisis as it stood, but a skirmish on April 25, 1846, between Mexican and American soldiers allowed him to call upon Congress to declare that a state of war already existed between the two countries. Congress declared war on May 13. Making full use of an increasingly professional, well-trained, and well-led U.S. military establishment, Polk aggressively carried out his war policies to conquer the lands in California and the Southwest that Mexico had refused to sell.

Polk's confidence, competence, and success as commander in chief must be rated highly. Although he had not served in either the army or the navy, Polk demonstrated that a civilian president could formulate national strategy as well as military strategy in the theaters of operation. Issuing orders, selecting field commanders, and coordinating the War, Navy, and State departments proved that Polk firmly held the levers of power.[6]

From 1861 to 1865 the Civil War appeared in many ways like an armed conflict between nations. The Confederate States of America sent out diplomatic representatives, printed money, operated a postal system, contracted for loans and purchases overseas, and held elections. In short, the Confederacy behaved like a sovereign nation and asked to be recognized as such by other powers.

Viewing the crisis differently, President Abraham Lincoln wanted outsiders and Americans to consider the conflict an internal matter, a rebellion or insurrection, no matter what its scale or duration. Lincoln recalled the oath he and every U.S. president had taken "to preserve, protect, and defend" the Constitution, and he never lost sight of that goal. But if it was internal and unique among American wars, how could the Civil War serve as precedent for subsequent American presidents who led the nation into wars against foreign powers?

Lincoln resolved early on that it was vital to U.S. interests to prevent direct European involvement in the fighting, especially by Britain and France. He took a risk by declaring a blockade of the South rather than the milder measure of "closing the ports" of rebellious states. Declaring a blockade was an act of war and carried important

4

legal connotations. Most important, such a declaration bestowed belligerent status on the Confederacy and thus allowed other powers to have official dealings with it in commercial and diplomatic matters. Lincoln's proclamation prompted British leaders to adopt a wait-and-see attitude on both the legal effectiveness of the Union blockade and the viability of the Confederate States of America.[7]

Some Southern leaders believed that Britain and France would have to side with the Confederacy to maintain the flow of cotton to European textile mills. Acting on this belief, Southern leaders discouraged (some said embargoed) the shipment of cotton. The South's so-called King Cotton diplomacy played into the North's hands. The South threw away the chance to show the weakness of the Union blockade and thereby demonstrate its legal ineffectiveness. As a consequence of following a flawed policy, President Jefferson Davis and his cabinet suffered a diplomatic defeat, one that undermined the credibility and financial foundation of their new government.[8]

Ably assisted by Secretary of State William H. Seward, Lincoln was winning at diplomacy and also took a series of increasingly drastic steps to marshal Northern resources and subjugate the South. Lincoln rolled up an impressive—even disturbing—record of executive actions taken without consulting Congress. Contemporaries, especially Democrats and Confederates, categorized many of the president's choices as improper or unconstitutional, and some of his actions were challenged in federal courts. Even when Lincoln called Congress into special session on July 4, 1861, he simply asked the national legislature to approve the extraordinary steps he had already taken.

In addition to his blockade proclamations of April 19 and 27, Lincoln directed on April 20 that nineteen new war vessels be put into service. His call on April 15 for 75,000 militia to suppress an insurrection in the Southern states was in accord with his constitutional powers, but he exceeded his authority on May 3 by unilaterally increasing the size of the regular army by 23,000 soldiers and the navy by 18,000 sailors. Only Congress could authorize such increases in the regular military establishment, but Lincoln wanted these things done without any quibbling from Congress. Furthermore, the president reached beyond his recognized authority in other ways. For ex-

5

ample, on April 20 he ordered the secretary of the Treasury to spend thousands of dollars for military purchases that the House of Representatives had not initiated and Congress had not passed, as the Constitution stipulated must be the case in financial matters. Subsequently, in several instances, Lincoln suspended habeas corpus, used soldiers to arrest persons accused of inciting to riot and disrupting rail lines or those suspected of other crimes, and directed the army to put some of them on trial in military courts. Whether the number of persons caught in this extraordinary federal web was large or small, the high-handedness of such events and the precedents they set were disturbing to many citizens. Finally, among Lincoln's executive actions were his proclamations regarding emancipation and black soldiers. Arriving at the conclusion that the institution of slavery and slave labor had aided the Confederate war effort, Lincoln issued the preliminary Emancipation Proclamation in September of 1862 and directed the Union forces to recruit blacks in January 1863. These controversial executive orders undercut the foundation of the Confederate society and economy and simultaneously broadened presidential powers.[9]

Lincoln made these and other presidential decisions during a conflict that was the greatest threat to the existence of the nation—a blend of civil war and international war—and he took it upon himself to decide how certain federal resources and powers would be employed to quell rebellion and prevent the breakup of the Union. In using obvious presidential prerogatives and drawing on other, less obvious, powers from the Constitution, Lincoln opened the door for subsequent presidents to act in similar ways, even if later wars did not present the same immediate menace to the nation or were short-term military deployments conducted simply by executive fiat. As Lincoln eventually postulated in reference to the Confederates, "as commander-in-chief . . . I suppose I have a right to take any measure which may best subdue the enemy." Since 1865 jurists and scholars—both conservative and liberal—bemoaned the broadened scope of presidential powers. The examples tested by Lincoln's creative mind fell into the hands of other presidents to use or abuse. Or, as Ludwell H. Johnson III phrased it, "The question of peace or war has thus come to depend on the president's perception of what constitutes a threat to the nation's security."[10]

Future chief executives saw less to emulate in the accomplishments of Lincoln's counterpart, Confederate President Jefferson Davis. Davis possessed a wealth of military and political experience, dedicated himself to the Confederate cause, and gave detailed attention to running the new administration. Indeed, some critics asserted that he became immersed in details that would have been better left to clerks or cabinet secretaries. But Davis courageously called for increasing action from the Confederate national government. He moved ahead of many Southern politicians and newspaper editors by supporting a host of innovative and sometimes drastic measures—among them approving a national draft law, starting up government-owned munitions factories, and instituting a variety of economic regulations. In short, though Davis remained conservative in some ways, he concluded that the Confederacy needed centralized government controls and may have taken as much power as the Confederate Constitution would allow its chief executive.[11]

Unlike Lincoln, however, Davis sometimes seemed reluctant to make full use of his authority. As the war intensified, Davis's political skills seemed to erode rather than grow. Arguing with cabinet members such as Secretary of War George W. Randolph, dealing with states' rights governors such as Zebulon Vance and Joe Brown, and bickering with thin-skinned generals such as P. G. T. Beauregard and Joseph E. Johnston wore down the president's health, forcing him to take to his bed for days at a time. After two years of war, Davis still refused to reassign old friends such as General Leonidas Polk in order to promote deserving younger officers to ranking field commands. Likewise he refused to remove Adjutant General Samuel Cooper and replace him with a more talented officer, such as Braxton Bragg. Although some historians have complimented Davis, or at least questioned the unending acclaim for Lincoln, the majority have found more to criticize than praise in Davis's presidency.[12]

Like Jefferson Davis, William McKinley has not attained high rank among nineteenth-century presidents. McKinley's lack of a favorable or deep impression on Americans can be attributed to several factors, including McKinley's own soft-edged personality, the fact that he left fewer personal documents than other presidents, and the fact that his assassination in 1901 catapulted a flamboyant successor—Theodore Roosevelt—into the office.

But as Lewis L. Gould argues convincingly in chapter 2, McKinley's guiding hand steered diplomacy during the Spanish-American War. Moreover, the president kept close track of military developments and demanded considerable effort from his commanders and cabinet secretaries. McKinley benefited from the advice of U.S. Army Adjutant General Henry C. Corbin, who stepped in as unofficial army chief of staff during the war. Secretary of War Russell Alger wanted to please his commander in chief but failed to surmount the numerous problems of a War Department unprepared for raising and supplying large forces in a short time. On the other hand, McKinley's secretary of the navy, John D. Long, proved to be competent and assertive, although he had the advantage of administering a navy that was technologically and logistically better prepared than the army. Had the war been protracted or fought against a stronger enemy, the results could have been damaging to the reputation and status of the U.S. military establishment. To his credit, McKinley made strategic choices that he believed would end the conflict as quickly as possible. Therefore Gould reckons that, for several reasons, McKinley must be judged a better commander in chief than most historians have previously thought.[13]

Before entering World War I, the United States, under Woodrow Wilson, had become a full participant in the imperial game. U.S. troops had intervened in Mexico and several other Latin American countries before the declaration of war against imperial Germany on April 6, 1917. In an astute move before the declaration of war, Wilson arranged for the purchase of the Virgin Islands from Denmark to prevent Germany from gaining a naval base in the Americas. Wilson could also justify this purchase as necessary to protect the recently completed Panama Canal, which passed through a zone under U.S. control.[14] But national military strategy should not be put aside until war begins. Despite taking some intermediate measures, such as the National Defense Act of 1916, Wilson and his cabinet neglected the martial preparations necessary before initiating war against a powerful belligerent.[15]

In chapter 3, Robert Ferrell points out numerous deficiencies in Wilson's leadership and that of his appointees.[16] According to Ferrell, Wilson's secretary of war, Newton Baker, displayed shortcomings in the War Office. Moreover, Secretary of the Navy Josephus Daniels was a political appointee who knew little about naval warfare. Ferrell also argues that Wilson performed poorly as national administrator on the home front. Few of the federal agencies he established functioned smoothly during the Great War. Thus Ferrell concludes that Wilson deserves low marks for military-related cabinet appointments and below-average ratings for his management of national resources during wartime.

By contrast, in the category of military appointments, Wilson outshone McKinley. Although Tasker H. Bliss and Hugh L. Scott performed poorly as army chiefs of staff, John J. Pershing and William S. Graves performed superlatively as expeditionary force commanders, and Peyton C. March invigorated the role of chief of staff.[17]

While a number of historians have not given Wilson high marks as commander in chief, his wartime leadership merits approval on some counts. Obviously, he saw the importance of the Western Front, but he devoted appropriate diplomatic attention to the Balkans and particularly to Russia, although the American and Allied interventions in the Soviet Union embittered East-West relations and formed a backdrop to the Cold War. The total war of 1917–1918 was far more sweeping in scope, intensity, and duration than McKinley's conflict with Spain. It presented thorny problems of dealing with coalitions and associated powers, tasks that Wilson handled well.[18]

Franklin D. Roosevelt surpassed any accomplishments of McKinley and Wilson as commander in chief. According to Henry L. Stimson, FDR was "without exception the best war president the United States has ever had." Although Stimson believed that Roosevelt seemed disorganized at times and lacked routine administrative skills, his strengths outweighed these deficiencies. A visionary thinker and fine public speaker, as adept at dealing with bureaucratic logjams as he was with allied nations, Roosevelt also possessed a keen intelligence and dynamic personality. All these traits combined to make him the superior commander in chief of the twentieth century. Furthermore, in Henry Stimson and Frank Knox, Roosevelt assembled the best tandem of secretary of war and secretary of the navy in American history, certainly the best since Edwin M. Stanton and Gideon Welles in Lincoln's Civil War cabinet. Seldom have talents and administrative abilities been so well suited to these offices as those of Stimson and Knox. Roosevelt seemed to keep track of everything civil, military, diplomatic, industrial, economic, social, and cultural. Of course, he picked able administrators to head the many federal agencies that managed the garden-variety details and problems. As Warren F. Kimball persuasively concludes in chapter 4, in Franklin Roosevelt the nation had its premier national coordinator.[19]

Harry S. Truman succeeded to the office of president on April 12, 1945, upon FDR's death. Truman finished prosecuting the great crusade against fascism. For advice he depended on Roosevelt's cabinet and, increasingly, upon General George Marshall. As D. Clayton James points out in chapter 5, controversy will always attend Truman's decisions to drop atomic bombs on Japan, a decision resulting in long-lasting political, military, diplomatic, and social consequences.[20] After the first bomb was dropped on Hiroshima, the Soviet Union entered the war in the Pacific. Soon thereafter a second atomic bomb was dropped on Nagasaki. The combination of Soviet entry into the war and American use of shocking new weapons forced Japan to surrender.

More than either Wilson or Roosevelt, Truman contended directly with the perceived ideological and economic menace of communism. While supervising military governments and planning economic aid to many nations, Truman tried to explain the collapse of Chiang Kai-shek's Nationalist regime in China and the ascendancy of the new communist government led by Mao Tse-tung. Moreover, Roosevelt's earlier decision to exclude Russia from atomic secrets and the debate over opening the second front in Europe had created antagonisms between the United States and the USSR. President Truman kept his attention focused on Europe and in 1947 announced the Truman Doctrine and the Marshall Plan, designed to contain communist influence and expansion and to rebuild the war-torn continent. Partly in reaction to the Soviet blockade of Berlin (June 1948–May 1949), the president called for the creation of the

North Atlantic Treaty Organization (NATO). By 1950 the capitalist Western Allies and the communist powers (including most of Eastern Europe) were divided into two rival camps.[21]

In the meantime, U.S. military strength had declined. For instance, U.S. Army and Army Air Forces contained more than 8 million men and women in 1945. No one at home or abroad expected the United States to maintain an army of that size, but by the end of 1946 those forces had been reduced to less than 2 million; in 1950 they stood at less than 1 million.[22]

Truman had presided over the typical American practice of rapidly demobilizing after a war, but in the late 1940s the United States had assumed new international responsibilities unlike any it had ever taken on before. To meet these responsibilities as well as to streamline and reorganize the military establishment, Truman and Congress agreed upon the National Security Act of 1947. This act produced far-reaching effects. First, it did away with the office of secretary of war and created the new cabinet position of secretary of defense, who would be superior to a trio of subcabinet officials—the secretaries of the navy, army, and air force. Second, the act gave birth to an air force independent of the army. Furthermore, the National Security Act officially set up the Joint Chiefs of Staff, which had come into being on an ad hoc basis during World War II. The act also authorized the Central Intelligence Agency (CIA). Finally, this law created the National Security Council (NSC)—an agency comprising the president, the secretaries of state and defense, and selected defense experts—to formulate policy and strategy. Using this new military establishment, Truman, as most late twentieth-century presidents, decided to rely on the air force and the new atomic superweapons for strategic action, coupled with the navy for its defensive and offensive capabilities. At the same time Truman and Secretary of Defense Louis A. Johnson expected that the strength of both the army and the marine corps could be significantly reduced. By 1950, the federal budget had cut funding for army training, severely reduced stockpiles of ammunition, and reduced funds for research and development for equipment and vehicles.[23]

How a president, cabinet, and Congress decides to equip, arm, and organize American military forces in peacetime greatly affects wartime performance. In Truman's case, he faced a variety of demands in domestic programs, and he chose to cut the army budget. His choice left the United States in a seriously weakened military position by 1950, looking toward the prospect of further reductions in 1951.

The Korean War, a significant turning point in American foreign and domestic affairs, changed the military spending patterns of the United States for the next four decades. The North Korean invasion supported the claim by American anticommunists that communism was aggressive and would try to expand. As D. Clayton James shows, when the fighting began in Korea Secretary of State Dean Acheson convinced Truman to apply the containment policy to Asia as well as to Europe. The president needed better military advice than Louis Johnson had offered, and therefore he made George Marshall secretary of defense in September 1950; Marshall's close associate, Robert A. Lovett, assumed the office the next year and held it until the end of Truman's term. Among military commanders available for directing U.S. forces in Korea, Truman elected to keep General Douglas MacArthur, one of America's most distinguished army officers. In chapter 5 James thoughtfully reexamines the disagreement between the general and the president and offers a new view of the confrontation.

Truman's decisions to go to war in 1950 and to make it a limited war (even though millions of U.S. and UN troops served in Korea from 1950 to 1953) were controversial then and have been ever since. Truman's presidential decision for war in Korea made it easier for Presidents Kennedy and Johnson to involve the United States in Indochina a decade later. Unlike McKinley, Wilson, or Roosevelt, Truman in the summer of 1950 declined to ask Congress for a declaration of war. Given that fighting had already broken out in Korea and several hundred U.S. soldiers were caught up in the North Korean invasion, Truman could have phrased his request to prompt a congressional response. Instead of a congressional declaration, Truman took the extraordinary step of seeking the involvement and approval of the UN, in the meantime relying on his powers as commander in chief under the Constitution to dispatch reinforcements to aid American forces being attacked in Korea.

The president expected the war against the communist North Koreans to be short and in some way beneficial to the United States—at least restoring South Korea's boundary and government. Soon he gambled on the possibility of rolling communism back to the Yalu River. Had he won the gamble and the war, Truman would have increased his chances in the election of 1952 and helped solidify the Democrats' hold on the presidency. Instead the Chinese intervened, the Korean War grew increasingly unpopular, and Truman's support at home dropped precipitously. He decided not to seek renomination. The unpopular, costly, and unpredictable war ended Truman's political career and opened the way for a Republican to win the presidency.[24]

In an adroit political move, the Republicans persuaded General Dwight D. Eisenhower, hero of World War II, to run as their nominee. Eisenhower promised to go to Korea and end the war. Adlai Stevenson and the Democrats went down to defeat in November 1952. Using implied threats and stern diplomacy Eisenhower brought the war to an end eight months later.[25] In most of the cases the president presented Congress with an implicit challenge: Let the war continue or cut off funds that the military forces needed to sustain themselves in combat.[26]

Certainly, Truman's actions for war in June 1950 were not the first in American history made without the consent of Congress. In other crises Congress willingly let presidents use their diplomatic and military powers, thus reducing congressional influence in the decision to commit the country to war. As Norman Graebner emphasizes in chapter 1, Congress has possessed the power of the purse but seldom has used that power to deny the financial support the executive needs to carry out military ventures. So long as the incursions or undeclared wars of the nineteenth and early twentieth centuries remained brief and inexpensive and failed to produce a direct confrontation with a major power, Congress—especially a partisan Congress of the president's own party—allowed great latitude to the executives in carrying out their foreign policies. In contrast, major presidential deployments of naval or land forces since 1940 have involved the United States in World War II, the Korean War, the Cuban Missile Crisis, the Vietnam War, and the Persian Gulf War of 1991.[27]

The post–World War II containment policy and the presidents' ability as commander in chief to send sizable forces overseas led directly to U.S. involvement in the Vietnam War (1964–1973). Fully agreeing with President Kennedy's public pronouncements on defending Laos and South Vietnam against communism,[28] Lyndon Johnson gradually authorized the steps that brought on a broader war in Indochina.[29]

Johnson had devoted most of his political career to domestic issues. His knowledge of military matters was limited; he may have been one of the U.S. presidents least prepared to deal with a war in a little-known part of Asia. The president spent much time and energy advocating a wide-ranging domestic program that he called the Great Society. As Frank E. Vandiver describes in chapter 6, Johnson sought advice on foreign policy and military matters from holdover officials from JFK's coterie, including National Security Adviser McGeorge Bundy, Deputy National Security Adviser Walt W. Rostow, Secretary of State Dean Rusk, and Assistant Secretary of State William Bundy. This group was characterized by David Halberstam's ironic phrase, "the best and the brightest."[30] Johnson also retained the services of Kennedy's secretary of defense, Robert S. McNamara, whose controversial stress on quantification, systems analysis, and "new management techniques" unsettled the Defense Department and perturbed military officers. McNamara has had his defenders and detractors, but his policies jolted the U.S. military establishment during the Vietnam years.[31]

The war in Vietnam, however, was an extraordinary combination of guerrilla and conventional warfare. At different times and various places open combat occurred on a regimental scale; in nearby provinces little fighting took place between units, but the communists carried out occasional military operations such as ambushes, raids, or surprise attacks on selected outposts. Across Indochina the communist forces used deception, stealth, and political subterfuge against the Americans while simultaneously intimidating, assassinating, and obtaining supplies from the local populace—a potent union of military, political, and economic terrorism. Few American military officers of the 1960s, including General William C. West-moreland, had experienced such warfare or given attention to it in their study of military history.[32] Therefore their education, equipment, and training did not prepare them for such a volatile mixture of unfamiliar cultures, terrain, and tactics as they found in Vietnam.[33]

By the time President Richard Nixon took office, political-military complexities of the Vietnam War had ruined the efforts of civil-military advisers in Vietnam. In contrast to the peninsula of Korea, which could be physically isolated and politically controlled, Vietnam shared borders with Cambodia and Laos. Furthermore, the corruption in the officer corps of the Army of the Republic of Vietnam (ARVN) was virulent and unquenchable, in contrast to a thoroughly reorganized South Korean officer corps based on merit. Moreover, the key to the process of completely restructuring ARVN was to place it under American generals as had been done in Korea after the North Korean invasion. On the contrary, as Vandiver points out, President Johnson and his advisers had decided not to bring U.S. and ARVN forces under a unified command system. Nevertheless, American advisers trained ARVN forces and in most respects created a conventional military establishment in the image of that of the United States. ARVN was designed to fight a conventional war, including an overt invasion from North Vietnam, not the multifaceted war that prevailed.[34]

By deciding to gradually withdraw American forces from Vietnam and at the same time open new diplomatic initiatives with the Soviets and Chinese, President Nixon performed a political highwire act in both the domestic and foreign policy arenas. Furthermore, as Stephen Ambrose also indicates in chapter 7, Nixon's decision to change the military draft to a lottery stemmed the torrent of protest in the United States against the war. The president's advisers on military and foreign affairs included Secretary of State William P. Rogers, National Security Adviser Henry A. Kissinger (who later replaced Rogers at State), and Secretary of Defense Melvin R. Laird. While Nixon slowly ended American involvement in the Vietnam War, his use of strategic bombing in Cambodia and North Vietnam created new controversies. Although it was the Watergate scandal that ruined his presidency and cast a shadow over his policy of détente with Russia and China, congressional leaders had already begun to consider how to place restrictions on executive power.[35]

Before Arthur Schlesinger, Jr., coined the term "the imperial presidency," Charles Tansill in 1930 recognized "that the power to formulate American foreign policy is one whose exercise might well involve the nation in war." After World War II but before the Korean War, Charles Fairman maintained "it is a commonplace that a President could so exert his constitutional powers as to make a declaration [of war], on one side or the other, inevitable." Declarations of war in the late twentieth century became elusive, if not archaic. Replacing them were UN resolutions, as in the Korean War, or a congressional substitute, such as the Tonkin Gulf Resolution. For what were expected to be brief encounters, the president merely made an announcement to the public, such as the one on the morning U.S. forces landed in Panama in December 1989.[36]

Such incursions as Grenada and Panama could well prompt Thomas Cronin to ask again, as he did in 1979, "How can the presidency be made more effective and more accountable at the same time?" In the early 1960s few observers believed that it was necessary to bring the president to account. In the days before the Vietnam War, Senator J. William Fulbright held the opinion that "for the existing requirements of American foreign policy we have hobbled the president by too niggardly a grant of power." Subsequently, Fulbright, a chief supporter of the Tonkin Gulf Resolution, turned 180 degrees to be one of the harshest critics of freewheeling presidential power in Indochina. By the early 1970s a concerted effort began in Congress to limit presidential war-making powers.[37]

Debated in various versions in Congress and speculated about for months in the press, the War Powers Resolution finally passed in November 1973, over President Nixon's veto. The resolution intended to prevent presidents from bringing on war without either a congressional declaration or a direct attack on the nation or one of its far-flung bases. But even this broadly worded resolution could not prevent presidents from sending U.S. troops into dangerous circumstances without congressional approval. The resolution specifies that the executive must immediately report any troop deployment to

Congress, and that sixty days later, if Congress has not supported the president's action with a declaration of war, the deployed troops must be withdrawn. According to the War Powers Resolution, if the president delays or refuses to recall the troops, after ninety days (by which time the nation could be engaged in a full-fledged war) Congress has the authority to call for the president to remove the military forces.[38]

Despite Congress' attempt to curb the president, commanders in chief continued to act unilaterally after the War Powers Resolution was passed. Important examples of belligerent action by executives include President Jimmy Carter's orders in April 1980 sending select military units into Iran in an attempt to rescue U.S. diplomats held hostage in Teheran, President Reagan's directive dispatching American military and naval forces to the Caribbean island of Grenada in October 1984 to quash a procommunist government, and President Bush's decision to crush the dictatorship of Panama's General Manuel Noriega in December 1989. These actions, however, were mere military maneuvers when contrasted with the Persian Gulf War of 1990–1991.

On August 2, 1990, following a period of strained relations between Iraq and Kuwait, an Iraqi army invaded and overwhelmed the tiny emirate in a few hours. Iraqi soldiers systematically looted Kuwait and took other steps indicating intent to occupy Kuwait indefinitely. While consolidating in Kuwait, the Iraqi forces nevertheless clearly threatened Saudi Arabia as well as nearby small coastal emirates, which together provided a primary source of the West's oil supplies. Was the Iraqi invasion simply a minor, localized incursion that could be pacified by innocuous platitudes and reversed after a few weeks of delicate negotiation, or was a major international crisis at hand?[39]

The Iraq-Kuwait dispute had been heating up for several months, but the invasion itself caught the U.S. government flatfooted. Sophisticated satellite reconnaissance photographs had revealed an Iraqi military buildup that posed an obvious threat to the contested Rumaila oilfields, but analysts had discounted the likelihood of a sweeping invasion and wrote off the bellicose pronouncements of Iraqi president Saddam Hussein as mere bluster. When Iraqi tanks rolled into Kuwait, President Bush, Secretary of Defense Richard Cheney, and General Colin Powell, chair of the Joint Chiefs of Staff, were either out of Washington on holiday or about to leave on vacation. The American ambassadors to Saudi Arabia and Iraq had been recalled earlier for consultations. Suddenly the American leaders faced a diplomatic dispute that had turned into a military confrontation.

President Bush could have responded with a series of diplomatic protests condemning Iraq's invasion and worked behind the scenes to encourage "an Arab solution" to Iraq's grievances against Kuwait. The president decided, however, that strong measures were necessary. Bush promptly concluded that the United States, and other Western nations along with Japan, could not risk even the small possibility that Iraq would invade Saudi Arabia and thereby control 40 percent of the world's known oil reserves. Therefore the president decided that the aggression would not go unanswered and a coalition of powers must protect Saudi Arabia and its petroleum. Since Saudi Arabia's military was only a modest force, its archconservative leaders could only hope to placate Saddam Hussein with bribes and tribute, but financial sops offered no guarantees of Saudi sovereignty. Moreover, the Saudis and other regional leaders already had misjudged Saddam once—believing that he would not swallow up Kuwait. Only military forces of other nations could deter Saddam and guard Saudi Arabia, though introducing Western armies into the region recalled bygone days of the European empires and might cause antiforeign protests and disruptions throughout the Middle East and North Africa. Aware of the dangers of bringing Western soldiers to the Arabian peninsula, the Saudi leaders nonetheless were convinced that Saddam's army was capable of invading and that he might launch an attack.[40]

Beginning on August 2, Bush combined diplomatic, economic, and military measures to defend Saudi Arabia and encourage Saddam to withdraw from Kuwait. Bush signed an executive order freezing Iraq's assets in the United States, halted all U.S. trade with Iraq, and urged the international community to do the same. He backed up the expected diplomatic protests by sending additional U.S. Navy ships to the region and putting U.S. airborne forces on alert. In tandem with these steps, he gained the diplomatic support of several other nations, including Arab states, in calling for an Iraqi pullout and restoration of Kuwait's emir. Evidently basing his actions on the examples of Abraham Lincoln, Franklin Roosevelt, Harry Truman, and Lyndon Johnson, President Bush concluded that he could order a symbolic quick-reaction force to Saudi Arabia to provide a "shield" for its oil resources. In its first days the shield was thin, but after a few weeks a nucleus of American forces provided the structure to build an offensive capability if Saddam kept his troops in Kuwait.[41]

Saddam had numerous options. He could have declared a great victory over a treacherous neighbor, paraded his captured gold and other booty, and taken his army home. He could have stopped short of complete withdrawal and occupied the Rumaila oilfields inside Kuwait's territory. (It would have been highly problematic for Bush to have built an international military coalition and continued intense diplomatic and economic pressure on Iraq if the invaders had abandoned all of Kuwait except the contested oilfields.) Instead, during August 1991 Saddam further reinforced his occupation forces in Kuwait, announced on August 8 that Kuwait would become the "nineteenth province" of Iraq, and demanded the closure of all foreign embassies in the occupied emirate.[42] Saddam was banking on help from the Soviet Union, Bush's reluctance to take military action, and the opposition of other nations, particularly Arab countries, to the use of force by the United States to oust Iraq from Kuwait. Saddam misjudged the course of events on all counts.

First of all, the Soviet Union failed to render its support. On August 2 the Soviets announced that they were stopping shipments of military supplies to Iraq. In the days that followed, Soviet leaders joined those of other nations in calling for Iraqi troops to pull out of Kuwait. Although the Soviets proposed several diplomatic initiatives that some interpreted as favoring Saddam Hussein, the Soviet ambassador to the UN did not veto the series of strongly worded UN resolutions against Saddam's government—resolutions that provided the firm foundation for President Bush's progressively belligerent policies. A more astute leader than Saddam might have understood the chilly Soviet attitude and realized that little help could be expected from Moscow.[43]

Secondly, within seventy-two hours President Bush made it clear that he would employ military force if Saddam did not withdraw his armies from Kuwait. Using the telephone day and night, Bush contacted numerous presidents and prime ministers, gathering widespread support for a hardnosed stand against Iraq's aggression. Significantly, leaders of such nations as Egypt, Turkey, and Syria were among Saddam's harshest critics. As early as August 6 Bush began ordering American combat infantry from the 82nd Airborne Division to Saudi Arabia. On August 10 some Arab leaders announced their intentions to contribute ground units to an international force to defend Saudi Arabia. Within two weeks of the invasion the lineup of multinational forces in the Middle East, on the way there, or proposed for commitment provided another message to Saddam that President Bush has been successful in assembling an extraordinary coalition against Iraq's aggression. Adding to his already significant actions, on August 17 Bush called up several U.S. military reserve components needed to supplement American combat strength overseas, yet another signal that Iraq should take his and the UN's admonitions seriously. Instead, Saddam trotted out Western hostages for television cameras and threatened to use the prisoners as human shields for Iraqi military bases.[44]

In the remaining months of 1990 the crisis intensified. Saddam refused to back off from his annexation of Kuwait and took no heed of the growing signs of international unity, including the military forces arrayed against him. By September 15, 1990, Bush had sent 150,000 U.S. military personnel to Saudi Arabia. As it grew, the international force, including British and French units, developed the capacity for offensive action against Iraq. Moreover, Japan and Germany pledged billions of dollars to defray the costs of Bush's well-coordinated Desert Shield. As the UN economic embargo started to take effect against Iraq, Turkey's president declared that he would allow NATO nations' air squadrons to use Turkish bases, and several other countries indicated that they would dispatch naval, air, ground, or medical units to the Persian Gulf. Saddam rejected a diplomatic exit, promising high American casualties in the "mother of all battles" if the growing coalition under Bush's leadership tried to free Kuwait and sending additional Iraqi reinforcements to the occupied emirate.[45]

Back in Washington, on August 9 Bush had sent a formal note to Congress, describing his initial steps, conforming with the minimal requirements of the War Powers Resolution by explaining the deployment of some U.S. troops into a dangerous situation. Although the president had discussed Middle East developments with members of Congress, he had acted on his own. Within four or five weeks many Americans sensed that a war was possible in the Persian Gulf. Confirming this possibility, on September 20 the Defense Department made American service personnel in Saudi Arabia eligible for "imminent danger" pay. Rather than call the president's hand on this extraordinary deployment of American forces, Congress declined to debate the issues and instead passed a joint resolution on October 1 sustaining Bush's actions to "deter Iraqi aggression." Democrats declined to make the likelihood of war and the military buildup in the gulf the issue in the off-year congressional elections, and the president also downplayed the matter. Congress adjourned on October 28.[46]

On November 8, two days after the congressional elections, Bush proclaimed that he intended to double the size of American military forces in the Middle East by sending 200,000 additional troops. He also proceeded with his successful diplomatic steps to isolate Iraq and forge an international military juggernaut. The president continued to overspend congressionally authorized limits on military matters by employing a musty piece of Civil War legislation, the Feed and Forage Act of 1861. Secretary Cheney called more marine and army reservists to active duty in November and December, sent National Guard brigades to regular army posts for combat training, and extended tours of duty or delayed retirement for thousands of military personnel. Although Saddam refused to believe it, by late December the United States had moved to a war footing. Indeed, these martial preparations led forty-five members of Congress to file suit in federal court calling for the president to obtain congressional approval for war. Turning away the members of Congress, a U.S. district court ruled that the suit had no legal standing.[47]

By the end of December American military deployments in the gulf region had grown to awesome proportions—300,000 soldiers, sailors, marines, and aircrew. Several thousand more soldiers received notification for deployment from Germany to the Arabian peninsula. On December 29 the UN Security Council adopted Resolution 678, setting a deadline of January 15, 1991, for Iraq to withdraw from Kuwait. Saddam Hussein had played the string out almost as far as it could go: he still could have retreated and called it a victory, but he seemed convinced that the U.S. Congress might yet foil Bush's military plans or that the Soviet Union might propose an acceptable diplomatic solution.

President Bush was reluctant to submit the issue of war to Congress. He and Secretary Cheney both had stated their belief that the executive could act independent of the legislative branch in such a crisis. Grudgingly, however, on January 8, 1991, Bush called on Congress to debate the issues and uphold the UN resolutions, including Resolution 678, which also called for "all necessary means" to oust the Iraqis from Kuwait. The president implied that the UN's imprimatur already gave him the authority to send American forces into combat. Speeches by members of the House of Representatives and the Senate ranged from complete support of Desert Shield to qualified misgivings for the dispatch of troops to unqualified opposition to the deployments and the exceptional international commitment President Bush had orchestrated. On January 12, by close votes—52 to 47 in the Senate, and 250 to 183 in the House—Congress upheld Bush's Persian Gulf policy. The national legislature endorsed the series of UN resolutions demanding that Iraq remove its 300,000 troops from Kuwait and that the ousted emir's government be restored. Especially significant, House members and Senators agreed that the congressional vote amounted to a declaration of war.[48]

On January 17, after Iraq spurned last-minute pleas to withdraw by the French foreign minister and the Pope, Bush ordered massive air attacks against Iraq and its forces occupying Kuwait. American and coalition air forces bombarded Iraq and Kuwait for thirty-nine days, with an astounding display of airpower. Day after day Saddam waited for his opponents' ground forces to attack into the teeth of his defensive lines, across Kuwaiti beaches filled with mines and covered by machine guns. Instead of a ground offensive, the relentless air bombardment continued. Saddam retaliated by firing Soviet-built Scud missiles into Saudi Arabia and Israel, apparently trying to provoke Israel into entering the war and thus fracture Bush's delicately balanced Western-Arab coalition. While the coalition's air forces pounded Iraq, U.S. troop strength in the gulf area surpassed 500,000. On February 24 the coalition's ground attack began, carrying the Desert Storm into Kuwait and Iraq. The counteroffensive ended one hundred hours later (8:00 A.M. on February 28) with Kuwait liberated and Iraqi forces routed. Tens of thousands of Iraq's soldiers surrendered.[49]

Bush's willingness to use military force in the Persian Gulf engendered surprisingly little popular controversy in the United States. Any number of reporters and commentators sounded alarms about similarities between Desert Storm and the Vietnam War.[50] But in contrast to Vietnam, the Persian Gulf War was brief—nine months long, including the buildup, the air campaign, ground fighting, and stand down (August 1990 to April 1991). The combat phase lasted less than six weeks. Also in contrast to Vietnam, in short order a powerful American-led multinational force deployed, prepared for battle, fought, and inflicted a clear defeat on the enemy, using conventional linear warfare. Only Bush's order to halt the ground offensive prevented virtual annihilation of most of Saddam's army, which might have taken another two weeks. Most Americans seemed bemused by the quick military success and bewildered at the campaign's sudden end. A few critics soon piped up with the opinion that Bush had used a sledgehammer to mash a wasp—that the United States had sent over too many soldiers, marines, tanks, planes, and ships. A smaller force could have done the job just as well, these critics implied. Of course, that view came only after the stunning victory had cast serious doubts on the training, leadership, and quality of Saddam's huge, Soviet-supplied army, reputed to be the fourth-largest in the world.[51]

Whatever analogies can be drawn between the wars in Korea and the Persian Gulf should not be stretched. Truman and Bush openly and rapidly sent large numbers of air, naval, and army units to a distant war zone, where each conflict had opened with an unexpected invasion. The UN played a crucial role in the Korean and gulf crises, and the Security Council passed resolutions that Truman and Bush used to justify their deployment of American forces. In both cases, several other nations quickly contributed military units under the UN mandate, unlike the case of Vietnam. By contrast, however, the Persian Gulf War was fought by all-volunteer American regular forces supported by some reservists (also volunteers), whereas both the wars in Korea and Vietnam involved sending thousands of draftees into combat. Unlike Lyndon Johnson, Bush activated several thousand military reservists, who served in crucial logistics and air transport units. Moreover, except for Kuwait City, the ground combat in the Gulf War occurred in lightly populated, open terrain, a fact that matched U.S. military strengths, rather than campaigns in rugged mountains or dense jungles, as in Korea or Vietnam. Ironically, the political benefits Bush gained from his outstanding display of wartime leadership appeared to be short-lived; the nation's economy turned sour in the latter half of 1991 and became a primary focus of the 1992 presidential campaign.[52]

Bush's role as commander in chief in the Gulf War and his use of war powers will no doubt be the subject of much debate—a debate complicated by the fact that some critics of the Reagan-Bush policies had supported leading Democratic presidents, such as FDR and John F. Kennedy, who acted without direct congressional approval. Some have seen Kennedy's deployments as laying the groundwork for American involvement in the Vietnam War, while others believe he was disinclined to escalate further. In other words, presidential decisions are subject to interpretation by journalists, scholars, politicians, and citizens, who will continue to debate the role of the president in wartime and related constitutional issues.

As has been the case since George Washington's time, the United States will depend on the education, experience, and intelligence of its president as well as the cabinet members, military officers, and unofficial counselors they turn to for advice. The chapters that follow show the talent, decisiveness, and character of modern American commanders in chief.

1

THE PRESIDENT AS COMMANDER IN CHIEF: A STUDY IN POWER

NORMAN A. GRAEBNER

Traditional claims to executive primacy in military affairs have kept pace with the expansion of the country's international role since its founding in the eighteenth century. The assumption that the control of external relations is the responsibility of the president is based on the sentence in Article 2 of the Constitution that reads, "The Executive power shall be vested in a President of the United States of America."[1] As early as 1906 Senator John Spooner of Wisconsin, in defending President Theodore Roosevelt's Caribbean interventions, asserted that the executive power in the Constitution gave the president exclusive control of almost every aspect of foreign affairs. "So far as the conduct of our foreign relations is concerned," he declared, "the president has the absolute and uncontrolled and uncontrollable authority."[2] In the significant Supreme Court decision of *United States v. Curtiss-Wright Export Corporation* (1936), Justice George Sutherland observed that the president is "the sole organ of the federal government in the field of international relations," and throughout the twentieth century, successive presidents have claimed a constitutional monopoly in determining the employment of the country's armed forces. Such official certainty regarding executive primacy in the management of the military services contrasts markedly with the Founding Fathers' definition of the president's role and the reality of power in the American constitutional system.

At the opening session of the Constitutional Convention in May 1787, Resolution 7 of the proposed Virginia Plan accepted the general admonition that a government of checks and balances required an independent executive with the "authority to execute the National Laws [as well as] the Executive rights vested in Congress by the Confederation."[3] When the convention, on June 1, turned to this provision, it readily accepted the notion of a national executive but rejected the prescription that the United States, in the British tradition, would consign all powers over foreign affairs, formerly embodied in Congress, to the national executive unless the convention were prepared to limit those powers by a strict definition. Charles Pinckney of South Carolina opened the discussion by advocating a vigorous executive but said he feared that "the Executive powers of (the existing) Congress might extend to peace & war &c which would render the Executive a Monarchy, of the worst kind, to wit an elective one."[4] John Rutledge, also from South Carolina, added that he favored a single executive, "tho' he was not for giving him the power of war and peace." James Wilson of Pennsylvania argued that only a single executive could give the office the necessary dispatch and responsibility. He did not, however, "consider the Prerogatives of the British Monarch as a proper guide in defining the Executive powers. Some of these prerogatives were of a Legislative nature. Among others that of war & peace &c. The only powers he conceived strictly Executive were those of executing the laws, and appointing officers, not (appertaining to and) appointed by the Legislature."[5]

When Edmund Randolph of Virginia retorted that a single executive would lead to monarchy, James Madison observed that the issue of a single or plural executive was less important than determining the extent of executive authority. In remarks recorded by Rufus King of Massachusetts, Madison agreed with Wilson that executive powers "do not include the Rights of war & peace &c, but the powers shd. be confined and defined—if large we shall have the Evils of elective Monarchies." Madison then moved to strike out the clause in the seventh provision relating to executive power and to substitute the words "that a national Executive ought to be instituted with power to carry into effect the national laws, to appoint to offices in cases not otherwise provided for, and to execute such other powers as may from time to time be delegated by the national Legislature." Pinckney believed that Madison's motion gave the executive too much authority; he declared that the national executive should have only the power "to carry into effect the national laws." The convention, in accepting Pinckney's argument that the legislature might delegate improper powers, amended the resolution proposed by the Virginia Plan to limit the executive power to that of executing the national laws and appointing "to offices in cases not otherwise provided for."[6]

Not until June 15 did Madison raise the question of executive authority in military affairs. Madison suggested that the executive, in addition to carrying out the national laws, might direct all military operations provided that no member of the federal executive "shall on any occasion take command of any troops, so as personally to conduct any enterprise."[7] In his noted address of June 18, Alexander Hamilton observed that the executive should have control of "the direction of war when authorized or begun." For him peace and war were not executive prerogatives; to the Senate he would give the sole power to declare war.[8] The constitutional powers over war and peace were taking final form. In its report of August 6, the Committee of Detail assigned to the legislature the power to make war, raise armies, build and equip fleets, and call forth the militia to enforce treaties, suppress insurrections, and repel invasions. To the executive it extended the power to direct all military operations as "commander-in-chief of the Army and Navy of the United States, and of the militia of the several states."[9]

On August 17 the convention took up the question of war powers as defined by the Committee of Detail. Several days earlier Randolph had argued that the power to originate war should rest solely in the House of Representatives; such power should not exist in a body as small as the Senate.[10] Pinckney opened the debate on August 17 by asserting that the House was ill-suited to carry the responsibility for making war. It was too large and proceeded too slowly. The Senate, he believed, should have the responsibility for war, just as it had the responsibility for peace. Senators would be better informed on foreign affairs than House members; therefore they were more capable of making quick and rational decisions. If the small states possessed a disproportionate share of power in the Senate, they would have as much at stake in cases of war as the large ones.[11] Oliver Elsworth of Connecticut retorted that making war was not the same as making peace. Any frame of government should create impediments to entering a war but none to terminate it. Making war comprised a simple, overt declaration; making peace required intricate and secret negotiations. George Mason of Virginia agreed. He, like Elsworth, favored a procedure that would clog rather than facilitate the making of war.[12] The greater inefficiency of the House merely guaranteed that Congress would impede any decision for war. Pierce Butler of South Carolina declared that he distrusted the House no less than the Senate. Butler said that he was "for vesting the power in the president, who will have all the requisite qualities, and will not make war but when the Nation will support it." Elbridge Gerry of Massachusetts responded that he "never expected to hear in a republic a motion to empower the Executive alone to declare war."[13]

Amid the debate over the war powers, Madison and Gerry moved to substitute "declare" for the term "make" war, leaving to the executive the power to repel attacks without a congressional declaration of war. Roger Sherman of Connecticut agreed that the executive should be empowered to repel attacks but not commence war. He opposed the word "declare" because it dangerously narrowed Congress's authority. In his opinion, Congress alone should have the power to make war.[14] Mason, like Madison, preferred "declare" to "make." Rufus King agreed. To make war, he warned, might be understood to conduct it, and that was an executive function. The motion to limit Congress's power to declaring war passed easily, eight to two, but nothing in that vote questioned the authority vested solely in Congress to engage the country in war.[15]

Early in the debate on the war powers Mason expressed the hope that the country would have no standing army in time of peace except for a few garrisons. The convention refused to accept any limitation on the size of the standing army. On August 20 the convention considered the proposition that the military should always be subordinate to civil authority and that the legislature could make no appropriations for a standing army for more than one year at a time. To assure greater continuity in defense policy, the convention voted to extend military appropriations for a period of two years.[16] Such limitations on a standing army compelled the convention to consider the creation of an effective militia. On August 23 the convention took up the recommendation of the special Committee of Eleven, which granted to the federal government the power to "make laws for organizing, arming & disciplining the Militia, and for governing such parts of them as may be employed in the service of the U.S. reserving to the States respectively, the appointment of the officers, and authority of training the militia according to the discipline prescribed by the U.S."[17] Eventually the convention adopted the entire proposal. In September the Committee of Style defined the war powers: "The President shall be Commander-in-Chief of the Army and Navy of the United States, and of the Militia of the several States when called into the actual service of the United States."[18] For the framers, Congress, not the president, was the true representative of the people. They placed in Congress the powers to tax, control commerce, raise armies and provide for their use through a declaration of war. The president shared none of these powers.

In *The Federalist*, written in 1787 and 1788 to support the Federalist cause in New York, Madison and Hamilton explained the military clauses in the Constitution with no effort to reinterpret them in favor of the executive. Madison, in *The Federalist No. 41*, observed that all societies, in their defense against foreign dangers, confided the necessary powers of declaring war and raising and equipping the military forces to the central government. The power of government over peace and war, as well as the raising of armies, was total because Congress could not determine the policies or limit the exertions of other countries in their relations with the United States.[19] For those who feared a large standing army the Constitution had limited the term of military appropriations to two years. Furthermore, in *The Federalist No. 24*, Hamilton reassured his readers that the "whole power of raising armies was lodged in the *Legislature*, not the *Executive*; that this legislature was to be a popular body, consisting of the representatives of the people periodically elected."[20]

Hamilton, in *The Federalist No. 74*, asserted that the president was to be "Commander-in-Chief of the army and navy of the United States, and of the militia of the several states *when called into the actual service* of the United States." For Hamilton this constitutional definition of the president's role was so reasonable that it required no further explanation. Hamilton explained why the direction of war required the exercise of power by a single person. "The direction of war," he wrote, "implies the direction of the common strength; and the power of directing and employing the common strength, forms a usual and essential part in the definition of the executive authority."[21] In *The Federalist No. 69*, Hamilton made a clear distinction between the war powers of the president and those of the British king. *"First,"* Hamilton wrote, "the president will have only the occasional command of such part of the militia of the nation as by legislative provision may be called into the actual service of the Union. The king of Great Britain . . . [has] the entire command of all the militia. . . . *Secondly.* The President is to be commander-in-chief of the army and navy of the United States. In this respect his authority would be nominally the same with that of the king of Great Britain, but in substance much inferior to his. It would amount to nothing more than the supreme command and direction of the military and naval forces . . . ; while that of the British king extends to the *declaring* of war and to the *raising* and *regulating* of fleets and armies,—all which, by the Constitution under consideration, would appertain to the legislature."[22] Such language reflected both the intentions of the makers and the provisions of the Constitution.

Nothing in the Constitution or the intent of the framers gave the president the power to commit the country to war. Such responsibility was too great to be entrusted to a president and his advisers, especially since others would carry the burden of fighting, dying, and paying the costs. A declaration of war would scarcely limit executive-legislative dissension over the framing of strategy, the selection of officers, or the management of the war effort, but such controversy would be a matter judgment, not constitutionality. Two special circumstances could contribute to the president's constitutional war-making power: where the threat was too trivial to require congressional approval and where the threat was too immediate to permit time for congressional consent. Even in the nineteenth century the president, on numerous occasions, employed the armed forces against pirates, Indians, border ruffians, and rioters without asking permission from Congress. When the British struck Washington in 1814, President James Madison had no time to call Congress into session to determine a proper national response. These extreme conditions where the president's war-making power was beyond chal-

lenge continued into the twentieth century. But between these ex-
tremes two bodies of constitutional authority came into conflict—the
president's power as commander in chief and the Congress's power
to declare war and to set the level of expenditure. Normally the refusal of Congress to declare war would be sufficient to prevent or at
least terminate any military engagement.

Still, in the two centuries that followed George Washington's inauguration in 1789, American presidents decreed the employment of
the nation's armed forces more than 170 times; Congress declared
war only 5 times. Since 1945 more than 100,000 U.S. military personnel have died in undeclared wars; more than 400,000 have suffered battle injuries. These presidential military ventures were not
limited to the protection of the nation's citizens from direct assaults
by pirates or marauders; many engaged the country militarily
against foreign states in Asia, the Middle East, and the Caribbean.
Only once, in 1812, did Congress actually debate the issue of war; in
the other four cases Congress, with limited discussion, agreed that a
war situation already existed. The careful division of powers between the executive and Congress in matters of war and peace has
been exceedingly ineffective. In practice presidents have often assumed the power to ignore Congress or override opposing congressional sentiment with apparent impunity.

Such immense power did not derive from the U.S. Constitution.
From the outset the relative power of the executive and Congress in
matters of peace and war flowed not from the separation of powers,
but from the organization of the federal government, the conditions
of national and international politics, and the authority inherent in
the chief executive's responsibility to recognize and respond to actual or perceived external threats to the nations's welfare and security. Nothing in the Constitution discourages a president from acting directly and decisively as commander in chief or as head of the
federal bureaucracy. Nor does the Constitution in any way limit the
power of a president to place the armed forces of the United States
wherever he chooses. But a president's real power to advance his foreign policy agenda always rested not on any exclusive constitutional
mandate but on his capacity to build and sustain, through qualities
of leadership, the necessary base of congressional and popular sup-

port. Indeed, the Constitution always permitted the executive to do whatever the public would approve. When assured of strong public support in his clash with congressional critics, a president faced almost no limits to his control of external policy. In placing the country's armed forces where he believes they will best protect the interest and security of the American people, a president can create a war situation that often leaves Congress only the choice to recognize it, if not with a declaration of war, at least with military appropriations.

In practice, the president could dominate the congressional and public mind most readily when the country was in a crisis mood—when external conditions appeared to demand strong national leadership. James Madison warned the country that the gravest dangers to its liberties would lie in "provisions against danger, real or pretended, from abroad."[23] Madison reminded delegates to the Constitutional Convention that governments in time of war gave immense discretionary powers to the executive. "Constant apprehension of War," he continued, "has the . . . tendency to render the head too large for the body. A standing military force, with an overgrown Executive will not long be safe companions to liberty. The means of defense agst. Foreign danger, have been always the instruments of tyranny at home."[24] What gave the president his ultimate advantage over his detractors as commander in chief was the broad assumption that the executive branch, because of its massive foreign affairs and military establishments, possessed knowledge superior to that available elsewhere in the country. In times of crisis, whether real or contrived, the executive often behaved as if that assumption were correct and, through arguments and assertions that played on national insecurities, went to extreme lengths to demolish his congressional opposition. Because opinion was the essence of executive power, a president could scarcely claim constitutional privileges when public or congressional sentiment turned against him. As a last resort, however, he could seek an escape from the limitations of law and adverse opinion by adopting forms of evasion and operating secretly through White House operatives employing funds from previous appropriations or private sources. Such behavior simply underscored the limited control that the American constitutional system exerts over the presidential conduct of external policy.

If the president's war-making power, as defined by the Constitution and *The Federalist*, comprised little but that of defending the country against imminent invasion when Congress was not in session, it did not deny executive primacy in determining the general direction of the country's external relations as long as any resulting actions made limited demands on Congress and the American people. When executive decisions created significant dissention or required extensive funding the executive had no choice but to engage Congress in a struggle for control of the country's mind and resources. Thus the president's institutional advantages over Congress did not eliminate Congress's power to compel changes in an established course. The president might dominate a divided Congress, but a united Congress could command any policy through its control of the purse and its power to pass legislation over presidential veto. Congress's control of the purse is a far greater power than the president's as commander in chief. Still Congress from the beginning exhibited great reluctance to use its superior powers to confront executive policy directly. Members of Congress, no less than the American people generally, have recognized the responsibility that the chief executive, as official spokesman of the nation, carries for the defense of the country's interests abroad. This responsibility Congress might share, but hardly bear. With good reason successive Congresses have shunned any action that might injure the executive office.

Members of Congress have always been conscious of the president's many advantages in commanding public opinion. They have hesitated from the beginning to risk their political lives by challenging the notion of presidential primacy in matters of external policy, especially when the country was in a crisis mood. Any congressional effort to compel a president to abjure a resort to force, unless supported by adequate public sentiment, could unleash charges of weakness and irresponsibility. If another country appeared to gain strategic advantage from America's failure to act, members of Congress would carry the burden of a failed policy. Nothing in the Constitution can prevent a determined executive from pursuing a successful policy without congressional approval, but no policy over time can remain so successful and cost-free that it does not require congressional and public approval.

President James K. Polk, in his management of the Mexican War between 1846 and 1848, demonstrated how completely a vigorous president could govern the question of war. In submitting a war message to Congress and asking for a declaration of war against Mexico, Polk followed all the constitutional forms. Still the president had dispatched U.S. forces to contested territories along the Rio Grande where predictably they would draw fire from Mexican detachments. When they did, Polk requested Congress to accept his war. Senator John C. Calhoun of South Carolina complained that the president had "stripped Congress of the power of making war, and what is more and worse, it gave that power to every officer, nay, to every subaltern commanding a corporal's guard."[25] As the Mexican War, a successful military venture, gained more popular support, Congress, despite its doubts regarding the war's legitimacy, exercised its power over the purse, not to end the conflict, but to sustain it. Polk's control of the country's external relations never rested on the Constitution or on the special complexity of international affairs, but rather on his successful management of public and congressional opinion. Abraham Lincoln saw this clearly when, near the end of the war, he wrote to his friend William H. Herndon:

> Allow the president to invade a neighboring nation, whenever he shall deem it necessary to repel an invasion, and you allow him to do so, *whenever he may choose to say* he deems it necessary for such purpose—and you allow him to make war at pleasure. Study to see if you can fix *any limit* to his power in this respect. . . . If, to-day, he should choose to say he thinks it necessary to invade Canada, to prevent the British from invading us, how could you stop him? You may say to him, "I see no probability of the British invading us" but he will say to you "be silent; I see it, if you don't."[26]

Several years later Lincoln, as president, created another war situation by exercising his executive prerogatives. In April 1861 he dispatched a small expedition to relieve Fort Sumter in Charleston harbor, suspecting that citizens of seceded South Carolina would fire on it to set off a civil war. With the fort nearly out of supplies, Lincoln had little choice; there is a difference between accepting a war and commencing one. Following the attack on Fort Sumter, Lincoln declared an "insurrection" and took a series of war measures. He called up 75,000 state militia members, thus bypassing a declaration of war. Still it would have seemed unreasonable to declare war in a civil conflict under any circumstances. Before the end of April Lincoln had proclaimed two blockades, the first of the Deep South states from South Carolina to Texas, the second including Virginia and North Carolina. On May 3 he decreed an expansion of the regular army beyond the total authorized by law, an act unprecedented in the nation's history. When Congress assembled on July 4, Lincoln sent it a message in which he acknowledged the illegality of his actions. "These measures," he wrote, "whether strictly legal or not, were ventured upon, under what appeared to be a popular demand, and a public necessity; trusting . . . that Congress would readily ratify them." Congress responded to Lincoln's request for the regularization of his acts with a resolution proclaiming that "all the acts, proclamations, and orders of the President . . . respecting the army and navy of the United States, and calling out . . . the militia or volunteers from the States, are hereby approved and in all respects legalized and made valid."[27]

Since the Civil War, American presidents have repeatedly sent U.S. forces abroad without congressional approval, not necessarily to engage in war. President Grover Cleveland in 1888 dispatched American servicemen to Samoa to join the Germans there in restoring order in the islands. After 1901 both President Theodore Roosevelt and President William Howard Taft intervened in Caribbean affairs with military power to protect perceived American interests in trade and security. In 1903 Roosevelt ordered marines to Panama to assure the success of the Panamanian revolution against Colombian rule. Roosevelt's Corollary of 1904 to the Monroe Doctrine formalized such interventionism to assure the fulfillment of international obligations by the Caribbean states. Eventually the United States established a half dozen protectorates in the Caribbean, all backed by U.S. armed forces without formal congressional approval. In 1914 Woodrow Wilson dispatched marines and soldiers to Vera Cruz to undermine the Huerta regime of Mexico; in 1916 he sent an expedition under General John J. Pershing into Mexico in an unsuccessful attempt to capture General Pancho Villa. To prevent Japanese aggression against Russia, Wilson in 1919 placed U.S. forces in Siberia. In 1941 President Franklin D. Roosevelt not only ordered the American occupation of Iceland but also employed U.S. warships to protect convoys in the Atlantic, where they quickly encountered German submarines. After the attack on the destroyer *Greer* southwest of Iceland, Roosevelt ordered the navy to engage German submarines actively. These many presidential ventures were not universally popular, but they all transpired well within a national consensus that regarded them as reasonable, if not necessary.

President Harry Truman's decision to commit American forces to Korea in June 1950 without a formal declaration of war presumed the necessary public and congressional support to permit a successful prosecution of the war. Certainly the country was well prepared emotionally to underwrite the initial commitment. For a year the concept of danger to all of East and Southeast Asia from a Kremlin-based communist monolith had dominated official American statements on events in China and Indochina. South Korea, like Formosa, had been purposely left outside the American offshore defense perimeter, and Washington officials had cautioned South Korean President Syngman Rhee to expect no American aid against his internal or external antagonists. With the unexpected North Korean invasion of June 25, however, the Truman administration detected in the blatant aggression a summons to take a stand. At the president's Blair House meeting on June 25 General Omar N. Bradley, chair of the Joint Chiefs of Staff, declared that "the Korean situation offered as good an occasion for action in drawing the line as anywhere else." Admiral Forrest P. Sherman, chief of naval operations, agreed. "The present situation in Korea," he said, "offers a valuable opportunity for us to act."[28] Two days later Truman informed those gathered around his council table that "we could not let [the Korean] matter go by default." By June 27 the president had committed U.S. air and naval units to the Korean conflict. Three days later he ordered General Douglas MacArthur in Tokyo to employ all available American forces in Korea except those required for the defense of Japan.[29]

President Truman's decisions invoked almost universal approval. Democrats in Congress praised the president for his decisive leadership. Senator Estes Kefauver of Tennessee admonished members of Congress to close ranks and "stand behind the president in the vital decision he has made." Most Republicans accepted the war with equal enthusiasm. Senator Styles Bridges of New Hampshire addressed his colleagues: "Now is the time to draw the line. Now is the time to tell the world . . . that America will not surrender, equivocate, appease or hesitate."[30] Senator Robert A. Taft of Ohio agreed with the president's decision to enter the war, but he warned Congress to exercise its authority to declare war or lose that constitutional right.[31] Tom Connally, Democratic chair of the Senate Foreign Relations Committee, advised Truman on June 27 that he need not consult Congress. When the president finally met members of Congress on June 30, he did not seek their advice but merely explained his decisions.[32] That refusal to confer with Congress did not disturb Senator Arthur H. Vandenberg of Michigan, who lauded the president in a letter of July 3: "When the time came for you to act in behalf of free men and a free world, you did so with a spectacular courage which has revived the relentless purpose of all peaceful nations to deny aggression."[33] Truman's support in Congress seemed assured. Republican Congressman Dewey Short of Missouri observed on June 30 that almost the entire Congress would support any presidential request related to the Korean involvement. Historians have agreed with that judgment.[34]

Conscious of the widespread approval of the Korean decision, the administration saw no need to ask Congress for a formal declaration of war. In defending the president's prerogative to conduct the war as an executive venture, Democrats argued that the American conflict in Korea was a police action, not a war, and therefore did not require formal congressional acceptance. Senator Paul Douglas of Illinois noted the distinction before the Senate on July 5. War, he said, "is the anarchic use of force by one nation against another for the purpose of imposing its own will, and in the absence of international authorization." In Korea the United States was acting as the agent of an international authority in an effort to protect the peace of the world.[35] That argument, often repeated, offered a cloak of legal respectability to an undeclared war and suggested reassuringly that the war was exceedingly limited after all. As the struggle continued at increasing cost, Secretary of State Dean Acheson acknowledged that the distinction was irrelevant; the United States was at war.[36] Another argument, equally specious, insisted that the United States was acting under the auspices of the UN; therefore the decision to intervene lay outside the jurisdiction of the U.S. Constitution. In fact, however, the president's decision to enter Korea with military force preceded the Security Council's vote to support the war through collective action. Thereafter the United States furnished well over 80 percent of the allied ground forces, more than 90 percent of the naval forces, and almost all of the air power. Moreover, the United States from the beginning assumed total command of the war. General MacArthur admitted later that his role as commander of UN forces in Korea was identical to what it would have been had all the forces been American.[37]

Actually the decision to avoid a declaration of war was based on more fundamental considerations. Truman's close advisers encouraged him to accept full responsibility for the war as commander in chief. Acheson assured him that he had the power to deploy U.S. forces anywhere without congressional approval. Indeed, the secretary instructed the State Department to prepare a memorandum on the president's authority to repel the Korean attack, using the many precedents in the nation's history where presidents had dispatched American forces to distant lands to protect the interests of the United States.[38] In an age of airplanes and atomic weapons it was even more essential that the president have the authority to respond quickly to foreign dangers. Under the imperative to act instantaneously, Congress, by permitting debate, could lead the country to disaster. Members of Congress received the State Department memorandum in early July. Truman himself readily accepted the supposition that his power as commander in chief gave him "the authority to send troops anywhere in the world."[39] He contended in speaking to reporters that the complexities of international affairs had eliminated Congress's power to declare war. But equally important in Truman's decision was the knowledge that a formal declaration of war denotes a major threat to national security and calls for a limitless exertion of power and will. For Truman it was essential that the United States engage in no actions that would provoke Russia or China to inaugurate a wider war. War limited to the Korean peninsula would demand no all-out effort and would bring victory without the need of fighting either China or the USSR.[40]

Whatever the bipartisanship during the early months of the Korean War, it quickly evaporated after the Communist Chinese entered the conflict in November 1950. The rapid deterioration of the American military situation in Korea undermined the public's general approval of the war effort. The national consent that had granted the president the authority to pursue his Korean venture without a formal declaration of war presumed a limited and temporary involvement. Republican leaders sensed the changes in public support as well as the narrowing choices and greater demands confronting American policy. Robert Taft warned his Ohio constituents that the new requirements of war "may well . . . involve taxes higher than we have levied on our people before. These sacrifices result directly from the fact that this administration has lost the peace after the American people won the war."[41] Capitalizing on the war's growing unpopularity, Republicans discovered the argument that rendered the war the unnecessary consequence of faulty policy. The United States had invited the North Korean aggression by failing to create an adequate army in South Korea and by withdrawing its own troops, leaving no force sufficient to discourage an invasion from the north. Finally, in January 1950, Secretary Acheson, defining publicly the defense perimeter that the United States would maintain in the Pacific, had pointedly excluded both Korea and Formosa. The North Koreans had merely taken the secretary at his word. "They knew that we had permitted the taking over of China by the Communists," said Taft, "and saw no reason why we should seriously object to the taking over of Korea."[42]

By January 1951 the specter of an expanding war in East Asia and the absence of a national effort to fight it created a crisis in Washington over purpose and strategy, leaving the administration only inadequate choices. Senator William E. Jenner of Indiana suggested two, neither of them feasible but both politically potent. If Congress, he asserted, had any "courage and patriotism left, they will lay down an ultimatum to the president, demanding either a declaration of war or the bringing back of American GI's to home shores." Clearly, as Senator Everett Dirksen of Illinois observed, the American people had no interest in a larger commitment to a war that was going badly. It was doubtful, he concluded, that the administration could obtain a declaration of war even if it tried. The war would continue, undeclared. Under the leadership of General Matthew B. Ridgway the Eighth Army in Korea had, by February, recovered from its long southward retreat and again demonstrated its capacity to drive the Chinese and North Koreans back across the 38th parallel.[43] As long as the war continued, Republicans and Democrats would support it. Taft acknowledged in March that congressional disapproval of the American involvement in Korea did not give Congress the right to deny adequate financial support for the war effort, because such behavior "might result in strangling the American forces in Korea. No Congress," he added, "is ever going to exercise the power of the purse to that extent."[44]

What aggravated the partisan attacks on the administration after March 1951 was the Truman-MacArthur controversy over strategy, with the latter offering a plan that promised total victory in Korea with little additional risk or expense. President Truman's dismissal of MacArthur in April and the subsequent congressional hearings in May did not alter the administration's strategy of holding the line in Korea, but in succeeding months they gave the war's critics endless opportunity to belabor the administration for its failure to either leave the war gracefully or win it.[45]

Throughout the Cold War era executive-congressional relations hinged on the willingness of Congress to underwrite policies—even military interventions—that successive administrations regarded as essential to defend the nation's security against unwanted communist encroachments. What mattered was the perennial power of the executive to control the congressional and public opinion that would assure the necessary appropriations. In 1955 President Dwight D. Eisenhower sought and obtained a congressional resolution authorizing him to use armed force to defend the Nationalist Chinese off-shore islands of Quemoy and Matsu should a mainland Chinese attack on them appear to be the first step in an assault on Formosa. In 1958, however, Eisenhower ordered troops into Lebanon to support that country's pro-Western government without any reference to Congress. Similarly President John F. Kennedy, in 1962, inaugurated the process of sending thousands of American military advisers into South Vietnam without congressional authorization. Also that year Kennedy used naval vessels, again without formal congressional approval, to establish a "quarantine" of Cuba and thereby prevent the movement of additional Soviet missiles to that island. This presidential action raised the specter of nuclear war. Yet the perceived security threat created by Soviet missiles in Cuba produced an overwhelming public support for the president's decision. In 1965 President Lyndon B. Johnson landed marines in the Dominican Republic to prevent an alleged communist takeover. This intervention, unlike its predecessors, created a minor storm of controversy between the executive and Congress, one identical in concept to another already under way over the country's burgeoning involvement in Vietnam.[46]

Before 1965 the American commitment to Vietnam created scattered doubts regarding its wisdom and future, but little more. When in the spring and summer of that year President Johnson converted the South Vietnamese struggle against the forces of Ho Chi Minh into an American war, the criticism mounted as rapidly as the war's escalation. By 1968 the widespread and highly vocal opposition, which now included all media networks, the country's leading newspapers, former generals, members of Congress and the American academic community, dominated all public discourse on the war.[47] Still Johnson and, after January 1969, President Richard M. Nixon, without formal congressional approval, ordered air and ground action in Vietnam of increasing magnitude and destruction. To those who saw no danger in North Vietnamese behavior to the security of the United States, the presidents and their advisers, in words reminiscent of Abraham Lincoln, replied that the danger was clear to them. In confronting Congress and its critics elsewhere the executive claimed superior knowledge, much of it kept secret. This claim gave both presidents a sharp advantage over their critics, enabling them to ignore countering arguments and to exploit the willingness of most Americans to accept executive judgments as valid. Neither Johnson nor Nixon had the power to silence Congress; yet their power to send troops into combat seemed to have no visible limit.

The reason is clear. The essence of their power lay less in the Constitution or their role as commander in chief than in their successful management of public and congressional opinion. With their comparatively silent public support both presidents had the power to make their demands on Congress, in part because the arguments that held the public majorities in line also captured much of Congress as well. Thus in supporting presidential policy members of Congress, in large measure, voted their convictions rather than their fears of public retribution. But whatever the motives of congressmen, it was in essence their willingness to support executive decisions, and this alone, that granted the presidents an authority, as Lincoln said, without visible limits. With access to television at prime time, with the power to control press conferences, and with batteries of gifted speech writers, executives could make words accomplish almost impossible feats. Never before had Washington officials dominated the news so completely. They determined the wording and the timing of official information, searching always for the arguments and phraseology that would play on national insecurities.[48] In their book, *Presidential Television*, Newton H. Minow, John Bartlow Martin, and Lee M. Mitchell insisted that their effective use of television gave presidents the power to tilt the constitutional balance in favor of the executive. Self-restraint alone appeared to be the ultimate limitation on presidential power.[49]

After 1969 it was Nixon's control of public opinion, not his constitutional control of the armed forces, that permitted him to defy his critics in Congress and allowed his spokesmen to trample on congressional committees at will. This relationship of the president to Congress explains why the great debates on executive powers are never simple executive-congressional confrontations. A congressional majority underwrote the war in Vietnam from 1961 until 1973 through its power of the purse; that war always belonged to Congress as much as to the presidents. They fought it together. Not even

Nixon's bombing of North Vietnam from early 1971 until the end of 1972 and his subsequent bombing of Cambodian targets belonged to him alone. These decisions were sustained by congressional majorities and by those Americans outside Congress who supported the bombing or a least had no interest in voicing their disapproval. The central question, therefore, was not the executive's limitless power over external affairs but why Congress refused to exert its far greater authority through the power of the purse. When the majority of Congress after June 1973 opposed presidential policy in Southeast Asia, that policy ceased to exist. Yet nowhere did Congress infringe on the president's power as commander in chief.

As the American war in Vietnam, never declared, faced ever-increasing opposition in Congress, administration spokesmen insisted that the president's command of the armed forces eliminated the need for any congressional approval of the war. "There can be no question in present circumstances," declared Leonard C. Meeker, legal adviser to the State Department in March 1966, "of the president's authority to commit U.S. forces to the defense of South Vietnam. The grant of authority to the president in Article II of the Constitution extends to the actions of the United States currently undertaken in Vietnam."[50] Under Secretary of State Nicholas Katzenbach informed the Senate Foreign Relations Committee in August 1967 that "the expression of declaring war is one that has become outmoded in the international arena." Under modern conditions it was for the president alone to determine when and how the armed forces of the United States should be used. President Johnson made even greater claims for executive authority when he informed a news conference in August 1967 that the administration did not require congressional authorization to commit armed forces. He had asked for the Gulf of Tonkin Resolution in 1964, he said, because "if we were going to ask them to stay the whole route . . . we ought to ask them to be there at the takeoff."[51]

Such official claims to executive primacy in matters of war and peace continued under Nixon's presidency. When the Senate in 1969, by a vote of seventy to sixteen, passed the National Commitments Resolution, which was designed to limit national commitments to agreements between the executive and legislative branches, the administration replied: "As Commander-in-Chief the President has the sole authority to command our armed forces, whether they are in or outside the United States. And, although reasonable men may differ as to the circumstances in which he should do so, the President has the constitutional power to send U.S. military forces abroad without specific Congressional approval."[52] In denying that he required any congressional authorization for his invasion of Cambodia in 1970, President Nixon declared that he was meeting "his responsibility as Commander-in-Chief of our armed forces to take the action I consider necessary to defend the security of our American men."[53] Throughout the Vietnam War executive branch lawyers stressed the vagueness of the Constitution on questions of foreign policy and war powers; they insisted that the question of authority to act or to restrain be left to the requirements of the moment in accordance with, as Katzenbach expressed it, "the instinct of the nation and its leaders for political responsibility." Those who viewed the Constitution as imprecise argued that the president must be left unencumbered to use the armed forces and to commit the United States as he saw fit, seeking congressional approval only when it appeared useful or convenient.

In the end such arguments could not deny that Congress still possessed the ultimate power over foreign affairs. After supporting the American involvement in Vietnam for eight years, congressional Democrats, in 1973, were determined to terminate the war by exercising Congress's power of the purse. Twice during the Ninety-second Congress the Senate passed amendments that would have eliminated funds for the war and compelled the president to withdraw American forces. The House refused to go along on the ground that such restrictions were an improper abridgement of the president's authority to conduct the country's foreign policy.[54] During January 1973 House Democrats, by a vote of 154 to 75, and Senate Democrats, by a vote of 36 to 12, resolved to pass legislation that would end the American involvement in Vietnam.[55] After the Vietnam cease-fire of January 27, 1973, Senate leaders, Republicans and Democrats alike, agreed that the administration's continuing air war in Cambodia had no constitutional or public support. They now began to introduce measures to cut off funds for any military action in Cambodia not specifically approved by Congress. Then in May a Gallup Poll revealed that almost 60 percent of the American people disapproved of the Cambodian bombing and that more than 75 percent believed that the president should seek congressional approval before carrying out any additional military action in Southeast Asia.[56] Clearly the president's policy in Cambodia was doomed.

Republican leaders in the House hoped to head off a vote that would curtail the president's authority, but in mid-May the House voted 219 to 188 to prevent the Pentagon from using funds previously appropriated to carry on the bombing. Then by a vote of 224 to 172 it forbade the use of any money in a $2.9 billion supplemental appropriation bill to be used anywhere in the vicinity of Cambodia.[57] Early in June the Senate attached a restrictive rider to a $3.4 billion supplemental appropriation bill, which, its backers believed, the president dared not veto. The House passed the measure and then attached it to the even more vital appropriation bill for funding the operations of government. The president vetoed the first bill, declaring that it would undo his efforts to obtain an honorable peace in Indochina. "We are now involved," he warned, "in concluding the last element of that settlement. It would be nothing short of tragic if this great accomplishment, bought with the blood of so many Asians and Americans, were to be undone now by Congressional action." It was this argument that had sustained his control of Congress and the public through four years. This time it failed. Congress moved unrelentingly toward a showdown with the president. It began to attach riders restricting the use of federal funds in Cambodia to increasingly essential financial legislation until the administration had either to capitulate or see the whole government grind to a halt. Finally the House and Senate agreed to the president's proposal of a cutoff on August 15.[58] On that day the American war in Vietnam came to an end. For eight years Congress could have terminated the war but for reasons of its own chose not to do so.

Determined to limit the executive's war-making authority and prevent a recurrence of the Vietnam experience, Congress, still quite conscious of its vulnerability to presidential policy-formulation, passed the War Powers Resolution over the president's veto on November 7, 1973.[59] What the successive war powers measures, beginning with Senator Jacob Javits's first war powers bill of June 1970, sought to accomplish was the restoration of balance between the president's control of the armed forces and the right of Congress to determine their use. The various bills attempted to delineate the circumstances in which the president could first act unilaterally and those that required the prior authorization of Congress. Under these measures even the use of armed forces under emergency conditions required congressional approval within thirty (later ninety) days. If the president, after as little as thirty days of fighting, could not convince a solid majority of Congress that his decisions were valid, those decisions would already have laid the foundation for a major uprising within the American populace and would be foundering militarily, if not morally, along the battle fronts. In practice the war powers measure of November 1973 would not limit presidential power if in future crises the executive could establish its dominance over congressional and public opinion as easily as it did in the Vietnam War.

Both Jimmy Carter and Ronald Reagan perpetuated the idea that the president possesses an inherent power over external affairs. Still the experience of their administrations demonstrated again that executive power rests on the capacity to control the public mind. Carter's failure to protect his policies from burgeoning congressional and public criticism reflected the adage that presidential power benefits from perceptions of national insecurity. Before the Soviet invasion of Afghanistan in December 1979, Carter sought to exorcise the Cold War by refusing to dwell on the Soviet problem at all. His search for relaxation of tensions proved to be his undoing when the Soviets broke the spell by invading Afghanistan. Reagan, by stimulating fears of Soviet expansionism in Central America, Africa, and the Middle East, was permitted to venture into external affairs far beyond what his critics regarded wise or prudent. Because of his extensive public and congressional following, Reagan managed to sustain a full spectrum of widely criticized policy objectives against his detractors in Congress and the public. At the same time the lingering Vietnam syndrome, both inside and outside the military forces, discouraged a resort to arms. Nevertheless, a majority tolerated, even applauded, the invasion of Grenada in October 1983 and the air attack on Libya in April 1986; that the public would condone a greater display of force was not apparent. In short, Congress and the public seemed willing to accept foreign adventurism as long as it did not involve the United States in war.

In the American constitutional system the struggle to control external policy is as endless as the challenges of an ever-changing world. But aside from certain formal arrangements, such as the Senate's authority to approve treaties, the Constitution cannot govern the exertion of influence by either the executive or the legislative branch of government. This compels Congress and the president to seek the power they require within the political system. In any executive-congressional contest over specific foreign policy issues, public opinion, the ultimate source of power in a democratic order, determines the winner. After mid-century, successive administrations won the struggle with Congress, often with ease, by exploiting Cold War insecurities. If Congress would strengthen its role, especially when that role appears vital for the proper performance of the country's external relations, it has no choice but to discover some effective means to challenge the president's special access to the public mind. For that reason the ultimate check on the unwise use of presidential power rests on the public's acceptance of a more sophisticated concept of national interest and a greater awareness of the limits of national will than it has often displayed in the past. Public understanding is crucial to the design and conduct of successful foreign relations. An administration treads on dangerous ground when it frames strategy without informing the American people under what circumstances and against what dangers it intends to use force. Karl von Clausewitz observed that a war without public support has little future. Ultimately any decision to use armed force must be explicable to the public's satisfaction. The critical issue in the perennial struggle between the president and Congress for control of external policy is the quality of the policies that the government pursues and the merit of the arguments used to sustain them.

2

WILLIAM MCKINLEY: "THE MAN AT THE HELM"

LEWIS L. GOULD

Among the presidents who have exercised the responsibilities of commander in chief during wars of the United States, the name William McKinley is not usually the first to come to mind as an important figure. The war that he waged was so brief and its outcome so overwhelming that it hardly seems a genuine conflict at all. The combat phase of the fighting with Spain began in late April 1898 and ended a little more than three months later; the peace treaty was signed on December 10, 1898. Given historical perspective, "the splendid little war," in John Hay's famous phrase, does not appear to have been an event in which the commander in chief was all that crucial to the victory of the United States.[1]

The character of President McKinley has also made an accurate evaluation of his performance in office difficult. A leader in an imperialist cause, a Republican who seemed to represent big business, and an executive who left only a fragmentary paper trail of his decision making, McKinley was not the kind of president historians are likely to esteem and respect. It has been easier over the years to fill textbooks and lectures with clichés about a presidential backbone that was like a chocolate eclair, a man who received a message from God about the Philippines, and a politician who deferred to Marcus A. Hanna and the business community.[2]

Although the majority of scholars agree regarding McKinley's irrelevance and ineptitude, there has been a dissenting minority of historians who consider that the president was a more effective and purposeful war leader than legend would have us believe. Margaret Leech, H. Wayne Morgan, David Healy, and David Trask, among

others, have argued the case for McKinley's importance and achievements during the past quarter of a century, but their findings have not overturned the commonly accepted view that McKinley was not a consequential president in war or peace.[3]

Closer examination, however, reveals that McKinley was a much more activist and innovative executive than the conventional impressions about him indicate, and his conduct of the war expanded the possibilities of what presidents could do as the leader of the nation's armed forces. By 1900, for example, the president was using the war power as a rationale for sending American troops into China at the time of the Boxer Rebellion, even though the United States was not at war with the Chinese or any other foreign power. The record supports the accuracy of the contemporary opinion of a well-informed reporter who concluded in October 1898, "No president since the time of Washington—not even Andrew Jackson himself—has ever exercised his constitutional functions as commander-in-chief of the army and navy so literally and consistently as William McKinley."[4]

McKinley came to the presidency with considerable military and executive experience. He had risen from the rank of private in the 23rd Ohio Volunteers during the Civil War to the brevet rank of major, had served in the U.S. House of Representatives for a decade and a half, and had spent four years as governor of Ohio, from 1891 to 1895. Not given to discursive letter writing, the president left only fragmentary evidence about his goals and intentions, but the record of his administration indicates that he was a quick study, read more widely than he let on, and had an effective grasp of the way that the government worked. Secretary of War Elihu Root summed up his boss very well: "He was a man of great power because he was absolutely indifferent to credit. His great desire was 'to get it done.' He cared nothing about the credit, but McKinley *always had his way.*"[5]

In the White House, McKinley was not given to musings on the nature of presidential power. The closest that he came to a statement of his view of the reach of his office was during a speech in Boston in February 1899: "Congress can declare war, but a higher power decrees its bounds and fixes its relations and responsibilities," he told an audience at the Home Market Club. "The President can direct the movements of soldiers on the field and fleets upon the sea, but he cannot foresee the close of such movements or prescribe their limits." In practice, the president proved to be an advocate of the principle that he should, in the words of a cabinet member, exercise "a close personal direction, not only of the organization of the forces but of the general plan of operations." McKinley became "the man at the helm," and one journalist called the conflict with Spain "the president's war."[6]

Circumstances soon disclosed the necessity and wisdom of that policy. The nation went into war in April 1898 with a good navy and a small, professional army that was ill prepared for the tasks it would soon be called upon to perform. Neither the leaders of the army nor the cabinet secretary who supervised them were well suited to the demands of modern war. McKinley had chosen the secretary of war, Russell A. Alger of Michigan, in 1897 at a time when fighting a foreign foe seemed improbable. A Civil War veteran, lumber magnate, and Republican stalwart, Alger had political claims on a cabinet post but little aptitude for military leadership. When he was appointed, a newspaper editor said, "We certainly tremble to contemplate the outcome of a war conducted under his direction." The national interest would have been served had McKinley fired the inefficient Alger at the outset of the fighting, but that drastic move would have posed political risks at a time when the president was easing Secretary of State John Sherman out of the cabinet.[7]

The commanding general of the army, Nelson A. Miles, was a posturing blowhard whose inability to put aside his own ego, or to give up his improbable dreams of becoming president himself, made him another source of irritation to McKinley. As one reporter delicately put it, "a generation of peace had failed to develop any one military officer of abilities so conspicuous and character so balanced as to entitle him to unquestioned leadership." McKinley eventually found a reliable military adviser in the adjutant general, Henry C. Corbin. "In all the work of organizing, planning, and operating, the President relied on his judgment," a cabinet member later recalled. However, the president remained the primary agent for shaping overall military policy.[8]

To manage a war that spanned both oceans, McKinley and his advisers soon found themselves in need of a constant flow of reliable, up-to-date information. The White House took on the appearance of a military command center. An office on the second floor became the War Room, where twenty telegraph lines, connected to a switchboard, enabled the president to be in touch with his field commander in Cuba within twenty minutes. The walls were covered with maps and charts on which officers tracked the movements of all ships in the war zones. "The War Room was never closed," noted a reporter, "and by the President's orders he was to be awakened at any hour of the night if important intelligence should come in."[9]

Within the White House direct telephone lines were installed between the president's office and the executive departments, the House, and the Senate. For a chief executive who preferred to keep his written directives to a minimum, the telephone proved to be a convenient innovation, and he relied on it extensively during the summer of 1898. As a student of presidential crisis management has observed, McKinley was employing "remote voice communication for the first time to project presidential presence into the battle zone on a near real time basis while he remained in Washington."[10] McKinley controlled the way the government learned about events, and he also supervised the manner in which his policies were conveyed to the public. "The President watches the war situation most earnestly and intently," his secretary, George B. Cortelyou, wrote in mid-June. "In the evenings before retiring he goes to the war-room and studies the dispatches before going to his room." The early, crude development of the institutions of crisis management would be one of the lasting contributions McKinley's war leadership made to the evolution of the modern presidency.[11]

How did McKinley approach the war itself and what were his goals for the United States in 1898? Although David Trask overemphasizes the extent to which domestic political goals drove the president's policy, he is correct in his judgment that McKinley did not want an open-ended conflict, nor did he have expansive overseas goals. His purpose was to end the war as quickly as possible and to persuade Spain of the wisdom of peace talks. The strategy he pursued was, in Trask's words, to pose "multiple threats to Spain's colonial empire." In essence, McKinley was fighting a limited war for limited purposes, and he did not want to expend American lives to achieve ends that the nation could not support in the long run. As a veteran of the Civil War who had "seen the dead piled up," McKinley was reluctant to subject the nation to a protracted war that would demand major societal sacrifices for victory. He became a consistent advocate for speed in the pursuit of victories that would bring Madrid to the negotiating table and end the war.[12]

McKinley's leading role in the war effort began as soon as hostilities commenced. The president conferred almost daily with his civilian secretaries and military commanders to discuss the evolving situation. As his secretary observed on June 8, "In all movements of the army and navy the President's hand is seen." One of the most important decisions was made during the early days of the conflict. On Sunday, April 24, the secretary of the navy, John D. Long, brought a draft order directing Commodore George Dewey and the Asiatic Squadron to "commence operations at once, particularly against Spanish fleet. You must capture vessels or destroy [them]." Contrary to the legend that credits Theodore Roosevelt's actions in February 1898 for Dewey's presence at Manila Bay, McKinley's decisive attack order was in line with the long-standing naval war plans to attack Spain in the Philippines.[13]

Dewey's decisive victory on May 1, 1898, led the president to take further actions to increase the American commitment in the Philippines. The number of troops assigned to the islands grew from 5,000 in early May to 20,000 by the end of the month. In his directives to the American commander, McKinley exercised the war power to outline an extensive program of military government for the areas of the Philippines under control of the United States, including the creation of a new legal system, the collection of taxes, and the confiscation of property. The strategy of attacking Spain on the periphery of its empire was now leading McKinley and his country into an Asian involvement that deepened as the war went on. But the president was the directing force of American action. He was not the "rubber-stamp" commander of Ernest May's description but rather played a decisive role in shaping policy toward the Philippines in 1898.[14]

The president's major concern as commander in chief, however, related to the liberation of Cuba. The impression in the United States before the war broke out was that defeating the Spanish in Cuba would be an easy proposition. Once the fighting began, the dimensions of the military's task came into focus. The public expected a rapid invasion of the Caribbean island and a prompt triumph over the Spanish forces there, but raising an army of sufficient size to deal with the 100,000 Spanish troops in Cuba would require weeks or even months to accomplish. Secretary Alger talked expansively of raising an army of 400,000 men within ten days, but he soon backed off from that unrealistic goal. During the early days of the war, conferences at the White House concluded that the navy should blockade Cuba and defeat the Spanish fleet. Meanwhile the army would raid the islands and extend aid to the indigenous rebel forces.[15]

Part of the blame for the lack of preparation lay with the president. During the crisis with Spain in the first three months of 1898, McKinley had regarded the army as an offensive instrument and had prevented it from using congressional appropriations to mobilize for war. Of course, an attempt to build up the army between January and April 1898 would have threatened McKinley's delicate diplomacy with Spain and left him open to the charge of insincerity in his efforts to prevent war. In any event, the ills of the army were long-standing, having grown out of a national unwillingness to use the army for more than breaking strikes and fighting Native American tribes during the Gilded Age.[16]

The administration tried to remedy these deficiencies during the spring of 1898 with a call for 125,000 volunteers and expansion of the regular army from 25,000 to 61,000 men. The surge of volunteers and the appointment of officers to lead them allowed the president to use the war as a means of promoting national unity. He named such prominent former Confederate officers as Joseph Wheeler of Alabama and Fitzhugh Lee of Virginia as major generals in the volunteers and ensured that both Democrats and Republicans were represented in the available staff positions. Even William Jennings Bryan held a volunteer commission, but McKinley made sure that his electoral rival did not get near actual combat. The president never lost sight of the political dimensions of his role as a war leader.[17]

The first month of fighting revealed the problems that the nation faced in bringing its armed strength to bear on the Spanish in Cuba. The troops lacked the wagons needed to move men and supplies, and ammunition was in short supply. Soldiers did not have enough uniforms, tents, cartridge belts, and mess kits. An effort to supply beef led to a major postwar controversy over the quality of the army's meat supply. The public looked on in dismay as troops crowded into camps across the country only to find inadequate facilities to feed, house, clothe, and train them. In one typical camp a volunteer detachment reported that "disorder prevailed, and it was impossible to learn anything regarding future movements."[18]

The confused situation of May 1898 did not last. As the weeks went by, Secretary Alger and General Corbin saw order emerge out of near chaos. Officers in the camps imposed direction and purpose on their men, and efficiency increased. By the end of July the army had achieved a state of readiness that had seemed unlikely during the tumult of May. Alger told reporters in early June, as public complaints grew, that "when war was declared, we were unprepared, yet obstacles almost insurmountable have been overcome." Alger was right, but the popular impression of military bungling had become fixed. The war had to produce some victories lest the president and his administration come under criticism for failure to achieve battlefield success.[19]

Plans to land American troops in Cuba and link up with the rebels went forward in late April until the presence of the Spanish fleet in the region led to a postponement of the expedition. Troops continued to assemble in Tampa, Florida, at the end of a single rail line amid reports of logistical delays. "No words could describe to you the confusion and lack of system and the general mismanagement of affairs here," wrote Theodore Roosevelt. Pressure was building in Washington, however, for a more ambitious assault on Cuba. The navy's capacity to maintain a blockade had been overestimated, and there was fear of European intervention if the United States pursued a passive strategy. In early May McKinley decided to authorize an invasion of Cuba, with Havana as the target. The planning of this campaign, however, rested on wildly optimistic assumptions about the army's readiness, and circumstances soon caused modifications and an eventual postponement.[20]

By the middle of the month, there were reports that the Spanish fleet had taken refuge in the harbor of Santiago de Cuba, on the southern side of the island. During the two weeks that followed these reports were confirmed, and by June 1 the American fleet, under Rear Admiral William T. Sampson, had the Spanish trapped. This news prompted an important war council meeting at the White House on May 26, when participants decided to abandon plans to attack Havana in favor of a strike against Santiago de Cuba and an expedition to seize Puerto Rico. Four days later Corbin instructed the commander of the American land forces, Major General William R. Shafter, to "capture or destroy the garrison at Santiago de Cuba." Reflecting the president's aim, Corbin reminded Shafter "of the importance of accomplishing this object with the least possible delay."[21]

Getting Shafter's force under way proved to be a formidable undertaking. As the days passed in Tampa, which was a tangle of men, supplies, and animals, the telegrams went out from the White House asking Shafter "when will you get away?" Finally, the president issued a peremptory instruction on June 7, 1898, as the troops were being loaded, "to sail at once with what force you have ready." Despite this presidential prodding, more delays ensued. The expedition did not sail until mid-June, and the troops did not reach Cuba until June 22.[22]

The commander in chief now followed the army's combat operations over the telegraph in the War Room. There was a brief skirmish at Las Guasimas on June 24 and a sharp clash at San Juan Hill on July 1. Shafter did not keep the White House informed during the day's fighting. The only message came late in the evening to disclose that he held the "outer works" of the Spanish and had suffered substantial casualties. For most of July 2 and into July 3 Shafter said nothing until he finally wired Washington that he was preparing to pull back five miles. He did not say that he had sought the surrender of the Spanish commander.[23]

Shafter's message came at a time of some anxiety for McKinley. Unsubstantiated reports in Washington hinted that the Spanish fleet had escaped from the harbor, while other messages indicated a sweeping American victory. As a result, Shafter was informed in language that McKinley had probably authorized that "of course you can judge the situation better than we can at this end of the line. If, however, you could hold your present position, especially San Juan Heights, the effect upon the country would be much better than falling back."[24]

As the dimensions of the navy's victory emerged and Shafter's resolve stiffened under White House prodding, American dominance over Spain on the battlefield became clear. Two more weeks of talks between Shafter and the Spanish commander ensued with McKinley intently watching his general. By now the president was skeptical of Shafter's capacity to fight on to victory. When the general said that his health was not good, McKinley told him to "determine whether your condition is such as to require you to relinquish command." The White House also sent General Miles to aid Shafter in the negotiations.[25]

On July 8 the Spanish general offered to evacuate Santiago de Cuba if he and his men could take their equipment and weapons to another location. Shafter recommended acceptance of the proposal as a means of saving American lives, and he warned about the possible effects of yellow fever on his forces. McKinley drafted the response to Shafter's ideas personally, and the copy in his handwriting survives in the Cortelyou papers. The president reminded Shafter of his earlier statement that he held an impregnable position and that the Spanish would eventually have to surrender unconditionally. "Under these circumstances," McKinley wrote, "your message recommending that Spanish troops be permitted to evacuate and proceed without molestation to Holguin is a great surprise, and is not approved." Another presidential telegram soon followed: "What you went to Santiago for was the Spanish army. If you allow it to evacuate with its arms you must meet it somewhere else. This is not war." As David Trask correctly comments, "McKinley wanted an early and definitive victory at Santiago de Cuba, and nothing had yet come to his attention to make him question the feasibility of such a triumph."[26]

During the week that followed the transmission of McKinley's July 9 orders, the Americans and the Spanish tried to find a formula that would allow the Spanish to surrender honorably. By July 13 the administration was again warned of the dangers of yellow fever to the troops in Cuba. In a lengthy meeting at the White House that day, McKinley decided to keep pressing the Spanish and rejected the notion of any concession to the enemy about the terms of surrender. The president, recalled one participant, expressed "himself not only vigorously, but with a certain vehemence very foreign to his usual manner." A settlement was finally arrived at that allowed the Spanish officers to keep their sidearms and specified that the United States would bear the cost of sending the defeated soldiers back to Spain. On July 17 the Spanish capitulated. Meanwhile, General Miles moved on to attack Puerto Rico, which was easily conquered during the remainder of the war.[27]

The architect of combat success had been the president. His decision to send the expedition to Santiago de Cuba had been a gamble because of the army's lack of readiness. His plans to keep maximum pressure on the Spanish in order to achieve an early and economical end to the fighting had seemed to justify the risk. When the opportunity for a decisive victory appeared, the president kept the pressure on his commanders in turn for a clear and unequivocal result. As his friend Charles G. Dawes noted, "The normal effect of the victory of Santiago might have been wholly lost if it had not been for the President's firmness." The strength of McKinley's actions during the summer of 1898 belie the historical stereotypes of his presidential performance.[28]

While pursuing military success on the battlefield, McKinley also had to use diplomacy to bring the war to an end. A negotiated settlement that achieved American war aims had always been the preferred solution. He told his diplomatic adviser, John Bassett Moore, that he wanted "not only to bring the war to a speedy conclusion, but so to conduct it as to leave no lasting animosities behind to prejudice the future friendship and commerce of the two countries." Nonetheless, McKinley expected that Spain would have to take the first step toward ending the war. As the British ambassador in Washington put it, "these people want peace ardently, but they don't want a middleman."[29]

Preparations for possible peace talks in late July 1898 put the issue before the administration of what it wanted to get out of the war. McKinley had written a brief memorandum to himself at the start of the fighting: "While we are conducting war and until its conclusion we must keep all we can get; when the war is over we must keep what we want." By the time the Americans began negotiations through the French ambassador, the fate of Cuba had been sealed. Spain had lost the island. The president then insisted that Puerto Rico and most notably the Philippines should also be part of deliberations for a peace treaty.[30]

The Philippines had become a central issue for the president because of the growing American presence in the islands, the possibility of foreign challenges to U.S. interests, and the problem of the Philippines nationalists who wanted an independent republic after Spain was ousted. Within the United States—and especially within the Republican party—a consensus seemed to be forming in favor of an expansionist policy. Henry Cabot Lodge warned that if the islands were returned to Spain "the Democrats will unite in attacking us for doing so as false to freedom & humanity & we shall have no answer."[31]

The president carefully guided the discussions in the cabinet meetings during the last week of July 1898. At his urging the cabinet decided to leave the ultimate status of the Philippines to the peace commissioners who would be negotiating with the Spanish. The administration also concluded that "no man will be put on that commission who is hostile to the acquisition of outside territory." Throughout these deliberations the president worked to ensure that his scenario would determine the outcome. When Secretary of State William R. Day suggested settling for a naval base at Manila, McKinley did not put the idea to a vote in the cabinet. He explained, half in jest, to his old friend, "I was afraid it would be carried."[32]

In the framing of the peace terms, as in the conduct of the war, Cortelyou wrote in his diary, the president's "guiding hand will be seen at every point in the negotiations." The young secretary realized this fact on July 31, when he said to McKinley that the way in which the diplomatic reply to Spain had been shaped "was a good example of the development of a public paper under discussion—that there had been material changes by himself and the Cabinet since the first draft was made." The president then let Cortelyou read the memorandum that he had prepared five days earlier setting out the American position. "These terms as thus stated by the President were exactly those which were finally transmitted to the Spanish Minister for Foreign Affairs, through the Ambassador of France."[33]

McKinley conducted the negotiations with the French ambassador during late July and early August in the face of military problems in Cuba that undermined the American's diplomatic position. The issue was the health of the soldiers on the island. First, the president received disturbing news regarding the conditions on two ships that were transporting troops to New York. Shafter informed Washington that "at any time an epidemic of yellow fever is liable to occur." McKinley moved quickly to help the soldiers on the transports, but moving the remaining American forces would not be easy. The administration did not yet realize the extent to which illness had crippled the forces led by Shafter, who had not received the evacuation orders he had sought.[34]

The general called his officers together and then informed Washington that the men should immediately be sent back to the United States. "If it is not done, I believe the death rate will be appalling." Shafter included statements from his medical officers and commanders to support his decision. These documents did not get to Washington, but other news from Shafter impelled the administration to start moving ships to Cuba. "We are doing everything possible to relieve your gallant command," Secretary Alger wrote.[35]

While the negotiations with Spain were still under way, the White House did not want news of the troops' predicament to leak out. Some of Shafter's officers, including Leonard Wood, Joseph Wheeler, and Theodore Roosevelt, gave a copy of what became known as the round robin to reporters in Cuba. In a separate letter, Roosevelt observed that the army was "ripe for dying like rotten sheep." The reports produced a sensation when they appeared in the national press on August 4, 1898.[36]

The episode outraged the commander in chief. McKinley drafted a letter to Shafter that described the round robin as "most unfortunate from every point of view." He added that "the publication of the letter makes the situation one of great difficulty. No soldier reading that report if ordered to Santiago but will feel that he is marching to certain death." McKinley was beginning to realize that he would have to do something about Alger and the War Department. "Unless drastic measures are resorted to," Cortelyou wrote, "the Administration of that great branch of the federal service will be one of the few blots on the brilliant record in the conduct of the war."[37]

But luck was with the administration, and the Spanish could not exploit the situation of Shafter's troops in Cuba. Their response to the American terms conceded the eventual loss of Cuba and Puerto Rico to the United States in the peace treaty and sought only to salvage something in the Philippines. To buy time, Spain fell back on the need of its government to consult the Cortes, the legislative branch. That ploy did not sit well with McKinley, who would not "lend myself to entering into these considerations of domestic government." Spain gave in, and the armistice was signed on Friday, August 12, 1898.[38]

During the months after the war ended, McKinley moved adroitly to limit the political damage of the public's unhappiness with the performance of the War Department. He allowed Alger to take most of the public blame for the problems, in part because the secretary had also taken credit for many of the positive aspects of the war. More substantively, McKinley set up a commission, headed by General Grenville M. Dodge, to examine the War Department's record and investigate the charges against it. The effect of this tactic was to stave off a congressional inquiry into the administration's war record.[39]

His actions as commander in chief during the summer of 1898 had a decided impact on McKinley's conception of the presidential office. At the end of the year, as he signed an order to transfer American installations that lay outside the United States, he observed, "It seems odd to be directing the transfer of navy yards, naval stations &c in Cuba." The rationale for these unprecedented actions was his status as commander in chief, and the war power was a primary resource on which he relied in 1898.[40]

His dependence on his standing as commander in chief continued during the rest of his administration. He used this authority to govern Puerto Rico, Cuba, the Philippines, and the Pacific dependencies for several years after the fighting with Spain had ended. These interim military governments continued for some time—eighteen months in Puerto Rico, more than two years in the Philippines, and three and a half years in Cuba. The army officers and civil administrators who acted as the president's agents exercised broad powers over political, economic, and social institutions in these foreign lands. The record of what occurred led one scholar of military government to observe in 1904, "In America we were supposed to have started out with an Executive with carefully defined powers, but we are now developing one with prerogatives which must be the envy of crowned heads."[41]

The war in the Philippines represented a striking extension of McKinley's responsibility as commander in chief. In December 1898, when the peace treaty with Spain had been signed but not yet ratified, he informed the army commander that the capture of Manila and the capitulation of the Spanish forces had "practically effected" the conquest of all the islands. He ordered the extension of military government "with all possible dispatch to the whole of the ceded territory." By the time the Senate ratified the treaty, fighting between the Americans and Filipinos had begun. The president continued to exercise his military power to rule the islands.[42]

In December 1899 McKinley, after ten months of governing the Philippines, informed Congress that "it does not seem desirable that I should recommend at this time a specific and final form of government for these islands." While the Filipinos were in revolt, the executive, acting through the military, would be supreme. When the insurrection was over, a condition that the president would proclaim, then Congress could act. Meanwhile, said the president, "I shall use the authority vested in me by the Constitution and the statutes to uphold the sovereignty of the United States in those distant islands as in all other places where our flag rightfully floats." It took another year for Congress, with the blessing of the White House, to pass the Spooner Amendment. That measure substituted legislative authorization in place of the war power as McKinley's justification for his continuing actions in the Philippines, but it also left him with "all military, civil, and judicial powers necessary to govern the Philippine Islands." A scholar of presidential commissions noted more than forty-five years ago that "the first and second Philippines Commissions show rather well the lengths to which the President can go under the inherent powers which he derives from the fact that he is Commander-in-Chief."[43]

Another case of McKinley's use of such powers occurred during the summer of 1900 when Boxer rebels and Chinese troops surrounded the foreign legations in Peking. The United States dispatched five thousand soldiers and marines as a part of the international relief expedition. With Congress out of Washington and an election campaign soon to begin, McKinley "on his own sole authority as Commander-in-Chief" dispatched American forces from the Philippines and the United States. There was some criticism of his actions at the time. A Philadelphia newspaper called the move "an absolute declaration of war by the executive without the authority or knowledge of Congress, and it is without excuse because it is not a necessity." McKinley turned aside calls for a special session of Congress because he believed that the war power gave him the right to send troops to China.[44]

By the end of McKinley's presidency, some interesting comments were circulating about the extent to which the power of his office had expanded during his administration. Perry Belmont, a Democratic critic, said that "since the inauguration of President McKinley there has been an enormous extension of Executive power," a development that Belmont linked to the president's invocation of the war power as commander in chief. McKinley had shown himself to be an adroit innovator in the use of his authority as commander in chief to achieve victory during the war with Spain and to govern the empire that the nation acquired as a result. David Healy is correct in his judgment that McKinley was "in many respects the first modern American Commander-in-chief." The evidence seems equally persuasive that McKinley's performance as commander in chief was part of a larger role of executive leadership that also made him truly the first modern president.[45]

3

WOODROW WILSON:
A MISFIT IN OFFICE?

ROBERT H. FERRELL

President Woodrow Wilson may have looked like a commander in chief, and because of the Constitution's description of the president of the United States he often found himself so described, but in truth the role was utterly foreign to his being. This remarkable chief executive has gone down in history as one of the great holders of his high office; yet his behavior during American participation in World War I was almost never that of commander in chief.[1] The reasons why Wilson did not fulfill this part of his constitutional role are many and relate partly to the time in which he lived, in part to his work as an educator—first as a professor at Bryn Mawr, Connecticut Wesleyan, and Princeton, then as president of the last institution—and partly to a personal outlook that brought him to a dislike of, almost an aversion for, military affairs and military men.

Wilson grew up in the high noon of the Victorian era when war seemed virtually abolished save for expeditions in Africa or Asia. To take part in a war between white men, between Anglo-Saxons as the word had it, would be race suicide—to use another description of the time. Words were what advanced humankind: the words of literature, the words of oratory. Wilson grew to manhood during this wonderful time, a sort of poised moment in the history of the world, and neither he nor his contemporaries had any idea of the reckoning that was about to take place. They believed in Western Civilization because what they saw emboldened them. All was right with the world. For Wilson, this outlook was reinforced by his experiences in academe, where he was quickly a huge success: most popular professor on the campus at Princeton and afterward the first nonclergy-

man to be president of that university. If the very fact of peace, he might have thought, could not remake the world of his time, it would be possible to educate the new generation to better ways. He lived at a time when people took the Latin root of the word *education* seriously. "Princeton in the Nation's Service," was the title of one of his best-known orations, and a century ago, Wilson and others believed in such words about education. Last, there was the view of life that came out of this president's Scottish and English inheritance, perhaps also out of Presbyterianism. Wilson wanted to believe that wars were a thing of the past—that war was against the nature of educated, modern peoples. For him even to consider himself a commander in chief was a kind of archaism from the eighteenth century. He was a student of English constitutional history as much as American, and in the English tradition the navy was important and the army was something to watch, for it could co-opt the state. European governments had fallen victim to the danger but not the English—except during the Cromwellian period, which was an interregnum in English history—and the American experience paralleled the English. George Washington had announced, although in the words of Alexander Hamilton, that the European experience was un-American. The only really large war in American history up to Wilson's time was the Civil War, and he did not believe that war was part of the nation's practical experience. As a native Virginian he justified it and said on more than one occasion (which incidentally endeared him when election time came) that the South had "absolutely nothing to apologize for,"[2] but he did not equate the War for Southern Independence with the kind of war the Europeans were talking about.[3]

It is a curious, almost forgotten fact that Wilson in 1917–1918 was a complete misfit as commander in chief, so far as the nation's war economy and mobilization of the War Department to conduct a fighting war on the Western Front in France were concerned. In regard to these vital elements of war making, his behavior was paradoxical, strangely apart from his fighting words but apart also from his reputation, which was greatly deserved, for being a leader of Congress and the nation. The president in 1917 was only a few years from his extraordinary triumphs at the beginning of his first term, when he had confounded the nation, and certainly the nation's informed electorate, by showing that he could come from governing a diminutive college and then a small state (New Jersey) to lead the country, that he would not merely propose—as had countless chief executives before him—great measures for passage by Congress but he could force Congress to do his will. Many years earlier he had written a doctoral dissertation, published in 1885 with the title *Con-*

gressional Government, in which he displayed how presidents after Lincoln had shown themselves subservient to Congress and thereby lacked leadership. Upon taking office Wilson displayed himself as no academic, no closet intellectual, but as a man who could enforce his will upon what had always been (and would, of course, be again) the most recalcitrant governing body in history. But in 1917 and 1918 his great leadership diminished virtually to nothing, save for a sudden and for him providential reassertion of authority during a few brief weeks in the spring of 1918—a reassertion that got him safely out of what was surely the most dangerous crisis of his presidency before the failure of the League of Nations proposal in the U.S. Senate some months later. The student of politics wonders what possessed the president to let things go, in regard to economic mobilization for war and in regard to the War Department, and to let everything cascade toward crisis.

In its top administration, economic mobilization was so badly handled that for a full year it was a travesty of what administrative action should be. The president seemed to believe that all he needed to do was make a public statement, form a committee, and forget the problem. A later generation would describe much of what happened as a public relations problem, and yet that would be unfair to the president; Wilson instead appears to have believed that motion equaled achievement. The first formal organization to oversee what would become the war economy actually was not Wilson's doing but that of the U.S. Navy, perhaps because that part of what was then a two-part armed forces was better acquainted with industry than the army, where manpower rather than machines dominated. The navy at that time had a far larger budget than the army, and most of its money went for ships and maintenance, only a small amount for the men who sailed the ships. The navy in 1916 organized a consulting board of scientists that included such prominent figures as Thomas A. Edison and Henry Ford. Its secretary, Grosvenor B. Clarkson, sent out inventory forms to discover the country's industrial resources, and though 30,000 forms came back, many did not. The consulting board and its secretary then disappeared into a perhaps well-deserved oblivion. The assistant secretary of the navy, young Franklin D. Roosevelt, privately sneered at its efforts and told an assistant that Ford was so ignorant of naval matters he thought a submarine was something to eat.

In August 1916, Congress—again, not the president, whose business it might have been—created a Council of National Defense (CND), another group of prominent citizens who worked without pay and whose private concerns limited their time spent on council duties. With war getting ominously close, the council met for the first time in December and, like its predecessor, appointed a director. After April 6, 1917, each member of the CND formed a committee presumably to supervise part of industrial mobilization. These committees themselves produced committees, and soon there were 150. Throughout 1917 the CND accomplished little or nothing except to have three successive heads, none of whom seemed able to control the council's amorphous body. At last a crisis in economic and military mobilization, the worst domestic crisis of Wilson's presidency, drove the nation's chief executive to appoint Bernard M. Baruch, a member of the War Industries Board—one of the CND's parts—as chair of that board, to which the president by executive order passed control of the entire work of industrial mobilization. By the time of Baruch's appointment in March 1918, America's participation in the war would be over in less than nine months.[4]

But it is in the details of economic mobilization in World War I rather than in administrative confusion that one sees the proof of maladministration, and it is instructive to turn to two major mobilization efforts, shipbuilding and powder manufacture. It would also be possible to look to other production programs, such as rifles, machine guns, artillery, tanks, planes, in which there were successes and failures—some success with rifles and machine guns, failure with the others. The efforts to produce ships and powder, however, best illustrate how Wilsonian administration affected economic mobilization, and thus the American war effort.

Undoubtedly some of the failure to turn out ships lay in the nation's near total unpreparedness for the task, for at the outset of the war it possessed a minuscule merchant marine, a very small number of ways on which to construct ships, and few workers and managers skilled in shipbuilding. The merchant marine had declined precipitously from the time of the Civil War, when attacks by Confederate raiders had driven much of the American merchant marine to foreign flags. The decline was visible indeed by 1917, when the total American ocean-going tonnage was a bare one million tons, which was about what German submarines sunk in the single month of April 1917. The number of American ways had declined to only sixty, for both steel and wooden ships, a grossly inadequate number considering the desperate need in 1917. American businessmen had taken up other enterprises, and ship construction had become a seldom practiced if not lost art.

More distressing than the long tradition of marine neglect were the officials whom the president installed to supervise the work of regeneration. None had experience in shipbuilding. Two of the men had industrial experience, and the president neatly balanced them with two who did not. Wilson first placed the Shipping Board in the hands of a city reformer named William E. Denman, an obscure individual who during a brief moment in the spring of 1917 enjoyed national prominence.[5] It is true that Wilson then balanced the inexperienced Denman with Major General George W. Goethals, the man whom Theodore Roosevelt had picked out of the army's Engineer Corps and told to go down to Panama and make the dirt fly. In building the Panama Canal, Goethals had supervised one of the world's greatest engineering feats and might have done the same with shipping in 1917–1918. Instead, he got into a public argument with Denman, who had little respect for the aging general, and Goethals submitted his resignation to the president in the summer of 1917. Wilson accepted with alacrity, also asking for and receiving Denman's resignation, as if the two officials were on the same plane of incompetence.[6]

The president then chose as head of the Shipping Board another unknown, Edward N. Hurley, who at least had some experience as a businessman. To take charge of the board's operating agency, the Emergency Fleet Corporation, Wilson chose another prominent figure, the steelmaker Charles M. Schwab—but not before he had tried a rear admiral, Washington Lee Capps, as Goethals's replacement; Schwab took over in April 1918. Presumably Hurley would deal with the president, Congress, and the public, Schwab with the work of shipbuilding. A former assistant to Andrew Carnegie, who founded the Bethlehem Steel Corporation, Schwab, who took over in April 1918, moved from yard to yard in a private railroad car urging shipyard workers around the country to get on with their assignments. But like his predecessors, Schwab did not have enough time to produce the results he and the nation desired before the war ended.

With regard to ships one must conclude that almost everything that could have gone wrong did. The nation had allowed the merchant marine virtually to collapse and had nothing on which to build. The personalities chosen for the task were inadequate; lack of talent canceled out talent. Planning also may have been on too large a scale, too grandiose. Planners decided to increase twentyfold the number of ways around the country, from 60 to 1,200. But time did not permit new construction. The Shipping Board had to make do with confiscating ships already under construction, appropriating enemy and neutral ships in harbor at the time of the declaration of war, and such legerdemain as bisecting lake ships to get them through the Welland Canal. The board planned to produce two million gross tonnage of new ships in the war's first year. It actually produced only 664,000 tons in 1917 and 1,301,000 in 1918, miserable figures considering the alarming needs.[7]

In examining the war economy it is also instructive to consider production of powder for the American Expeditionary Forces (AEF), gathering in France under the leadership of General John J. Pershing, and see how presidential prejudice, really presidential populism, produced a second disaster for the war economy. If the war had lasted into 1919, powder production, like shipbuilding, might have become a triumph. Had Pershing received the enormous reinforcements that he had requested—he seemed to be aiming for one hundred divisions, each consisting of 40,000 men, a number that included 12,000 support troops per unit—there would have been great need for powder, and Wilson's final arrangement for its production would have supplied it. But because of a contention with the country's most important powder maker, the Du Pont Company, the administration delayed for nearly a year in setting in motion an arrangement that would have guaranteed Pershing the ammunition he required in 1918. Fortunately the Allies, mainly the British, supplied it.

71

The story of powder in World War I is not well known, and yet it stands revealed in an authorized biography of Pierre S. Du Pont that has not attracted much academic attention.[8] The authors of the biography show clearly that the Wilson administration's basic problem with the company was that Pierre Du Pont's efficiency as a powder maker and his business acumen were too much for President Wilson and Secretary of War Newton D. Baker. At the outset of the war the Allies had gone to the Du Pont Company with huge orders, as it was far more economical to have Du Pont produce powder than to ship to Britain or France the four to nine pounds of raw materials required to make one pound of powder. The Du Pont Company of course took the orders, and knowing that the resultant new plants would probably have little use in peacetime, the head of the firm charged the Allies enough to amortize the entire complex of plants. Unlike his competitors, Winchester and Remington, who financed their capital expansion by borrowing money against payments they would receive in the future, Du Pont wrote off everything by charging for it. Certainly the company made a profit, and even with the Wilson administration's retroactive Du Pont–dedicated tax of 12.5 percent on profits in 1916, shareholders received more than $62,000,000 in dividends that year, exactly the face value of the company's common stock.

It was the Du Pont Company's success, and profits, though not from American orders, that excited the president and his secretary, and when the United States became involved in the war, these two executives of the nation's war effort virtually ignored Du Pont. Baruch, who in March 1917 had an advisory role in one of the Council of National Defense's committees, wrote personally to Pierre Du Pont and inquired about the status of all raw materials needed for explosives, but that was all; otherwise, silence descended. Confused by this situation, the company's head wrote Baker that the company's entire production had been taken up until September 15, 1917, inferring that if the U.S. government wanted powder it would have to arrange for new plants. Baker did not take the hint. One might contend that the secretary and his superior in the White House did not know at that time whether America's contribution to the war would be largely ships and supplies other than powder or perhaps only financing of Allied war orders. Baker and Wilson may indeed have been confused. But Wilson had sponsored a Draft Bill within days of the declaration, which became law in May, and a necessary sequel would have been to equip the levies so raised. In any event it would have been good judgment to have kept in touch with the nation's premier powder maker. The fault of omission seems, in retrospect, one of commission.

In the autumn word came from the president's confidant in London and Paris, Colonel Edward M. House, that a crisis was at hand: Collapse of the Russian front and the imminent dissolution of the provisional regime in Russia might well allow the Central Powers to transfer hundreds of thousands of troops to the Western Front and bring a breakthrough in the spring. When word came from House, the War Department got into action, though without getting in touch with the machinery of mobilization—the War Industries Board and, behind it, Secretary Baker and the president. Major General William Crozier signed up Du Pont for a $250,000,000 contract, the largest single contract ever granted by the American government up to that time, that included $90,000,000 for new powder plants. Within days Secretary Baker had canceled the contract, and for weeks afterward the Du Pont Company did not know what the government in Washington would do.

It gradually became clear that Wilson and Baker feared giving such a large contract to Du Pont, feared the reaction from the public, which knew about the company's huge profits the year before and would see only assistance to a so-called "merchant of death." At one juncture Baker remarked privately that he had "just come from the White House" and that the country was going to win the war without Du Pont. President Wilson appointed a western mining executive, Daniel C. Jackling, to head the government's powder program, and Jackling immediately went to Pierre Du Pont and asked for help. A big contract went to a construction firm with no experience in powder making, the Thompson-Starrett Company, which insisted that Du Pont take half of the contract. By this time Secretary Baker realized his error, saw the possibility of losing the war without Du Pont, and allowed the Delaware company to take half, and more, of the new contract. In the end Du Pont's plant, Old Hickory near

Nashville, Tennessee, was in production just as the war ended. On the war's last day the Thompson-Starrett plant, called Nitro at Charleston, West Virginia, began production.

Some years before World War I, in the 1890s, Professor Woodrow Wilson of Princeton taught a course on the theory of administration while a visiting professor at Johns Hopkins University in Baltimore and took his meals in the same boarding house as one of his young students, Newton Baker. This chance encounter was to have fateful results for the management of the War Department in 1917–1918. The student went to Cleveland where he assisted the reform mayor, Tom L. Johnson, was himself elected mayor and made a considerable reputation championing a three-cent ice cream cone, a three-cent streetcar fare, and a three-cent admission to a municipal dance hall where young men and women could meet under wholesome circumstances. He even arranged an annual contribution of $10,000 to the local orchestra, an unheard-of profligacy. Wilson watched Baker's rise with pride and in 1913 offered him a position as secretary of the interior, which the mayor declined. In 1916, with no experience with the military, Baker accepted the secretaryship of war, succeeding Lindley M. Garrison of New Jersey who had resigned after the president refused to reform the highly politicized National Guard.

Baker quickly made a reputation in Washington. Boyish in appearance, a man so short in stature that he was accustomed to sitting behind his massive desk in the War Department with one leg curled under him, he was almost inconspicuous standing next to the bulky generals. He was an attractive civilian figure in a forest of uniforms. On his desk was always a fresh flower. His ideas were those of a reformer; he was a close friend of Frederic C. Howe, with whom he had roomed in college. Although he made excellent speeches. He spoke so rapidly—225 words a minute—that stenographers had difficulty following him, his speeches made excellent sense and were gracious, thoughtful, and frequently witty.[9]

Baker's modus operandi in the War Department pleased his military subordinates. He seemed to hold a reverence for military men, liking all the officers he met, without exception. He especially liked

74

the two chiefs of staff in the critical year of 1917, Major Generals Hugh L. Scott and Tasker H. Bliss. Whatever these chiefs desired, Baker backed them up, once saying to General Scott: "You know all about this. I know nothing. You must treat me as a father would his son."[10] He later informed his first biographer, Frederick Palmer, that he had learned this subordination of the civilian to the military from his father, who had told him of an episode involving General Robert E. Lee and President Jefferson Davis. According to the story, once when Davis was giving Lee military advice, the latter unbuckled his sword and handed it to Davis, who immediately ceased the advice. Such an arrangement, the younger Baker believed, was far more beneficial to the Confederacy than the way in which President Abraham Lincoln, Secretary of War Edwin M. Stanton, and Major General Henry W. Halleck had constantly interfered in the operations of General Ulysses S. Grant.[11]

Baker thus was a remarkable contradiction, or a bundle of them, much like his chief, the president. Baker's private secretary, Ralph Hayes, believed that the reason Baker and Wilson got along so well, apart from their fond relationship of student and teacher, was that "their mental processes were either so much alike or so harmonious."[12] Baker looked and talked like the civilian he was. At the same time he let the War Department generals do what they wanted.

The reason Baker acted this way is not difficult to divine. First, he must have allowed Scott and the others to do what they wished because of a sense of his own inadequacies in military matters. Second, he did not believe, as Elting E. Morison has shown so perspicaciously, that it was his task as a public servant to run the enterprises he presided over. Morison has written that Baker acted as if he held "a sort of pastoral office." He considered that his duty was to exhort, to elucidate, and above all to persuade, not to order or command.[13]

It is possible that Baker learned this pastoral idea from Wilson's course on the theory of administration at Johns Hopkins. But one can only add that such a procedure in a brassy place like the War Department in Washington was fantastically wrong. A more recent biographer of Baker has written that the secretary of war was the head, not the figurehead, of a great and successful enterprise.[14] The first of these judgments seems difficult to believe. As for the latter, the enterprise was great, but Baker's contribution was great only in its ineptitude. Success came only after Baker, in a fit of efficiency, passed the duties of army chief of staff to Major General Peyton C. March in March 1918. This highly efficient general paid little attention to his nominal chief, who had an office adjoining that of the chief of staff. At the beginning of his tenure, March discovered that on Baker's desk was a buzzer that the secretary could press when he wanted the chief of staff. The first time Baker pressed it, March returned to his office and pulled out the wire, uprooting the buzzer.

But what had all this to do with Baker's superior, President Wilson? The most obvious connection, as previously mentioned, was the president's quixotic appointment of an erstwhile student. Having made this mistake, the president should have watched the result and taken measures to get Baker out of the War Department instead of keeping him there until March 4, 1921. Wilson always took every possible occasion to protect Baker. Colonel House, always deft and extremely careful, especially when approaching his good friend the president, suggested to Wilson just before the beginning of the war that Baker and his counterpart in the Navy Department, Secretary Josephus Daniels, should be relieved. House did not like either one. They were good men, he wrote in his diary, but their goodness could be effective only in peacetime, and they "did not fit in with war." The colonel also thought that they did not have public support and the mistakes they were sure to make would be laid upon the shoulders of the president. House believed that Wilson "had taken a gamble that there would be no war and had lost" and must proceed to bite the War and Navy Department bullets. In his exegesis the colonel resorted to the metaphor of wood and said—in his diary, probably not to the president—that Baker and Daniels were not good timber. To all this, or something close to it, the president "listened with a kindly and sympathetic attention and while he argued with me upon many of the points, he did it dispassionately."[15]

The most remarkable testimony to Wilson's ill judgment once he had appointed Baker, and a testimony about Wilson's idea of how a commander in chief should act, came some years later, and Baker in full innocence made it himself. The former secretary of war, back in Cleveland, wrote Pershing's principal supply officer, Major General

James G. Harbord, in 1929 that "I think the world and you would be very much surprised indeed if you could realize how completely President Wilson let me run the War Department without ever an order, and with only the rarest suggestion, from him." Baker said he tried to keep Wilson informed by reports, formal and otherwise, "but his time was much taken up with other things and I frequently found it difficult to keep him in touch with the larger activities of the Department much less the detail." Baker told Harbord that as far as the selection of officers was concerned, he did not consult the president about anything except the appointment of Pershing and the refusal to allow Major General Leonard Wood to go to France. He did give the president the lists of promotions to general officer, but then that information was required of him as the president had to nominate general officers to the Senate.[16]

In examining the Wilsonian War Department in 1917–1918 one turns finally to the army's first two wartime chiefs of staff, Hugh L. Scott and Tasker H. Bliss, who were as much misfits in their offices, for the purpose of war, as were the secretary of war and his chief, the president. How the president could have tolerated them is difficult to comprehend, other than by the fact that Wilson himself was so unwarlike, so unimpressed, even repelled one might say, by the work of war.

The case of Scott was almost alarming. He appears to have received the rank of brigadier general because immediately after Wilson's first inauguration in 1913 the president asked General Wood, then chief of staff, if he, as president, had the authority to appoint a general. Wood said he did. The president then promoted Scott, whose brother had been a member of the faculty at Princeton and had supported Wilson during disputes with the faculty over their membership in the eating clubs and the organization of the graduate school. Having thus attained general officer rank by preferment, Scott perhaps managed to become chief of staff through the same channel. He never should have gotten so far. For one thing, he was troubled with sleepiness. Secretary of the Interior Franklin K. Lane wrote privately in February 1917 that at a meeting Scott just fell asleep—"Mars and Morpheus in One!" Moreover, Scott knew little about the war raging in Europe. One day he asked a colonel on his staff, Robert E. Lee Mickey, about the Battle of the Marne. "Mickey," he said, "everybody's talking about the Battle of the Marne. What happened at the Battle of the Marne anyway?"[17]

Baker liked Scott very much and later described him fondly, although in 1918 under pressure from General March he concurred in Scott's relief from the command of a training camp at Fort Dix, New Jersey. March and Baker together had gone up to Dix and there listened with agitation—the war was on—while the old general took forty-five minutes to describe the meaning of the feathers in an Indian war bonnet. Scott had been an Indian fighter in the old days and once had stood on a high peak with Captain Frederick Benteen, of Custer fame, and there they had seen herds of buffalo that filled the plains for twenty miles. Those had been Scott's good days. In 1917–1918 he should have been on the front porch of the Old Soldiers Home in Washington, D.C.[18]

After her husband's relief from Fort Dix, Scott's wife wrote Baker plaintively asking that Scott receive the four stars that had gone to March as chief of staff and that Congress had also conferred upon Scott's successor as chief, General Bliss.[19]

Tasker Bliss did not fit the War Department's needs in 1917–1918 any more than Scott had, if for a different reason. Scott had written orders on little pads of paper, in a large, bold script, a sort of symbol of his inefficiency. Bliss was in comparison a scholar; he knew Greek and Latin and would have done well as a professor of classical languages and literature in a small college. Instead he seems to have believed that he could analyze not merely warfare but international relations as well, although he had no experience in either. Robert L. Bullard, who became commander of the Second Army under Pershing and was one of the two officers to receive the rank of lieutenant general during the war, despised Bliss, who he said was a theorist with almost no practical experience with troops. As for the international analyses, Bliss later made them when he was one of the five American commissioners at the Paris Peace Conference. He wrote dozens of memorandums about foreign affairs in Europe and elsewhere, memos that President Wilson may not have read carefully. But, to be sure, in dealing with the War Department it did not matter much if one wrote brief notes, as did Scott, or lengthy memos, as did Bliss. Neither of these officers was a sufficient mover of the bureaucracy, the extraordinary shuffling and paper-passing of which disgraced the department during the first year of American participation in World War I.[20]

As the weeks and months went by and the year 1917 drew toward its end, increasing criticism of the war effort, in regard to both economic and military mobilization, began to be heard across the country. The furies were gathering. At last, matters moved into a crisis, and President Wilson, as commander in chief, had to face that crisis.

Some of the criticism of the administration's handling of economic and military mobilization was, beyond doubt, personal and political. At the beginning of the war, former president Theodore Roosevelt had asked to lead a division, and the administration had properly turned him down—Roosevelt was still full of intellectual keenness but physically not up to such a task, no longer the young Rough Rider of 1898. Moreover, his division would have drawn off some of the best officers that the regular army possessed, which Baker and Wilson could not have allowed. In addition, his commissioning as a major general would have ruined the decision of the War Department to appoint most field-grade officers for the line, major and above, from the regular army. The result was that Roosevelt, who never had liked "that skunk in the White House," went into opposition and soon was writing editorials published and syndicated by the *Kansas City Star* that were increasingly critical of what he boisterously described as the slowness—he used other words—of the Washington leadership, civil and military.

There was a personal-political element about the criticism, and yet it was more than that. Wilson and Baker watched the criticism mount and consoled themselves—and actually believed it was the truth—that the critics were inspired by personal and Republican venom. But war mobilization had been so poorly led that the critics had much more in mind. Senator Henry Cabot Lodge expressed their feelings when he wrote Lord Bryce on December 24, 1917: "The fact is that the president has no administrative capacity. He lives in the sunshine. He wants nobody to tell him the truth apparently and he has a perfect genius for selecting little men for important places."[21] These critics had tired of William Denman and his argument with General Goethals, would have been outraged over the president's treatment of Pierre Du Pont had they known of its proportions, and were exasperated by Baker and Scott and Bliss. When Roosevelt criticized the president in the *Star* he undoubtedly had himself in mind as civil head of a new administration and Leonard Wood for the War Department. Many critics would have supported such changes, and the combination might have done great things—what a magnificent duo they would have been in wartime Washington!

At the beginning of the crisis over economic and military mobilization the president's opponents chose to focus, not on Wilson, although the target was tempting, but on the War Department. The president could exert all the power of his office against critics however well informed and patriotic, but Baker and Scott and Bliss had no such protection. It was also easier to take on the War Department rather than the incompetent management of the war economy, which was a scattered proposition compared to the better-organized War Department, conveniently concentrated in the old State, War, and Navy Building, a monstrous mountain of masonry next to the White House.

The department was in sad shape. Its principal administrative apparatus, the so-called bureau system, had simply broken down. Secretary of War John C. Calhoun had created the system after the War of 1812, placing each major activity of the department in a separate bureau, and by the time of the Wilson administration a general known as the bureau chief headed each of these satrapies. The system had collapsed before, under the strain of military operations against Spain in 1898, which for the army had put into Cuba in the vicinity of Santiago a force smaller than one of the divisions under Pershing's command in France.

During the Taft administration, Chief of Staff Wood had taken steps to enforce the intent of the Root reforms of 1903 and force the bureau chiefs into subordination to the then secretary of war, Henry L. Stimson. But the chiefs were clever fellows, long accustomed to sly maneuvering, and they soon bounded back in 1916 when an act of

Congress stipulated that no officer of the general staff could hold an administrative post. Secretary Baker benignly accepted this attenuation of the authority of Generals Scott and Bliss, which perhaps was not a bad idea for them, but the result when war broke out was that the department was again operating as a highly fragmented organization, each bureau chief doing what seemed right in his own eyes. Baker compounded the situation by giving each chief a "hunting license" to search out and obtain, or else make contracts for, scarce supplies. After the war a perspicacious War Department colonel wrote that the result was a "slowing down" that almost paralyzed the war machine in the winter of 1917–1918. James E. Hewes many years later, in an official study of army administration, excoriated the bureau system and Baker's part in enlarging its extraordinary inefficiencies. Baker, Hewes wrote, "had had little contact with the management of large-scale enterprises where the necessity for firm executive control was taken for granted." Hewes concluded, "Without effective leadership the War Department bumped its way from one crisis to another toward disaster."[22]

At this juncture a combination of acts of God, and an act by an administration official brought on the crisis that had been approaching. The war economy was creaking along, not seeming to be getting very far; Pershing had been in France for six months and had received only four of the thirty divisions Baker had promised him. Then the winter of 1917–1918 turned appallingly cold, the coldest in fifty years, −20 degrees Fahrenheit in Boston, −16 in Albany. The good Lord (Wilson's critics might have said) improved upon the winter cold by producing two huge snowstorms. On January 5, 1918, winds of fifty-five miles an hour brought the first, a fifteen-inch snowfall that blocked railroad terminals and all but stopped movement around the country. The second blizzard struck six days afterward. Then came one of the most inept orders by a federal administration official in the twentieth century, perhaps since 1789.

The president in his mobilization efforts had appointed a Princeton colleague and later the president of Williams College, Harry A. Garfield, son of the assassinated president, as head of the Fuel Administration. Garfield found a perfect mess, which in fact had been caused by the president himself. Wilson personally had fixed the price of bituminous coal at two dollars a ton, when a price of three dollars was necessary to keep marginal mines in operation. Production losses began late in the summer of 1917, and by December coal production was down by six million tons a month. At that time, when almost all energy was produced by coal—in houses and factories and to operate ships—the loss was impossible, and the unmercifully bad winter days of January 1918 immediately produced a coal crisis. Even before that, ships had been unable to depart from eastern ports because of empty bunkers, and freight cars full of war matériel had piled up all the way to Pittsburgh because of the inability to get the ships out of port. Things had gotten so bad that the army used ships for storage. Garfield appears to have had no presidential guidance, and on January 16, with the coal crisis upon him, he ordered a five-day embargo on the use of coal in almost all factories east of the Mississippi, beginning the next day, after which nonessential industry was to go on a five-day week, shutting for nine "heatless Mondays" from January 28 until March 25.

The storm that burst upon the administration was one of the two worst crises of Wilson's presidency. It was fortunate for the president that only after the coal crisis did the economic cost become evident—in lost wages and production the coal embargo cost an estimated $4.3 billion; a coal journal calculated that it saved 3.4 million tons, but measured against losses the cost per ton was $1,256.94. People sensed, if they did not know, these economics, and the political upheaval was almost unbelievable. Senator George E. Chamberlain of Oregon, chair of the committee on military affairs and a Democrat, spoke in New York two days later and called for a cabinet minister of munitions. Realizing soon afterward that such a secretary would be dominated by the other cabinet secretaries, the senator amended his bill to propose a war cabinet or council of "three distinguished citizens of demonstrated ability" to function independently of the cabinet, directly under the president, with almost unlimited control of the war, civilians and military alike. Had it passed, this proposition would have taken personal direction of the war out of Wilson's hands.

All the while the critics were moving relentlessly toward Baker, demanding his resignation. The criticism turned savage, people saying the country needed a butcher, not a Baker. Colonel George Harvey of *Harvey's Weekly*, once a Wilson supporter, discovered that if one rearranged the letters of Baker's name it spelled BRAKE. Colonel House—no more a colonel than Harvey but still a Wilson supporter—did not know what to do about Baker, whom he had tried to get out of office nearly a year before. A month earlier he had suggested to his chief that Baker might become private secretary to the president, but that raised in Wilson's mind the question of loyalty to Joseph P. Tumulty, the secretary who had been with him since the governorship in Trenton. The Texas colonel wrote in his diary that everything was in chaos and that Baker did not realize the seriousness of the situation. "He does not at all appreciate the fact that everyone who knows the situation in Washington has lost confidence in the organization." And how to tell the president? "Neither does the president appreciate this, so there you are."[23]

House always believed that his influence on the president varied with the subject; if it were foreign affairs, the president would probably accept what he proposed, but in domestic matters, he would only listen and possibly, even probably, do nothing. House was highly unsure of his ability to change domestic arrangements, and yet, somehow, by piecing together what House wrote in his diary and Baker's subsequent actions, one must conclude that it may actually have been the frail, quiet House, whom his critics described as "Colonel Mouse," who solved the president's unpleasant problem with the critics of economic and military mobilization. House got Baker up to New York and talked with him at length and may well have stirred the secretary of war to the action that turned the tide and virtually saved the day.[24]

Beginning January 12 the secretary had testified before the Senate military affairs committee for four days and had made some of the senators angry—speaking deliberately, smoking big black cigars, almost defiant in relating that all was well. Now, after talking with House, Baker went before the committee a second time, January 28, and spoke for four and a half hours, and by all testimonies did a superb job. Senator Reed Smoot, Republican of Utah and no supporter of the president, admitted that "all agreed it was a fine presentation of a very poor case." A British diplomat in Washington not altogether friendly to his country's associate wrote Foreign Secretary Arthur Balfour that the American secretary had done well, calling it "a masterly performance." The newspaperman David Lawrence, another of Wilson's former students at Princeton, sent the president an enthusiastic note saying he had just come from the Capitol after listening to Baker's entire speech and it was a masterpiece of convincing description.[25] Among other things, the secretary had said that although Pershing had few divisions at the moment he soon would have more—half a million men by early that year, a million and a half by the end of the year—and that the industrialist and partner in the Morgan firm, Edward R. Stettinius, who had been in charge of Allied purchases, would become "surveyor general" of all War Department purchases.

The president, too, was now showing steel. Senator Henry F. Ashurst of Arizona, a Democratic enthusiast to be sure, wrote in his diary that he "called upon W. W. and found him in a fighting mood. His jaw was set. His eyes shot fire."[26] The president said publicly that Senator Chamberlain's charges were "astonishing and absolutely unjustified distortions of the truth."

Then two more acts of God intervened, this time in Wilson's favor. Theodore Roosevelt was hospitalized for a serious illness, and a similar affliction took Senator Chamberlain out of the fray. With this respite, and with the counterattack beginning to work, the president in his own hand wrote out a bill that became the Overman Act, conferring virtually dictatorial power upon himself to organize and direct the nation's resources. Public opinion may also have begun to tire of all the accusation, and there were suggestions in the press that a few speechless days on Capitol Hill would help as much to win the war as the heatless days imposed by the Fuel Administration.

The administration thereupon made two brilliant moves to revive its fortunes. On the side of economic mobilization the president on March 4 appointed Bernard Baruch chair of the War Industries Board. Almost at the same time Baker brought General March back from France, where he had been Pershing's chief of artillery, and made him chief of staff of the army. During the half year that remained of war Baruch did what was possible, mainly a rewriting of War Department orders, and by largely voluntary measures—to which he gave the appearance both of patriotism and of immense personal power, even though he did not possess it—he brought some order into war production. March in turn took on the Baker-Scott-Bliss War Department and simply turned it upside down, doing a magnificent job in snatching order out of chaos. A little-known figure in American history books, March was a tall man with a pointed, wispy beard, imperious eyes, and a head topped with a thatch of gray hair. In short order, and with assistance of the equally efficient George Goethals, to whom he gave ever more authority to eliminate the bureaus through amalgamation, he turned the department into a machine that not only gave Pershing the troops Baker had rashly promised but another half million as well, forty-two huge divisions in France by the Armistice, twenty-six of them in the line. Peyton March, as much as Pershing, was responsible for changing the balance of divisions on the Western Front in favor of the Allies and bringing the defeat of imperial Germany.[27]

A triumphant outcome is not, however, a fitting conclusion to any measurement of President Wilson as commander in chief during the first major foreign war the United States ever fought. All was not well that ended that way. Looking back on 1917–1918 from a vantage of three-quarters of a century—with tens of thousands of World War I's once four million veterans still living, all of them in their nineties—the historian cannot help but conclude that blame for the egregious errors in mobilization, economic and military, should lie primarily with the commander in chief, for he, President Wilson, was officially responsible. To be sure, this does not mean that the president had to do everything himself or that he could have. It does mean that when he appointed subordinates he should have chosen men with experience if possible and, in any event, followed up on their appointments by watching their activities to see that they did their duty. It was quaintly irrelevant, as Baker liked to do, to cite the relations of Lee and Davis. Common sense, that aid to all good administrators, demanded supervision and, if necessary, admonishment and replacement.

The responsibility was Wilson's. And behind his actions, which as commander in chief were almost entirely inactions, lay the faults of his being—the confidence of the Victorian era, his successes as a university professor, and his dogmatic hatred of war itself.

4

FRANKLIN ROOSEVELT:
"DR. WIN-THE-WAR"

WARREN F. KIMBALL

Franklin D. Roosevelt, commander in chief. He loved the sound of it. Minor bureaucrats during World War II still remember answering a ringing phone to hear that instantly familiar voice say, "This is the Commander in Chief."[1] As we celebrate one after another fiftieth anniversary of the events of World War II, the image of Franklin Roosevelt threatens to overpower us all. But that image all too often depends more on the agenda of the interpreter than on Roosevelt himself. Is he "that most elusive of political personalities," as some would have it? Was he merely an opportunist reacting to events? Or did Roosevelt move consistently toward a set of goals that can be deduced from what he did, if not always from what he said? Was he somehow different as commander in chief than as president?[2]

A few weeks before the Japanese attacked Pearl Harbor and the Philippines, Roosevelt's secretary of state, Cordell Hull, told Henry Stimson, the secretary of war, "I have washed my hands of it [the crisis with Japan] and it is now in the hands of you and [Frank] Knox—the Army and the Navy." Two years later, in 1943, with victory predictable, if a ways off, the president seemed to echo that same preoccupation with military success. "Dr. New Deal" had done his job, he commented to a reporter, it was time to bring in "Dr. Win-the-War." Despite his attempt to be casual—the comment was made in an aside after the press conference had ended—the media seized on the remark as an indicator of a major shift in domestic policy.[3]

But Dr. New Deal was not gone for long, if he had ever left. Two weeks later, while Roosevelt's opponents were still chortling that he had killed his own child, the president made "the most radical

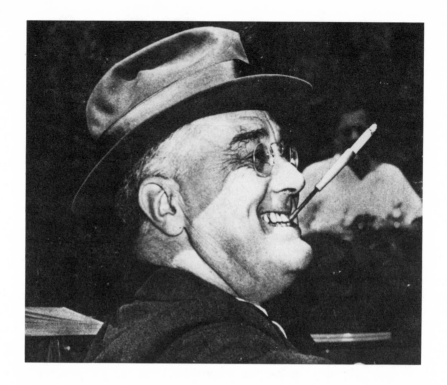

speech of his life," to use the words of historian James MacGregor Burns.[4] Clearly the dismissal of Dr. New Deal did not mean postponing domestic reform, but rather that the relief-and-recovery New Deal of the 1930s was no longer what the nation needed.[5] Once again, Roosevelt had exposed the connection in his own mind between his international and his domestic programs. The restructuring of the international scene was the woof, domestic reform the warp, of the pattern he tried to weave.[6] His vaunted "political opportunism" was much more than mere manipulation of the electoral and legislative politics in which Roosevelt both reveled and excelled. (How many presidents are associated with only a single major domestic political setback, FDR's so-called packing of the Supreme Court?—and that after thirteen years in office!) His political agenda concerned politics in the broadest and most positive sense—what generally falls under the rubric of leadership.

Roosevelt's definition of victory included the peace, not just a military defeat of the nation's foes. His politics, his political economy, his political vision—say it whatever way you wish—underpinned and informed his day-to-day responses to crises, even if those crises occasionally required action that seemed to contradict the longer-term ends he sought. What the military calls "fire-fighting" often takes precedence over broader, less pressing political goals, and in his relations with the military, in his actions as commander in chief, Roosevelt often had to fight fires. World War II was a fire to fight, while the postwar world posed fundamental, systemic problems. The very fact of war demonstrated to Roosevelt the need for reform of the international system. He had not wanted the war, but once it came it offered an opportunity to promote his international and some of his national goals. To analyze Franklin Roosevelt as commander in chief requires an awareness of those broader aims.

Yet, FDR as commander in chief has all too often been treated in isolation. One early image, promoted perhaps by wishful thinking on the part of the military, had Roosevelt leaving the running of the war almost completely to his military chiefs (with the exceptions invariably being mistakes). Those military leaders—General George C. Marshall of the army, Admiral Ernest J. King for the navy, plus others such as Henry "Hap" Arnold and Dwight D. Eisenhower (all hand-picked by the president, which suggests he planned to be in charge)[7]—claimed that Roosevelt had only rarely and cautiously interfered with their work, although whenever their favorite plans were shelved they invariably blamed politics and politicians, often Winston Churchill.[8] Of those at the top of the military pecking order, only Douglas MacArthur constantly whined, during and after the war, that the politicians in Washington always blocked his plans. That whining came despite Roosevelt's support for MacArthur in at least two major strategic disputes—the decision to split the Pacific into two commands (one of which was MacArthur's in the Southwest Pacific) and the decision to invade the Philippines. The very fact that the United States won World War II—or at least its part of it—prompted Roosevelt-haters and Republicans (often the same) to give the credit to the generals, the admirals, and particularly to "the boys on the front lines." After all, it was obvious to such critics that

FDR was just a political conniver, incapable of providing the kind of leadership needed to win the Good War.[9]

But that image of Roosevelt as a relatively aloof commander in chief was challenged effectively some thirty years ago, as historians, particularly those involved with the research and writing of the *U.S. Army in World War II* series (the justly praised Green Books), found and described Roosevelt playing a key role in decision after decision. Forrest C. Pogue, Kent Roberts Greenfield, Maurice Matloff, Martin Blumenson, Richard Leighton, Robert Coakley, Edwin Snell, William R. Emerson—that incomplete list reads like a Who's Who of American historians of World War II. Their work on the official histories gave them special access to archival materials that drove home the fact of Roosevelt's active and often crucial involvement in what had seemed like military decisions. Their voluminous writings ever since have continued to emphasize that point.[10] But apparently their message was forgotten or not heard, for a more recent study of FDR as commander in chief has, as its straw man, the "misapprehension that he left the conduct of the war largely to the military," concluding that "Roosevelt as war lord has been there all along, needing only to be recognized."[11]

Then there is the British/continental image of Roosevelt and the Americans as short-sighted and "unrealistic"—the ultimate insult. Churchill had three major disagreements with Roosevelt over wartime strategy in Europe. In each case the prime minister and his military advisers later found the president naive and quixotic. In one instance, the Americans rejected British arguments and refused to make the Italian campaign *a*, if not *the*, major thrust against Germany (and, to read Churchill's memoirs, against the Soviet Union). The second argument, over American insistence on an invasion of southern France (operation ANVIL/DRAGOON), generated the harshest language, as Churchill realized that the campaign prevented the British from undertaking a major effort in the eastern Mediterranean. The last dispute concerned the rejection by Eisenhower and Roosevelt of British proposals for a major drive toward Berlin in 1945, a thrust to be led by British General Bernard Montgomery that would have, argued Churchill, allowed the Anglo-Americans

(Churchill's emphasis was on Anglo) to get to Berlin before the Russians.[12]

In each case, the prime minister asked that the Americans make war the handmaiden of politics. In each case, Churchill had his own purposes, international and domestic. He recognized that Roosevelt likewise had his own motives, ones that reflected the president's understanding of American interests. Nor did Churchill always disagree. The British leader himself could not settle on a consistent policy toward the Soviet Union, and he never really challenged Roosevelt's cooperative approach until March 1945, after the Yalta Conference.[13] Yet, when the British wartime leader came to write his memoirs, expressly constructed to promote good Anglo-American relations,[14] he portrayed the president and the Americans as innocents for not realizing that balance-of-power politics would govern—with the British acting as brokers between the United States and the Soviet Union. The prime minister drew a much-exaggerated portrait of himself as the wise and prescient leader who foresaw Soviet expansion, while Roosevelt comes off as a pleasant Pangloss, unwilling to accept the facts of geopolitical power. The president's failure to support Churchill's position became an example of young "Jonathan's" admirable but foolish idealism.

In fact, Roosevelt understood well the connection between military and political goals. For example, in May 1942, he promised Soviet Foreign Minister V. Molotov a nearly immediate major offensive across the English Channel, saying that the Anglo-Americans understood "the urgent tasks of creating a second front in Europe in 1942."[15] The explanation Roosevelt gave to Churchill was openly political: "I am inclined to think that at present all the Russians are a bit down in the mouth. But the important thing is that we may be and probably are faced with real trouble on the Russian front." Both the prime minister and his general staff had made clear their belief that a 1942 invasion had no military value, but Roosevelt initially ignored their advice.[16] General Marshall gave ambiguous support to the president and agreed to a limited 1942 attack aimed primarily at diverting German air resources if the Soviet Union appeared about to collapse. But the general's real intention was to maintain pressure on the British to go along with his plans for a large-scale cross-Channel invasion in 1942 or 1943. Molotov's definition of a second front as a campaign that would draw forty German divisions away from the Russian front may have been unrealistic, but so was Marshall's suggestion for a diversionary attack in France. Certainly the American could not have imagined that draining some German air power away from the eastern front would have kept the Soviets from collapse.[17]

The British and then historians ever since have generally treated Roosevelt's promise as a placebo designed to pacify Stalin once Molotov failed to get agreement on Soviet absorption of the Baltic States, particularly since the Anglo-Americans were always worried that Stalin might, as he had in 1939, open negotiations with Hitler. But it was March 1942, more than two months before Molotov's trip to Washington, when Harry Hopkins wrote, in a memo to the president, "I doubt if any single thing is as important as getting some sort of a front this summer [1942] against Germany."[18] Concern about a Soviet accommodation with Germany could not be separated from the military reality that without the Soviet Union in the war, a second front would not have been possible in 1943, in 1944, or perhaps ever.[19] Was that not an appropriate question for a commander in chief to confront? Faced with adamant opposition from his British allies, who would have to provide the bulk of the manpower in 1942 or 1943, Roosevelt backed away from his vague promise.

Of course there were longer-term considerations, although Roosevelt never presented them in so many words. Support for the Soviet Union clearly fit within his political strategy of creating civilized Russians out of revolutionary Bolsheviks—a policy Roosevelt adopted even before the United States had formally entered the war. In any event, what were Roosevelt's motives? Military theater strategy? Grand strategy? Alliance politics? Postwar planning? Or all of the above?

From that "Second Front diplomacy" flowed Roosevelt's most famous and revealing override of his military chiefs—the decision to invade North Africa in autumn 1942 rather than husband resources in preparation for a major cross-Channel attack in 1943. Marshall, Eisenhower, Patton, Wedemeyer, and other generals repeatedly denigrated the decision as "political." They were committed to the principle of concentration of forces and viewed Churchill's periphery strategy as inherently flawed. An invasion of North Africa did not go in the direction of Germany or against the major elements of the German Army, hence it would act as a "suction pump," drawing Anglo-American strength away from where it ultimately had to go. Though the accusation was never hurled, the Americans clearly thought the British were afraid to take on the German Army. As Secretary of War Stimson put it, "The Shadows of Passchendale and Dunkerque still hang too heavily over the imagination of his [Churchill's] government."[20]

Most historians, writing in the afterglow of victory over the evil Nazis, have defended the strategic wisdom of Roosevelt's decision. Of course Marshall may have been right. But those who argue that a 1943 invasion of Western Europe might have shortened the war and forestalled Soviet "liberation" of much of central Europe ignore the pull of the Pacific. As Roosevelt and Hopkins understood, prolonged inaction against Germany could have created enough congressional and domestic pressure to force a shift of resources to the war against Japan. The president worried about "finding a place where the soldiers thought they could fight" and realized that only bloodying American troops in combat against the Germans would solve the problem.[21] Since the strategy of winners is justified by victory, we will never get beyond conjecture. Moreover, such conjecture misses the point. Roosevelt's decision, however wise or unwise, was made largely for political, not military, reasons. And those political reasons were substantial—not trivial, selfish, or opportunistic. The decision to concentrate on the war against Germany was military in that the sensible thing to do was defeat the strongest enemy first. But it was also a political statement that Roosevelt's schemes for postwar collaboration with Britain and the Soviet Union, the great powers, demanded a Europe-first strategy. If the United States left its Allies alone in Europe, how could it hope to lead in the postwar world? After all, politics, claims Clausewitz, is what war is all about.[22]

A final image of Roosevelt as commander in chief is a variation on the American-as-innocent theme. It begins with a neo-Clausewitzian assumption that politics should govern the decisions of a commander in chief and concludes that, in Roosevelt's case, political decisions were instead dictated by military events. Soviet domination of Eastern and Central Europe became simply a function of the Red Army's westward march. The president's defenders ask, what else could he have done, faced with the awesome power of the Soviet military offensive? His critics complain that the lack of a cohesive foreign policy left the initiative to the Red Army. In between are those who argue that whatever Roosevelt's wartime policies toward the Soviet Union, they made (or would have made) little difference given the reality of Soviet military power.[23] But from whichever way he is viewed, Roosevelt was passive and uncertain.

Similarly, Roosevelt seemed less than assertive in the case of his agreements with Stalin in East Asia that sanctioned a postwar Soviet presence in Manchuria. The president's early defenders insisted that he was hemmed in by military pressure for full-scale Soviet participation in the war against Japan in order to save American lives.[24] Critics then attacked FDR's failure to take an early anti-Soviet stance and criticized him for letting dubious military advice take precedence over support for Chiang Kai-shek's regime. That argument resulted in some fancy broken-field running by like critics, who often supported Harry Truman's decision to drop the atomic bomb and justified that decision on the same grounds of military necessity that they claimed Roosevelt should not have heeded. Then Marshall's biographer, Forrest Pogue, refuted the notion that Roosevelt made concessions to Stalin in the Far East because Marshall and the American military twisted the president's arm. Instead, Marshall and all the Americans at Yalta assumed that the Soviets would keep their pledge to enter the Pacific War and thus bear their share of the heavy casualties that were expected in any land war against the Japanese in Manchuria and northern China.[25] Nor did Roosevelt say anything at Yalta to indicate that he thought otherwise. That, and the president's long-standing concern about the postwar settlement, indicates that agreement to Stalin's territorial proposals was political—since the military issue of Soviet intervention was a done deal. The arrangement not only gave Roosevelt another opportunity to promote his postwar vision of a civilized Soviet Union but also a chance to foster a China that would accept American leadership—which required that a Soviet-supported Mao Tse-tung not emerge the winner.

That is not to agree with those who picture Roosevelt as a dupe and a fool who naively sold out Europe and Asia to the communists.[26] But it does accept that part of the argument that says Roosevelt, not just the Red Army, played a significant role in deciding the postwar fate of Europe and East Asia. For the president, the issue was not the simplistic Manichaean choice between good guys and bad. Granted, by mid–1944, a "get tough" approach with the Soviet Union was unlikely to displace the Red Army from where it was or would soon be. But Roosevelt's "good neighbor" approach began long before 1944. Unlike Woodrow Wilson twenty-five years earlier, Roosevelt was not haunted by the specter of rampaging bolshevism. Since 1917, the Soviet Union had gone little beyond revolutionary bluster. Even the 1939 Nazi-Soviet Pact, unpalatable as it had been, was viewed through the prism of "appeasement" and Anglo-French rejections of American appeals that they stand up to Hitler. The president rejected but understood Stalin's public defense that the Soviet Union had no choice since it had been left by Britain and France to stand alone. But irrespective of the background, the war created a new situation, and for Roosevelt the choice was for a peace accompanied by positive, systemic reforms—not a mere armistice that only set the stage for the next confrontation.[27]

The reality is that Roosevelt was far from passive and uncertain. He had a postwar vision that, vague as it was, he pursued with remarkable consistency. He was not a commander in chief who failed to recognize the relationship of military power and political goals. He was reluctant to use military force—the Good Neighbor Policy in Latin America and his avoidance, before the United States joined the fighting, of any commitment to large-scale U.S. involvement in the European war, are two examples. But this is the same Roosevelt who agreed with Churchill to keep the atomic bomb secret from the Soviets (as well as from everyone else); the Roosevelt who agreed with his military that there should be U.S.-controlled (the military wanted them U.S.-owned) bases in the Pacific after the war; the Roosevelt who spoke forcefully of how American security required control of the West African port of Dakar and who had incorporated

Greenland and Iceland into the Western Hemisphere by presidential fiat—the kind of creative geography that only popes had tried before.[28]

Roosevelt demonstrated his leadership even before the United States formally entered the war when he consciously and purposefully decided to treat the Soviet Union as a potential "good neighbor." His decision in 1941 to send that nation effective aid, taken against the counsel of most of his advisers as well as that of Churchill, was a forceful example of a president and commander in chief in action. The American military chiefs, believing the Red Army would melt away under Hitler's assault, had little liking for diverting matériel intended to build up either American or British defenses. The arguments they made sounded hauntingly similar to those made a year earlier against expanded aid to Britain—why send supplies to a nation on the verge of collapse? Roosevelt had overruled that advice in the summer of 1940 and did so again in the late summer and early autumn of 1941.[29]

Alliance and postwar politics—properly two halves of the same walnut—were simultaneously his major concern in that and almost every other case. Trying to analyze Roosevelt merely as commander in chief isolates too small a part of what he was and did. His impact on the war as commander in chief must be seen as part of his broader role as president; part of his broader self-perception as both a national and a world leader. To divide him up into little chunks—commander in chief, political party boss, head of government, head of state, domestic leader—distorts and misleads. Roosevelt was always a politician in the best sense of the word, constantly trying to fulfill goals he set for himself, the nation, and the nations of the world. Military victory was never the president's overriding worry once the tide of German and Japanese advances was stemmed at Stalingrad and Guadalcanal.[30]

In fact, there is little if any evidence that Roosevelt did not trust his military subordinates when it came to winning battles and campaigns. Rarely, if ever, did he involve himself for military reasons in battlefield operations or even theater strategy.[31] His military chiefs tell no stories of Roosevelt tinkering with their plans in the way that Churchill drove his chief of staff, General Alan Brooke, to distraction. George Marshall never had to complain about the president as did Brooke when he described the prime minister "sitting in Marrakesh . . . now full of beans. As a result a three-cornered flow of telegrams in all directions is gradually resulting in utter confusion. I wish to God that he would come home and get under control."[32] Roosevelt occasionally succumbed to romantic schemes like Merrill's Marauders and Chennault's Flying Tigers but never toyed with them the way Churchill constantly did with Wingate's Chindits.[33] The president was less susceptible to the lure of small-scale, clever plans that seemed to restore a sense of personal romance and adventure to war. Of course he had no "Dickie" Mountbatten whispering in his ear about Dieppe raids or converting icebergs into floating airfields, but there is little indication that such stratagems would have captured—and distracted—Roosevelt's imagination the way they did Churchill's (even if FDR once suggested to General Arnold bombing a Shanghai electric plant).[34] Roosevelt's uniformed palace advisers were two—General Edwin "Pa" Watson, whose major qualifications for his position as military aide were his skills as a raconteur and his ability to fob off unwanted visitors, and Admiral William Leahy, who owed his job, as chief of staff to the commander in chief, to General Marshall, who concluded (not always correctly) that Leahy would coordinate military advice without unduly imposing his own rather unimaginative views or being used by the president.[35]

Roosevelt's trust in his military subordinates extended even to the political sphere and, at times, seemed to foster results that went against his wishes. Unlike Churchill, who tended to see his military leaders as parochial and unable to grasp the broader requirements of national policy, the president allowed his military commanders on the scene to handle civil administration in liberated or occupied territory. He seemed confident that he and his generals held compatible views about how governments and societies ought to be reconstituted. Secretary of War Stimson, whose official memory reached back to the unhappy experiences of the U.S. Army during the Spanish-American War, insisted that military commanders be in charge of areas behind the line, and FDR was comfortable with that procedure. Thus American military commanders could act with a wide degree of political latitude. That latitude made possible MacArthur's reestablishment of the Philippine government, which Roosevelt held up as a model for other colonies; helped Eisenhower to set up the much-criticized Darlan deal with Vichy forces in North Africa, a plan Roosevelt fully endorsed; set the stage for the restoration of the Italian monarchy, which Roosevelt had gently opposed; and even lent support to the establishment of the Free French and Charles de Gaulle as the provisional government and leader of France, to which the president had seemed unalterably opposed.

But in no case did the decisions of his military field commanders fundamentally alter the president's policies. Victor Emmanuel of Italy regained his throne only in return for accepting the plebiscite that soon returned him to the ranks of the unemployed. At the same time, the United States avoided further controversy with Britain over the issue—and Britain was a keystone in Roosevelt's postwar structure. As for de Gaulle and France, the real cause of the president's reluctance to recognize the French general's leadership had always been the belief that postwar France would be racked by internal dissension. Choosing sides in that struggle would only put the United States in a no-win position that could get the country involved in endless squabbling. That was the problem, not Roosevelt's personal antipathy to the French general. By 1944, Roosevelt had no positive alternative to offer, and both the British and Eisenhower were working with de Gaulle, making it easy for the president to accept the Frenchman as a fait accompli.[36]

Roosevelt's style as commander in chief seemed intensely personal, as with all his governance. That style so disturbed and threatened General Marshall that he took steps to insulate himself. He worked through Hopkins, avoided informal visits to either the White House or Hyde Park, made a point of being referred to by Roosevelt as "General Marshall," not "George," and even carried things to the exaggerated extreme of consciously refusing to laugh at the president's jokes.[37]

Of course Roosevelt's breezy approach and casual manner were just as calculated as Marshall's defense. The president's affable exterior barely hid less pleasant qualities. He had cronies and playmates, but few friends. He used his "cuff-links" gang[38] to provide entertainment and companionship on fishing trips and around the

White House, but when they no longer served that purpose he could coldly discard them. His teasing jokes often cut to the quick. Loyalty for FDR was, at times, a one-way street. When Harry Hopkins, ill and overworked, married and left his quarters in the White House, he lost his place as confidant and adviser, even though he had come closest to being Roosevelt's alter ego. Marshall decided that his independence depended upon being able to evade Roosevelt's personal grasp. Even Henry Morgenthau, Jr., who had true affection for FDR, never felt secure about their relationship. But the president's control did not depend upon personality ploys. As all his contemporaries have testified, Roosevelt made the hard decisions on his own, insulated from outside influences by his own personality just as much as Marshall insulated himself with his.[39]

In some ways, Roosevelt's relationship with his military chiefs differed little from his approach to important political advisers. He ensured personal control of both by making certain that they reported directly and often privately to him and not through the civilian cabinet secretaries—whether State, War, or Navy. He selected most of them personally—having in his head the equivalent of George Marshall's famous "little black book," containing evaluations of U.S. Army officers. Roosevelt demanded that both diplomats and military personnel stay out of domestic and congressional politics—transgressors soon found themselves shipped off to places like the Paraguayan embassy or the Persian Gulf command. When Roosevelt selected George Marshall as army chief of staff, the decision contained a message from the commander in chief. The president passed over the other leading candidate, Major General Hugh Drum, who was politically and socially well connected. Drum's constant self-promotion had annoyed Roosevelt to the point that he reportedly complained, "Drum, Drum! I wish he'd stop beating his own drum!"[40] But more important, Roosevelt avoided selecting subordinates who had independent political support and never did so in his military appointments, save for the special and curious case of Douglas MacArthur.[41] Marshall, who understood and accepted his role, had no need of such a message. In fact, the general proved to be one of the administration's most effective advocates on Capitol Hill.[42] But Roosevelt's action stands as part of his definition of his role as commander in chief. It was acceptable to disagree with the Boss one-on-one. But it was definitely not acceptable to try to get outside help in an attempt to force Roosevelt to change his mind.

Nor was Roosevelt's trust in his military a result of disinterest. He rarely held formal, large-scale meetings with his joint chiefs, leading one army historian to claim that the meetings held aboard the battleship *Iowa*, en route to the Teheran Conference, were the only chance the chiefs had up to that time to talk in depth with the president about "politico-military issues."[43] But Roosevelt was always leery of formal meetings replete with records and minutes. He once had angrily told Henry Morgenthau not to bring a secretary to cabinet meetings to take minutes and reacted the same way when General John Deane, acting as a secretary to the military chiefs, tried to jot down comments in a notebook. But he talked regularly with his military chiefs individually and sometimes together, even though the meetings rarely appeared in the Usher's Diary of White House appointments. Moreover, Roosevelt met daily with Admiral William Leahy, whom Marshall and the others used as a conduit for ideas and information.[44]

Of course the American military's public protests that they were not politicians were belied by their private actions. As Marshall's biographers have demonstrated, he climbed the slippery pole to army chief of staff by making clear, consistent political moves, even if the bottom line was always his competence, integrity, and intelligence. His opposition to the North African campaign and the "Mediterranean suction pump" he knew would follow was always phrased in strict military terms—the cross-Channel invasion was the quickest and thus least costly way to win the war. But inferred was his belief that operations in the Mediterranean and Middle East were designed to shore up British imperial interests. Politics could have "a determining influence on military operations," wrote Marshall in his private notes. After the war he admitted that American military leaders "discussed political things more than anything else. . . . But we were careful, exceedingly careful, never to discuss them with the British, and from that they took the count that we didn't observe these things at all. . . ."[45] By 1943, as historian Mark Stoler has shown, the military chiefs were supporting Roosevelt's policy of co-operation with the Soviet Union. They argued not only that the Soviets were needed both to win the war and to keep American casualties at "acceptable" levels, but also that postwar collaboration was essential since the United States would not be able to challenge the Soviet Union's strength in Europe and northern East Asia.[46]

As all Marshall's biographers have noted, much of his success in getting FDR's support came from his awareness of what FDR would accept. After being slapped down over the North African invasion, the general was careful not to propose things unless he was reasonably certain Roosevelt would agree.[47] He guessed wrong only once more on a major issue. Marshall wanted to support General Joseph Stilwell's attempts to step up pressure against the Japanese in the China-Burma-India theater of operations and thought that the president was committed to major operations in Burma aimed at opening the land supply routes to Chiang Kai-shek's forces in south-central China. That seemed to be what Roosevelt had told Chiang at the first Cairo Conference, just before the Big Three met at Teheran. But when the president returned to Cairo after talks with Churchill and Stalin, he postponed his support for the Burma campaign. Marshall, not only loyal to Stilwell but suspicious that Churchill and the British had too much influence over FDR, was furious. There were, of course, military explanations for Roosevelt's action. The British had argued persuasively at Teheran that there were not enough landing craft to go around. Perhaps. But Roosevelt had never accepted supply and production as a limitation.[48] The more likely reason is the politics of strategy. Chiang Kai-shek, for whom Roosevelt had grand ideas, was proving a disappointment. Weak and anti-Western, Chiang appeared less and less suited for the great power role someone had to play in East Asia once Japan was defeated. It made no sense to make a costly commitment to a Chinese leader who seemed unlikely to handle the postwar job the president had in mind.[49]

But how does all this help us to understand and assess Franklin Roosevelt's performance as commander in chief? In 1959 and 1960, what was then the Office of the Chief of Military History published *Command Decisions*, a series of case studies on decision making based on research done for the series *The United States Army in World War II*. Being studies of perhaps, America's only unambivalent war (the opinions of Charles Tansill and Bruce Russett not with-standing[50]), it is no surprise that they are primarily rounds of applause. (In fact, the ambiguous legacy of U.S. wars apparently caught up with the panel of editors, which, in the preface to *Command Decisions*, looked forward to another book on the same subject, this time based on an idea for a series called *The United States Army in the Conflict with the Communist Powers*.[51]) What is striking about *Command Decisions*, as well as the Green Books from which it grew, is the role played by the president. The essays were written by army historians and aimed at army readers, but time and again it is the president, not army leaders, who makes the crucial decisions. Even in the disgraceful case of the mass evacuation and internment of Pacific coast residents of Japanese origin, the decision is laid on the president's doorstep.[52]

But equally significant are the cases where the president was absent. Time and again, when the issues are strictly matters of theater strategies or local operations, Roosevelt made no appearance. Even though Churchill alone of the major wartime leaders did not possess formal authority as commander in chief, it is hard to imagine a like set of case studies written by British military historians without the prime minister appearing in every essay.[53] Similarly for Hitler, who routinely examined military tactics and strategies—although we must be careful not to accept at face value the convenient vindication offered by the German military that it would have won that battle or this campaign had it not been for the interference of that "madman" in Berlin.[54] The true role of Stalin as commander in chief has yet to emerge from the fog of deification that has characterized military history in the Soviet Union, despite *glas'nost*-generated Stalin-bashing since the 1980s. Nevertheless, what materials are available suggest that Stalin was actively involved in military plans and their execution.[55]

But in Roosevelt's case, the failure of the dog to bark in the night highlights the difference between him and the other major government leaders acting as commanders in chief during the war. Roosevelt's interventions in matters military were, in fact, invariably political—political in the sense of alliance and international politics, not just domestic elections and public or congressional opin-

ion (although those were always factors). When the military decisions either supported or threatened no interference with the president's international politics, Roosevelt left the military to its own
devices. The one exception to that might be long-term logistics planning, where FDR's casual, even blithe optimism shocked both generals and industrialists.[56]

To return to the case studies in *Command Decisions*, of the twenty
that analyze American judgments (three concern Japanese or German decisions), only four fail to assign the president a crucial role.
Three of those pieces—essays on MacArthur's defense of the Philippines, on battlefield decisions made (or not made) at Anzio, and the
debate over the failure to close the Argentan-Falaise gap behind the
Germans at Normandy—examined only limited issues of battlefield
operations and tactics. Politics played no role. Another—an essay on
the decision to invade the main Philippines island of Luzon after the
Leyte Gulf landing, rather than bypassing it for Formosa—focuses
on the military issues and concludes that the "question was decided
primarily on its military merits." But in a quick, throwaway para-
graph, the author (Robert Ross Smith) admits that a "political implication" existed. MacArthur and others had argued that the United
States needed to liberate the Philippines in order to maintain credibility in Asia.[57] It was an American version of Churchill's insistence
that the Japanese be thrown out of Singapore by "European" troops.
Perhaps Roosevelt considered that argument, perhaps not. Either
way, MacArthur made a blatant appeal to nonmilitary factors.

What is left? A list of decisions that comprises many of the critical
points of policy for the United States during World War II. The Ger-
many-first decision, the dispatch of U.S. forces to Iceland in the summer of 1941, the North African invasion, the OVERLORD decision at
the Teheran meeting, the invasion of southern France—time and
again the subtitle reads "The President Breaks the Deadlock," "The
President's Decision," or "The President Disposes." Even the case of
General Mark Clark's decision to take Rome rather than attempt to
encircle the main German forces the *Command Decisions* piece
paints as a strictly military decision. Historians, however, have subsequently pointed the finger at Roosevelt once they learned that
Clark and Marshall spent a good deal of time talking privately to

the president just before Clark returned to Italy and made the march on Rome. There is no smoking gun to prove that FDR instructed Clark to take Rome first, but one can hear Henry II complaining, "Will no one avenge me of the injuries I have sustained from one turbulent priest?"[58]

And what were the president's goals? Certainly to win the war was the sine qua non. But setting that goal hardly took much thought or effort. The overarching goal for Franklin Roosevelt, from the moment the war began right up until his death, was to create a postwar structure that reflected his (and most Americans') view of a world system that would work: a world system that was universal only in the sense that every society was moving in roughly the same direction, even if they might never get to the same end. Whatever his playacting as commander in chief, Roosevelt always operated as president, not just military commander—balancing domestic politics, wartime strategies, and postwar goals. He may have played with toy boats in his tub, enjoyed model boats as an adult, and handled senior navy promotions on a personal basis (Marshall once sarcastically asked Roosevelt if he would stop referring to the navy as "we" and the army as "they"[59]), but *divertissement* should not be confused with serious concerns.

Even while World War II raged, legal scholar Edward Corwin began to debate Roosevelt's exercise of power under the commander in chief provisions of the Constitution. Legal niceties aside, Corwin raised a troubling point. Roosevelt, speaking in September 1942 and sounding a good deal like Abraham Lincoln in a similar crisis, threatened to ignore Congress and take certain actions unless the necessary legislation was passed. Although he justified his threat on the grounds that the Constitution and Congress gave him the power "to avert a disaster that would interfere with the winning of the war," he closed his speech on a different note. "When the war is won, the powers under which I act automatically revert to the people—to whom they belong." Whether the president could act without congressional authority in wartime is one question, but the implication that his war powers came directly from the people—not through the Constitution—suggests that Roosevelt put himself above the rule of law, which is, to use Corwin's devastating words, "a doctrine closely akin to the Leadership principle which our armed forces are combating today in the four corners of the globe."[60] Corwin was reaching a bit, for it is a long way from FDR's arm-twisting of Congress to Adolf Hitler's *Führer Prinzip*, yet the lies of the Nixon years should keep us cautious—even if there are those who think they can understand Richard Nixon without Watergate. Perhaps universalist prescriptions for world order, even in Roosevelt's cramped and ambiguous form, create the "political" commander in chief—certainly that seems to have been what lay beneath the policies of Harry Truman and Lyndon Johnson. But more likely the threat rests with the extraordinary power presidents assume they have been given by the U.S. Constitution and which both Congress and the public have reconferred—a power and authority with only individual restraint (benevolent authoritarianism?) and the structure of separation of powers acting as checks.

5

HARRY S. TRUMAN:
THE TWO-WAR CHIEF

D. CLAYTON JAMES

In the fourth century B.C., the philosopher Diogenes allegedly roamed Athens with a lantern searching in vain for an honest man. In the latest version of this legend Diogenes resumed his quest in post-Watergate America and finally found his man of candor in Harry S. Truman. The downfall of Richard M. Nixon in 1973–1974 produced a spate of scholarly and popular writings that led to a new appreciation of Truman as a president who was comparatively free of skullduggery and deceit. Like barnacles adhering to a ship's hull, new perceptions collected about Truman that reinforced the old images of the decisive, frank chief executive of "The buck stops here" and "Give-'em-hell Harry." Today's student of Truman must dig hard to scrape away his barnacles, and in no facet of his leadership is this more true than in examining his role as commander in chief during the final four months of World War II and during the first two and a half years of the three-year war in Korea.

In heading the U.S. armed services in two wars Truman, of course, did make many significant decisions, though that does not necessarily mean he was decisive or free of deceit. He is best remembered for three momentous decisions as wartime leader. First, he authorized the use of atomic bombs against Japan in order to bring about a quicker, less costly end to the Pacific war than could be achieved by the invasion of Kyushu, then set for November 1945. Second, he committed U.S. forces to the war in Korea in June 1950 in order to contain communist expansion and to avert appeasement of the leaders of the presumably Moscow-directed global communist menace. Third, in April 1951, he fired General of the Army Douglas MacAr-

thur as the head of the U.S. and UN commands in Korea and Japan because the general was guilty of insubordination, of threatening the hallowed principle of civilian supremacy over the military, and of trying to start World War III. These three common perceptions are widely held not only by the American public but also within the walls of academe, yet all three are misleading if they are not reevaluated and qualified. This chapter will reconsider these perceptions, and it will examine other, less-well-known decisions of Truman as wartime president that might have involved him more directly or have had more lasting importance.

In textbooks, television documentaries, commercial motion pictures, newspapers, and popular periodicals the common perception has persisted that President Truman used the atomic bomb against Japan to bring the war to a quick close and that his decision was necessary and wise. After the Hiroshima attack on August 6, 1945, Truman commented, "We have used [the atomic bomb] in order to shorten the agony of war, in order to save the lives of thousands and thousands of young Americans."[1] Ten years later he wrote: "The final decision of where and when to use the atomic bomb was up to me. Let there be no mistake about it. I regarded the bomb as a military weapon and never had any doubt that it should be used."[2] On several occasions he boasted that after making the decision he got a sound night's sleep and never had second thoughts about it. No evidence has surfaced to contradict either Truman's claim that the decision was his or the fact that he sincerely believed it was a military necessity.

The evidence also still strongly suggests that he turned to the best and brightest minds around him for counsel and that their predominant sentiment was in favor of resorting to atomic warfare. His inner circle of advisers on the issue was impressive, including as it did such figures as Secretary of War Henry L. Stimson, Army Chief of Staff George C. Marshall, Secretary of State James F. Byrnes, and Prime Minister Winston S. Churchill. Moreover, Stimson headed a distinguished eight-man advisory group called the Interim Committee that counseled the president on atomic matters. The president and the Interim Committee, in turn, were assisted by a scientific advisory panel made up of four world-renowned scientists.

On June 1, 1945, after obtaining the consensus of the scientific advisory panel, the Interim Committee unanimously recommended to the president that atomic weapons be used as soon after August 3 as feasible and without warning against military targets and war industries in Japan. On July 16 the first atomic bomb was exploded in the New Mexico desert, and eight days later Truman ordered an atomic bomb to be dropped on Japan as soon after August 3 as weather allowed. Stimson, the president's closest adviser on this matter, later maintained, "No man, in our position and subject to our responsibilities, holding in his hands a weapon of such possibilities, could have failed to use it and afterwards looked his countrymen in the face."[3]

The issue of military necessity has not appeared as cut and dried to scholars, leading to a large body of critical writing on the atomic-bomb decision. Early dissenters pointed out that even if the first bombing had been justifiable, there was no reason to devastate Nagasaki without giving the Japanese government time to assess what kind of new weapon had destroyed Hiroshima. Other critics emphasized that American intelligence data had demonstrated as early as February 1945 that Japan's economy could be brought to a state of collapse through naval blockades and strategic bombing raids and that it was disintegrating rapidly by that July. Still others charged that the president and his key advisers had discounted intelligence reports of Japan's frantic efforts to get the Soviet Union to act as a mediator in peace negotiations that final spring and summer of the war. Also, some claimed that Washington had failed to study in depth the possible impact on Japan's will to fight if the Soviet Union entered the Pacific war, even though three times between November 1943 and February 1945 Premier Joseph Stalin had pledged to enter the war against Japan within three months after Germany's capitulation. (No major research has yet been published on how influential the Soviet invasion of Manchuria and Korea was on the Japanese government's capitulation.) Some Truman detractors dwelled on the fact that the president and his chief policymakers ignored protests by scientists and engineers working on the Manhattan District project, such as the Szilard petition and the Franck Committee's report, which revealed dissent over moral and technical problems in introducing atomic warfare and proposed that other alternatives be considered.

Some of the Manhattan scientists wanted Japan to be invited to send observers to a deserted Pacific area to witness an atomic explosion before the weapon was actually used against a Japanese city. Military authorities objected, however, fearing that such a demonstration might be a failure. Admiral Ernest J. King, chief of naval operations, believed a naval blockade would bring about Japan's capitulation without the need to resort to invasion or atomic warfare. On the other hand, General Henry H. Arnold, commanding general of the army air forces, was convinced that the continued fire raids of Japanese urban areas by his Boeing B-29s would compel Japan to surrender soon and obviate the necessity of turning to other options. Plans for the invasion of Kyushu in November 1945 had attained a momentum of their own by that spring, however, and the president and most of his key advisers, including War Department leaders, believed an amphibious assault larger than OVERLORD would be required to break the enemy's will to fight. Estimates of casualties, based on the costly attacks on Iwo Jima and Okinawa, soared to 500,000 American servicemen, then to a million, with little substantiation beyond the heavy losses in securing those two islands. Truman surely was influenced by the prospects of high casualties in assaulting the Japanese home islands, as well as the humanitarian aspect and the certain outcry from his political opponents. Contrary to the charges of some detractors, his decision to employ the atomic bomb did not stem from vengefulness or racism. Truman had his flaws, but none of his principal biographers have attributed such venomous motives to him on this or other major decisions of his presidency.

By the early summer of 1945, the Joint Chiefs of Staff and their planners had concluded that neither a naval blockade nor an intensified strategic bombing campaign with conventional high-explosive and incendiary bombs would bring Japanese leaders to surrender. At the same time the president, unwittingly, made it more difficult for Japan to capitulate by remaining adamant on unconditional surrender and refusing to allow the Japanese to retain their imperial institution, a proposal strongly advocated by experts on Japan in the State Department. A man who had been imbued from childhood with midwestern rural values, Truman had repeatedly fallen back on two criteria when confronted with complex crises in the Senate and in the White House: what is the simplest course and what is right. In reaching the awful decision to inaugurate atomic warfare in July 1945, the president believed the simplest route to terminating the war with Japan and the right thing to do was to limit the number of American casualties by holding back the four armies MacArthur was preparing to send to Kyushu (and the next spring to Honshu) and, instead, to dispatch two B-29s to drop atomic bombs on Hiroshima and Nagasaki. Unfortunately, neither he nor his military chiefs anticipated before the latter city was decimated that the Japanese government in Tokyo had not yet had enough time to gather evidence of what had happened at Hiroshima—so complete was the communication breakdown—to make an informed decision about continuing the war.

Because only eight days passed between Truman's learning of the successful New Mexico atomic test and his order to use an atomic bomb on Japan, revisionists have long been disturbed about why the decision was made so quickly. Some concluded that Truman acted quickly to forestall the Soviet Union's participation in the Pacific war. Others carried this logic further, charging that he was bent on exploiting America's atomic monopoly to intimidate Stalin and thereby deter communist expansion in the Far East and elsewhere in the wake of World War II. Such "atomic diplomacy," these critics claimed, aggravated the already accelerating tensions between East and West, attributing to Truman a significant share of the responsibility for the beginning of the Cold War.[4]

Of all scholarly criticism of the conventional Truman-Stimson explanation, the accusation that Truman exploited the atomic weapon as an instrument for diplomatic fencing against Stalin has received the most attention. This is ironic since the atomic monopoly that the United States enjoyed from 1945 to 1949 brought no strategic advantages of consequence. It may well be the only period in history when one state had sole possession of a "superweapon," or instrument of war distinctly superior to any other, and was unable to convert that asset to political, diplomatic, economic, or strategic benefits. In fact, the American atomic monopoly did not even lead to psychological or propagandistic advantages since few other nations—and surely not the USSR—believed the United States would use atomic force except in a case of global war. The fact that Truman was the only leader ever to have actually employed atomic bombs in war, however, may have established his image in Moscow as more decisive, if also more impetuous, than Stalin would otherwise have thought.

However heated the scholars' arguments on the atomic-bomb issue, the frustrating fact remains that American generations, one after another, still learn only that Truman ordered the atomic bombs dropped to end the war by forcing Japan's surrender. Perhaps someday the post-1945 findings of scholars will be incorporated into the common perception of this complex issue. But what will be the composite evaluation of Truman and the atomic-bomb decision? Will he appear as the noble terminator of history's greatest war or the scheming instigator of the Cold War? Whatever the synthesis may be, his name will be linked forever with the start of the atomic age.

It is unfortunate that so little attention has been devoted to two other important contributions by Truman to the history of nuclear warfare. In the first place, it was during his administration—and not during that of Dwight D. Eisenhower—that the first corner was turned toward a "massive retaliation" policy. Under Truman the stockpiling of atomic bombs began in earnest, and the number that the United States possessed grew from 9 bombs in 1946 to about 650 five years later. This accumulation came at a crippling cost to America's conventional defense system from 1945 to 1950, which became painfully apparent when depleted, ill-prepared American forces went into action in the Korean War. Truman's second neglected contribution was his decision in March 1950 to order a crash program to build hydrogen bombs. A thermonuclear breakthrough in the spring of 1951 made the awesome superweapon possible. On the last day of October 1952 Truman's decision was dramatically implemented when an American hydrogen bomb exploded on the Pacific atoll of Eniwetok with a force equal to 10.4 million tons of dynamite, or about a thousand times the force of the atomic bomb dropped on Hiroshima.[5]

Some astute Japan experts in the State Department were convinced by early summer of 1945 that Japan's surrender could be secured by blockade, bombardment, and a presidential proclamation that the emperor would be retained, the last being of incalculable value in persuading Japan's civilian and military authorities to end the war. The State-War-Navy Coordinating Committee (SWNCC), an interdepartmental agency made up of officials from the three departments, had been established in early 1945 to provide guidance to the president and the Joint Chiefs of Staff on surrender terms and occupation policy for the military governments in postwar Japan and Germany. SWNCC prepared a draft of a surrender ultimatum to be sent to Japan by Truman and Churchill at the Potsdam Conference in July 1945 and included a passage providing for "a constitutional monarchy under the present dynasty."[6] Most members of SWNCC and its Far East subcommittee were confident that the retention of the emperor was vital to allay the anxieties of Japanese conservatives, the dominant force in the government in Tokyo. In fact, according to a leading authority on the subject, "the preponderance of advice to Truman from the State, War, and Navy departments, and the JCS, was to leave Hirohito on the throne—to use him for the surrender of the military and the initial phase of the occupation, to treat him as a symbol, and to let the Japanese decide on the ultimate disposition of the monarchy."[7] The final text of the Potsdam Declaration, however, was approved by Truman, Stimson, and Byrnes in consultation with British leaders at the conference after deleting any specific reference to saving the imperial institution. In high circles in Tokyo the Potsdam Declaration of July 27, 1945, was viewed with fear that the principle of unconditional surrender would be fully implemented, especially regarding the emperor. Japanese resolve stiffened anew, and the war would go on for nearly three more weeks, which included some of the worst bloodletting.

Nevertheless, when the American forces of General of the Army Douglas MacArthur arrived in Japan with token elements of British and Commonwealth units to implement the military occupation, new directives from Washington were forthcoming that would lead, in essence, to an indirect occupation in which the Allied supreme commander would "exercise his authority through Japanese governmental machinery and agencies, including the Emperor, to the extent that this satisfactorily furthers United States objectives."[8] Thus, ironically, the president, who thought he was shortening the war by introducing atomic weapons, may have prolonged it through its most horrifying phase by inexplicably omitting the assurance to the Japanese in the Potsdam Declaration that the emperor would not be removed from his throne. Many authorities on Japan still believe such a pledge might have led to Japan's capitulation without resort to atomic attacks or the Soviet war against Japan.

The most far-reaching action by Truman in the closing months of World War II may have been his determination to make the occupation of Japan a virtually total American performance in all important facets ranging from policy formulation to the military administration and field forces. On the way back to the United States after the Potsdam Conference, Truman said, "I made up my mind that General MacArthur would be given complete command and control after victory in Japan." Persuaded after his often tense encounters with Stalin at Potsdam as well as by the Soviets' increasing influence in Eastern Europe that spring, Truman concluded that "force is the only thing the Russians understand" and therefore "I would not allow the Russians any part in the control of Japan."[9] Before long, however, Truman was persuaded to try to block all meaningful participation in control over occupied Japan by *any* of the other eleven nations that were supposed to be represented in the alleged Allied occupation of Japan.

On September 6, 1945, four days after MacArthur presided over the formal surrender ceremony on the battleship *Missouri* in Tokyo Bay, the president approved a SWNCC-drafted document entitled "United States Initial Post-Surrender Policy for Japan," which was sent to the general as a directive from the Joint Chiefs of Staff. The dominant role of the United States in occupied Japan is set forth clearly in a section ironically called "Allied Authority." It states that "the occupation shall have the character of an operation in behalf of the principal Allied powers" in the war against Japan, and representation in Japan of their forces "will be welcome and expected," but all occupation ground, sea, and air units will be under "a Supreme Commander designated by the United States." The American government and the supreme commander, whom Truman had designated as MacArthur on August 15, would attempt, "by consultation and by constitution of appropriate advisory bodies," to develop policies satisfactory to "the principal Allied powers," but, "in the event of any differences of opinion among them, the policies of the United States will govern."[10]

To the chagrin of America's wartime allies in the Pacific but to the delight of a heavy majority of contemporary Japanese, the Soviet Union had no significant voice in the ensuing occupation, the British and Australian contingents were given minor roles, and the United States and Japan cultivated a strong friendship based on Cold War strategy and capitalistic profits. The credit and blame for an all-American show in occupied Japan must be shared by Truman as the key policymaker and MacArthur as the implementing commander.

The second common perception about Truman as commander in

chief is that he boldly committed U.S. forces to Korea in order to halt communist expansion and to avoid appeasing the leaders of the allegedly Moscow-sponsored aggression. In late June 1950, when war erupted along the 38th parallel in Korea, it soon became apparent that the South Korean Army could not stop the well-armed invaders from communist North Korea. Within a week of the first attack, American air, naval, and ground forces had been dispatched to South Korea by Truman's executive orders. The fighting would continue for more than three years and would cost more than 142,000 American casualties.

Although the president later referred to the intervention in Korea as his "toughest decision,"[11] the initiative for it actually belongs to Secretary of State Dean G. Acheson. When news of the fighting first reached the United States, the president was in Missouri, and it was Acheson who handled the early responses to the crisis. By the time Truman returned to Washington the following day, Acheson had asked the UN Security Council to call for a cease-fire in Korea and had prepared strategic recommendations for Truman to consider. "It looked as though we must steel ourselves for the use of force," Acheson had concluded. Before he went to Blair House that evening, Acheson said, his own mind "was pretty clear on where the course we were about to recommend would lead and why it was necessary that we follow the course."[12] Truman agreed with the secretary of state's basic proposals, and during the following days Acheson continued to coordinate the escalation of American involvement in Korea. Furthermore, he counseled Truman against seeking congressional approval for his actions.

Since the spring of 1945 Truman's relations with Acheson had become increasingly cordial and mutually respectful, and by the eve of the Korean War, Acheson was the president's most trusted adviser. In contrast, during the same period Truman's already well-developed antipathy toward the military establishment was reinforced as senior officers resisted administration pressure for rapid demobilization of conventional forces, draconian budget cuts, unification of the armed services, as well as by numerous other issues. General of the Army George C. Marshall and Fleet Admiral William D. Leahy were among the few military leaders Truman came to trust and admire.[13]

But the president's preference for Acheson's advice ranked well above that of all others.

Had Acheson opposed involvement in Korea instead of playing the role of chief advocate, Truman probably would have acceded to his judgment. The U.S. mission in South Korea, including five hundred military advisers, had been under the State Department's jurisdiction since the American XXIV Corps had been withdrawn in 1949. When the fighting broke out the next year, the Joint Chiefs of Staff were unenthusiastic about returning large regular army forces to Korea. For several years the joint chiefs had judged South Korea to be strategically useless, and they continued to consider it so even after the United States had entered the conflict.[14] They also knew that the forces at their disposal had been crippled by massive budget cuts since the end of World War II and were inadequate to protect all of America's global commitments. While the joint chiefs did not vehemently challenge military intervention in Korea, they would have been unlikely to champion such action in the absence of Acheson's advocacy, so powerful was his position with Truman.

The U.S. decision to enter the Korean War was greatly influenced by the widespread belief that global communism was monolithic and controlled tightly by the Soviet Union. The Truman administration immediately categorized the North Korean advance as a Soviet-sponsored challenge to the United States and to world peace and did not officially recognize the possibility that it was a civil war driven by internal political forces instead of by orders from Moscow. (Ironically, while the State Department had concluded in its White Paper in 1949 that the war on the Chinese mainland was a civil conflict that the United States should not enter, Truman, Acheson, and their key advisers did not consider the prospect that the Korean conflict was also a civil war.) Even after the Communist Chinese entered the war to bolster the North Koreans, the Truman administration still viewed Moscow as the main force behind the Korean War. One long-term result of the Korean War in fact was the exacerbation of tensions between Peking and Moscow in the later 1950s.

Also affecting the intervention decision were the analogies drawn by Truman and his advisers to place the Korean conflict in historical context. As Truman later explained, "It was my belief that if this aggression in Korea went unchallenged, as the aggression in Manchuria in 1931 and in Ethiopia in 1934 had gone unchallenged, the world was certain to be plunged into another world war." He added: "This was the same kind of challenge Hitler flaunted in the face of the rest of the world when he crossed the borders of Austria and Czechoslovakia. The free world failed then to meet that challenge, and World War II was the result."[15] One authority has suggested that "the naked military character of the North Korean attack and the fact that it involved a sudden, massive employment of official armed forces across a clear-cut territorial boundary appear to have been responsible for calling to mind the historical parallel [with Hitler's pre-1939 moves]."[16] Whatever the reasons behind the comparison, many Washington decisionmakers believed that failure to stop the Soviet-sponsored aggression in Korea would equal the appeasement of Hitler in the 1930s, with similar disastrous results. In retrospect, the application of the "Munich lesson" to the Korean invasion appears less valid the more scholars learn about the complexities of the mix of nationalism and communism in Korea in 1945–1950.[17]

The most disturbing features of the U.S. decision to enter the Korean conflict were the absence of a national strategy with clear objectives and the failure to evaluate the military capabilities of the country to carry them out. Not only did the abrupt reversal of the importance placed on South Korea directly contradict the Truman administration's position of the preceding years, but Truman and Acheson also apparently thought the intervention could succeed without a congressional declaration of war, without fully mobilizing the U.S. military, and without raising taxes. As brilliant as Acheson may have been, perhaps Truman would have been wiser to have sought his principal counsel elsewhere that fateful last week of June 1950. A prominent scholar on the episode concludes: "Had the President been less cock-sure either about the lessons of history or about their applicability in the Korean case, he might have had more qualms. Had his advisers not recognized and shared his certitude, they might have taken more pains to assess the advantages and disadvantages of alternative courses."[18]

The first two common perceptions of Truman, regarding the

atomic-bomb decision and the U.S. entry into the Korean conflict, involve conventional positions of the Truman administration that became embedded in the mythological side of American history but that have been substantially revised by scholars. The third common perception is different in that the views of Truman, the public, and the scholars coincide: the president relieved MacArthur in April 1951 because he was being insubordinate, he was challenging civilian supremacy over the military, and he was endeavoring to expand the Korean conflict into World War III.

In the hearings on MacArthur's firing conducted by the Senate's Foreign Relations and Armed Services committees in May and June 1951, the administration's array of top civilian officials and Pentagon brass appeared well briefed in presenting Truman's case against the general on these three grounds. By the time the lengthy investigation ended that summer Gallup and Roper polls showed that public sentiment had shifted from condemnation of Truman at the time of the dismissal in April to strong support, mainly because of his officials' effective depictions of MacArthur as insubordinate, defiant, and warmongering. Since then most historians and other academics who have written about the controversy have appeared reluctant to defend any aspect of the position of the general who was the darling of the right wing.

On a number of occasions from August 1950 until April 1951, MacArthur was indeed insubordinate: in his public statements criticizing the administration's policies on Korea and Taiwan, in his ignoring of the president's order to obtain approval before issuing communiqués regarding military or foreign policy, and in his evasive, mendacious, and arrogant dealings with the Joint Chiefs of Staff. A general with less political clout who acted so brazenly toward his superior would probably have faced a court-martial. Indeed, if Truman, beset by McCarthyism and manifold troubles in his own party, had possessed a more secure political base, he might well have had MacArthur court-martialed. There is little doubt that the president was correct when he later remarked, "MacArthur left me no choice—I could no longer tolerate his insubordination."[19] Even a commander-in-chief who was not feisty and contemptuous toward lofty, pretentious generals would have probably found MacArthur's conduct intolerable. General of the Army George C. Marshall, the secretary of defense, put it simply: MacArthur's removal became a "necessity" when he engaged in "wholly unprecedented" public criticism of the president's policies.[20]

Although clearly guilty of insubordination, MacArthur did not present a threat to civil-military relations in the United States. He was never an "American Caesar" who harbored dreams of gaining political power by force or other unconstitutional means. In 1944 and 1948 his name had been entered in several presidential primaries by conservative Republicans, but he was never close to getting the party nomination for president and never made an overt move to campaign actively. As for overturning the long-established principle of civilian supremacy over the military, MacArthur, a sharp student of American military history, knew well how widely affirmed the principle was by Americans. His at times arrogant attitude during the Korean War, likewise, did not constitute a menace to the American civil-military order. At the point MacArthur's behavior became intolerable to Truman, the president peremptorily and quickly relieved him of all four of the august commands he held and ordered General Matthew C. Ridgway to succeed him immediately.[21] The quick and decisive manner in which the president exercised his power as commander in chief when he fired MacArthur on April 11, 1951, stands as incontrovertible evidence that the principle of civilian control over the military was hale and hearty.

At the Senate hearings on MacArthur's firing as well as in later writings, his critics portrayed the general as wanting to start World War III. But often their arguments were based on the false premise that only two options were possible at the time, either a new world war or the limited war as it existed. In truth, other alternatives could have been considered, such as a controlled escalation of naval and air warfare that might have restored decision on the battlefield and ended the bloody stalemate, yet without provoking the Soviet Union to enter the conflict.

At no time did MacArthur advocate a ground invasion of Communist China by UN forces. His proposals on December 30, 1950, to blockade and bomb mainland China and to use Chiang Kai-shek's troops in Korea or in limited assaults against the Chinese coast opposite Taiwan were carefully considered by the joint chiefs.[22] All his points ultimately were rejected on tactical or logistical grounds, but not until the joint chiefs testified later at the Senate hearings did they suggest that they had interpreted his four-point plan as an effort to start a world war.

Actually MacArthur was firmly opposed to a war with the USSR at that time because he knew how unprepared the American military was and because he was convinced Stalin would not engage in full-scale warfare to defend North Korea or Communist China. As it turned out, MacArthur may have had a clearer idea of the Soviet Union's stance than the Truman administration did; the general was one of the first high-level American leaders to repudiate the notion of the communist monolith, with marching orders to its satellites supposedly emanating from its Moscow center.

It is a sad commentary on bias among historians that very few scholars have penetrated the curtain of emotionalism enshrouding the Truman-MacArthur controversy to rethink the issues that were at stake. There really was no crisis in civil-military relations and no threat of World War III, though there was insubordination and an unfortunate breakdown in communication in the American chain of command. If he were alive today, Truman, who always had a mischievous sense of humor, woulud chuckle over how the public and the scholars still buy his version of why he fired "our Big General in the Far East" or "the Right Hand Man of God," two of his favorite descriptions of MacArthur.[23]

Besides the two common perceptions of Truman as Korean War chief, there are other aspects of his wartime leadership that deserve attention. Mainly because of Truman's staunch advocacy of civil rights, the integration of the American armed services was under way by the time he left office. On July 26, 1948, he issued an executive order for the uniformed services to implement "as rapidly as possible" a policy of "equality of treatment and opportunity for all persons without regard to race."[24] His order also established the President's Committee on Equality of Treatment and Opportunity in the Armed Services to examine the personnel policies and practices of the military establishment to determine how they needed to be revised. At a meeting in September 1948 with the committee, which was made up mainly of nationally prominent African-American leaders, Truman stated that he hoped they could work quietly with the military in accomplishing desegregation "in such a way that it is not a publicity stunt."[25] The somewhat vague, confusing text of the order gave temporary hope to some of the reluctant brass who believed it could be evaded.

By the time the Korean War erupted some progress had been made, but a furor arose when thirty-nine soldiers in the all-black 24th Infantry Regiment were convicted of "misconduct before the enemy" and sentenced to long prison terms. Thurgood Marshall, special counsel for the National Association for the Advancement of Colored People, spent more than a month in Japan and Korea investigating the courts-martial of the suspiciously large number of 24th Infantry troops. Pressure from Truman and "Marshall's highly critical report" brought reduced sentences or reversed judgments in most of the cases.[26] Three months after Marshall's report and six weeks after his own relief as Far East commander, MacArthur commented on Marshall's findings, "I am willing to concede that these courts-martial may have been excessive."[27]

By late 1951 all the U.S. Eighth Army's outfits were integrated in Korea, but segregation still was prevalent among American troops in Europe and did not get under way there until the spring of 1952. The air force and the marine corps abolished their last all-black units in late 1952, and the navy had made some headway, though about half of the black sailors were stewards. It would be October 1954 before the army, which had the largest number of African-Americans by far of the armed forces, integrated its remaining all-black units. The journey to fair and equal conditions for blacks in the U.S. Armed Forces was by no means completed, but Truman could leave the White House with the satisfaction of knowing that thanks to his initiative and constant pressure on the Department of Defense, the Korean War was a landmark in the movement toward equality of treatment for all American military personnel.

If Truman's efforts toward military integration had far-reaching implications, his decision to authorize MacArthur's forces to liberate North Korea in the autumn of 1950 was an unprecedented incursion into the Cold War that culminated in Communist China's entry into the war. On September 27, 1950, twelve days after MacArthur launched his brilliant amphibious assault at Inchon, the joint chiefs, with Truman's approval, sent him a directive setting forth the new objective of "destruction of the North Korean Armed Forces." He was "authorized to conduct military operations north of the 38th Parallel in Korea, provided that at the time of such operations there has been no entry into North Korea by major Soviet or Chinese Communist forces."[28] Two days later General of the Army George Marshall, who had become secretary of defense on the 21st, sent MacArthur a cordial, supportive message that included a potentially dangerous carte blanche: "We want you to feel unhampered strategically and tactically to proceed north of the 38th Parallel."[29] MacArthur, who was feeling quite confident after his Inchon-Seoul envelopment had broken the back of the North Korean Army, replied cockily to Marshall: "I regard all of Korea open for our military operations unless and until the enemy capitulates."[30]

South Korean divisions began crossing the border into North Korea on October 1, while that same day MacArthur broadcast an unconditional surrender ultimatum to North Korea that brought no response. With Truman's strong support, Acheson and the U.S. delegation at the UN drafted a resolution that, in effect, would give UN sanction to MacArthur's forces conquering North Korea and establishing "a unified, independent and democratic government in the sovereign state of Korea." It was passed by the UN General Assembly on October 7 by the overwhelming vote of forty-seven to five, with seven abstentions.[31]

In the Cold War context of the time as well as the heady euphoria about MacArthur's capabilities following Inchon, it must have seemed to Truman like an unexpected opportunity to free an oppressed land. But Truman's decision involved two serious risks. First, he gambled on an escalation of the war that could cost him and the United States its allies, who feared that the American strategic priority would shift from Western Europe to East Asia. Second, he risked the chance to accomplish many goals in Fair Deal domestic programs that were much dearer to him than the unification of Korea. As one authority analyzed it: "Indeed, Korean unity was so low in Truman's order of priorities that it was off his list within three months of its adoption. It went off London's list on first sight of the Chinese in Korea; Truman was somewhat slower, to his cost."[32] In the media in allied nations as well as in the United States after the ensuing Chinese intervention in North Korea, the conflict was often tabbed "Truman's War." He had risked his prestige on a new, radical, and impossible war aim that would contribute not only to the demise of MacArthur's career but to the president's as well. Truman's gamble on liberating a communist nation would culminate in the first American war to end in a stalemate. To his dismay it became a war that he could neither win nor end.

In December 1950, while Communist Chinese armies were driving the UN Command out of North Korea, Truman announced the appointment of General of the Army Dwight D. Eisenhower as the first supreme allied commander of NATO forces. At the same time, the president stated that American forces in Western Europe would be considerably reinforced as the nucleus of the ground arm of NATO. MacArthur, who had been pleading for four additional divisions to stem the Chinese tide in Korea, was pleased when Senator Kenneth S. Wherry of Nebraska, the Republican floor leader, introduced a resolution in early January 1951 proclaiming that "it is the sense of the Senate that no ground forces of the United States should be assigned to duty in the European area for the purposes of the North Atlantic Treaty pending the formulation of a policy with respect thereto by the Congress."[33]

Thus was set in motion the three-month Great Debate, as it became known, that produced an acrimonious battle in the Senate and in the national media over Truman's right to deploy troops to NATO without congressional approval and, more important, over the priority for the United States of the security of Western Europe, especially when American forces were engaged in a war on the other side of the world. Senator Robert A. Taft of Ohio, "Mr. Republican" to party conservatives, strongly supported Wherry's resolution and helped to persuade the Foreign Relations and Armed Services committees of the Senate to begin hearings on the matter later in January.

The antiadministration forces during the Great Debate included fiscal conservatives, who warned that America's NATO commitment was becoming too costly; self-styled realists who would restrict American military assistance to nations where the communists had already used force, namely Korea and China; admirers of General MacArthur and, usually a different breed altogether, supporters of Senator Joseph E. McCarthy of Wisconsin; and, finally, those who favored aggressive interventionism in Asia and isolationism in Europe. With Marshall and Eisenhower lending their considerable prestige to the administration's campaign on Capitol Hill, Truman's plans to strengthen NATO militarily were not deterred by either the above-named factions or the news of increased fighting and soaring casualties in Korea.

In mid-February, with Truman's enthusiastic endorsement, Secretary of Defense Marshall announced that four U.S. Army divisions would be sent to Europe, and in April Eisenhower established the new supreme headquarters of NATO near Paris. Eventually the Senate tabled the Wherry resolution in favor of another one that endorsed Eisenhower's NATO appointment and the deployment of the four divisions to Europe but also advised the president to consult Congress before further reinforcing the American forces in Europe, to submit semiannual reports to Congress about NATO, and to get the other NATO nations to contribute more troops and funds to the organization's military arm. The formal end of the Great Debate came with the Senate's passage of this resolution a week before MacArthur's dismissal in early April.

Truman had stood his ground firmly and courageously in favor of Europe's priority over Asia in American strategic and security planning. He did not again have to face a formidable congressional attack on the Atlantic alliance that he had been zealously striving to form since the crises of 1947–1949 that resulted in the Marshall Plan, the Berlin blockade, and the founding of NATO. "The impact of the Korean War on European-American relations," observes an esteemed historian of diplomacy, "may make that event, rather than the signing of the North Atlantic Treaty in 1949, the watershed of American isolationism." He continues, "The conflict tested America's determination to turn away from the traditional abstention from European political affairs and from military obligations they might impose."[34] Truman thus played a crucial role, for better or

125

worse, in keeping strategic priority on Western Europe during a critical period when the Asia-first excitement in the United States was at its zenith.

This chapter has been only an introduction to the common perceptions that have been too uncritically accepted about Truman as wartime commander in chief and a glimpse at a few of his other strengths and weaknesses in that role. Space does not permit delving into his other important wartime military decisions, six of which would have been especially tempting to consider: (1) in contrast to FDR's shelving of the State Department in global strategic affairs, Truman's gradual but unmistakable shift of dominance in determining strategy and force deployments from the Pentagon to the State Department, especially under Marshall and Acheson; (2) his encouragement during the Korean War of Japan as a base of operations and logistics for UN forces, which precipitated the subsequent boom in that nation's industry and trade; (3) his endorsement of the basic principles of NSC-68, a National Security Council study of 1950, that led to high levels of military spending and unprecedented peacetime growth of the military-industrial complex in the United States; (4) his decision to open truce negotiations in Korea in July 1951 when American field commanders were reporting Communist Chinese troops surrendering in record numbers and enemy armies on the brink of collapse; (5) his involvement in reorganizing the intelligence community, especially in creating the CIA in 1947 and the National Security Agency in 1952; and (6) his ambivalence toward military leaders, viewing most of them with the contempt that a National Guard captain might feel toward a regular army general yet holding in the highest esteem General Marshall and Admiral Leahy among his principal confidants. For a president who professed to dislike virtually all things military, seldom has there been a White House occupant who relished more his role as commander in chief or whose fate it was to make so many critical military decisions.[35]

6

LYNDON JOHNSON:
A RELUCTANT HAWK

FRANK E. VANDIVER

Some presidents make history, others endure it, and some have it thrust upon them. Lyndon Johnson engaged history on all three fronts. Even his enemies concede that he bestrode his offices rather than filled them and that he bulked more egregious, louder, coarser, subtler, craftier, and more charming than most mortals.

Like all men of power, LBJ generated legends and myths and rumors that trail after him like dust devils on a Texas prairie. Some of them nearly match the man, but he is hard to pin down, to typify, to fit into any commonplace mold. McGeorge Bundy calls LBJ "the hardest man to trace."[1] There is something uncomfortable about a man so big—in Dean Rusk's eyes, Johnson "strode like a colossus over the Executive Branch,"[2]—and that sort of hugeness fuels an envy that delights in chipping away at monuments.

There is little doubt that LBJ wanted to be a monument, one fixed in the hearts of the American people as a talisman of America's promise of a better life for everyone. His Great Society ideas sprang from genuine concern for the "under-citizens" of the nation: the poor, the deprived, the racially mistreated. That he cared is evident from the things he achieved in the Senate and from the remarkable package of progressive legislation introduced during his presidency.

If LBJ loomed large, he also loomed as a "heavy" in the eyes of many people. Sometimes petty, sometimes crude in word and gesture, now and then mean, Johnson had warts to match his virtues. He is easy to caricature, much harder to characterize, and almost impossible to encompass, and much of the problem in sizing him up stems from Vietnam.

127

As the Asian imbroglio degenerated into a crisis and then into a disaster of unpredictable scope, people's perspectives shifted. Americans generally look askance at their leaders during peacetime—carping about their policies, narrow vision, small gifts, and large foibles—but during periods of crisis, particularly in time of war, Americans look to their leaders, especially the president, for solace and success. LBJ enjoyed a couple of good years of trust after he took office, as Americans, shattered and frightened by President John F.

Kennedy's assassination, sensed and shared LBJ's sorrowing, felt his awesome burden, and gave him affection and faith.

He already claimed a good deal of respect because of his selfless service as vice-president but especially because of his peerless performance as Senate majority leader. Most of his career had been spent in public service. A product of raucous Texas politics, LBJ loved the workings of suasion and authority and put his feelings about the presidency clearly: "I . . . used its powers and prerogatives as fully as I could to accomplish what I thought ought to be done."[3] Johnson spent power carefully, but Vietnam drained it daily.

Lady Bird Johnson remembers that Vietnam hung over her husband's administration like a black cloud. She watched as pressures mounted and mused that "Lyndon lives in a cloud of troubles with few rays of light."[4] The war sapped energy, quenched hope, and made faint hearts from strong, and it finally eroded LBJ's own considerable confidence to the point of his deciding not to run for reelection in 1968. Why? What happened to pull down an initially popular government and force a resignation?

There are all kinds of speculative explanations: the war as an aberration of time and place; the rising influence of a growing number of doves; deliberate media misperceptions that bled America's belief in its own virtue; fatigue; the ineluctable "body count." Reasons are rife as critics. Over them all hangs an important question: Did the commander in chief do a good job? That question, however, is hard to answer. Immediately comes a confusion of other questions: What does a commander in chief do? What is the scope of the job? How does one measure the person to the task? What is the incumbent commander's concept of command? How wise and honest are the commander's advisers?

Experience taught Lyndon Johnson the nature of the job. He knew the Constitution better than most, had often consulted with wartime presidents, and had worked closely with the Senate Armed Services Committee and with Pentagon officials on a good many budgets. Did LBJ have a personal idea of the job? Not a clearly enunciated one, other than that he knew as president he was the commander of the armed forces of the United States. His own experience in the Pacific, large or small, gave him some perspective on men at war. His Texas background lent pride in the martial doings of Texans from the Alamo to Gaines's Mill and on the Marne. President Harry S. Truman's troubles in Korea had been shared by LBJ, who had been majority whip for the Democrats from 1951 to 1953, and Johnson never forgot that the Chinese had crossed the Yalu River. As vice-president, he saw daily the growing American presence in Vietnam.

Johnson's Asian fact-finding mission for President Kennedy in May 1961 forged lasting views about Laos, Thailand, Cambodia, Vietnam, Taiwan, India, and Pakistan. Reporting on that trip, he told JFK bluntly that the Southeast Asia Treaty Organization "is not now and probably never will be the answer because of British and French unwillingness to support decisive action," and he warned that "country to country, the degree differs, but Laos has created doubt and concern about intentions of the United States throughout Southeast Asia. . . . The independent Asians do not wish to have their own status resolved in like manner."[5]

Shrewdly assessing his reception by various leaders, Johnson told President Kennedy that the mission may have stopped the decline of confidence in the United States but did not restore what had already been lost. Everyone showed the kindest courtesy, but LBJ saw behind the diplomatic masks. "If these men I saw at your request were bankers," he told JFK, "I would know—without bothering to ask—that there would be no further extensions on my note."[6]

As he flew back to Washington on Air Force One on November 22, 1963, the new president of the United States faced vast turmoil. Not until two days later did he fully pick up the mantle of commander in chief. When he did, war news was mixed. Still working out of his vice-presidential office in the Executive Office Building, the president sent for Secretary of State Dean Rusk, Secretary of Defense Robert McNamara, Under Secretary of State George Ball, CIA Director John McCone, and National Security Adviser McGeorge Bundy.

First, the president wanted to hear the collective view of how things were going in Vietnam; next, he wanted to assess what his ambassador to South Vietnam, Henry Cabot Lodge, had to say against some impressions he had formed of untidy conditions in the U.S. Embassy in Saigon. Lodge waxed optimistic. Although the recent ousting and assassination of South Vietnam's President Ngo Dinh Diem had resulted in a kind of desperate scrambling for a successor, the ambassador thought that on the whole the new government had advantages over the old. Military men now ran South Vietnam, and Lodge expected them to speed up their war effort.[7]

Unconvinced, LBJ asked John McCone what his Saigon reports indicated and heard a generally depressing evaluation: Vietcong activity had greatly increased in the weeks since the coup, and there were indications that North Vietnam intended to step up pressure against the South.[8] McCone offered scant comfort. "As long as the Ho Chi Minh Trail was open and supplies and convoys of people could come pouring in there without interruption," McCone said, "we couldn't say things were so good."[9] These conflicting reports brought LBJ to his first confrontation concerning Vietnam, a confrontation made difficult by its political dimensions.

Henry Cabot Lodge ranked high in public opinion. A Republican senior statesman, a man of proven patriotism and diplomatic competence, he had been appointed by President Kennedy as a demonstration of solidarity in Vietnam. With a respected Republican leader in Saigon, JFK hoped to show bipartisan commitment to South Vietnam's effort to resist communism. There may have been a bit of Irish cant to the appointment as well since overt failure could be laid on Republican shoulders. But Lodge generated a force of his own. Shortly after Lodge's appointment, the president and his advisers came to realize that their ambassador followed his own policies and programs, that he operated almost as the satrap of Saigon. With his high reputation, Lodge was hard to control, and undue pressure might generate political repercussions.

Lodge thus effectively eluded subordination, and that bothered LBJ. His trip to the Far East gave him fears about the embassy, about the way Americans in South Vietnam warred with each other, about the issue of coordination. With an unerring sense of timing, Johnson turned to Lodge and spoke of his own "serious misgivings." He was unhappy at reports of dissension at the Saigon mission. No more of that would be tolerated. Develop and manage a strong cooperative team, the president told Lodge; Washington would support him. As for priorities, supporting the new South Vietnamese govern-

131

ment would be first. If this seemed to expand Lodge's authority, it also firmly fixed his responsibility, especially since the president said that he would pick some members of the new team.[10]

There was a point to this meeting that Lodge's hauteur might have blurred, a point clearly understood by McGeorge Bundy. Lodge struck LBJ as a "soft man," one in need of stiffening. LBJ wanted the ambassador to know that his new chief was not weak, was not going to lose the war, and "neither was Cabot Lodge."[11] That meeting's ambiguities, the conflicting testimony, and the uncertainties seeping through dispatches from Vietnam set a fairly dismal trend for the years of Johnson's war.

A user of history, LBJ often recalled Truman's dedication to his doctrine of containment and remembered, too, the wages of appeasement earned by Neville Chamberlain and the authors of the Munich Pact. French experience in Indochina also figured in the president's Asian calculations, and he never forgot several of his predecessors' commitment to South Vietnam. "I do not believe that President Eisenhower had any real choice but to originate our commitment," he said later, adding that "I do not believe that President Kennedy could have done otherwise than deepen our commitment."[12] As president, Johnson saw no other alternative for himself and told Congress and the American people on November 27, 1963, that "we will keep our commitments from South Vietnam to West Berlin."[13]

Keeping those commitments involved devising ways to reach decisions on the war. From the beginning, the president was determined to keep JFK's people in their jobs—those who would agree to stay. Later, critics would suggest that this decision was a sentimental mistake, but his reasons were not altogether sentimental. Johnson wanted to heal the wounds of the assassination and thought a show of continuity would reassure the nation and the world. He also sincerely believed that most of Kennedy's people were outstanding performers.

For war policy, Johnson counted on Secretary of Defense Robert S. McNamara, an authentic "whiz kid" who cherished the precision of systems analysis and whose mind impressed Johnson as carrying more information "than the average encyclopedia."[14] He counted, too, on McGeorge Bundy, Harvard man and top-flight foreign policy expert, who continued to serve as national security adviser until 1966. Through these men came advice from others, especially from the Joint Chiefs of Staff, headed by the courteous and extremely efficient General Earle G. "Bus" Wheeler. The channels were good and apparently reliable.

Information and advice coming through these channels and from the State Department, headed by the scholarly, careful, and gentlemanly Dean Rusk, all confirmed the need to stick with South Vietnam.[15] If the United States dumped its ally there, erosion of faith could occur all over the world. The Domino Theory might well prove true. Noncommunist Southeast Asian nations might topple like tenpins, a possibility chilling to LBJ and his advisers.

For the new president, some changes in operational procedure were necessary. As vice-president, Johnson had attended JFK's National Security Council meetings with their large and varying membership, their unstructured, wide-ranging discussions, their interruptions and background murmurings. This method suited Kennedy perfectly; he wanted to hear everybody, to let conversations set their own pace, and from this bubbling caldron he fashioned a course of action. Not LBJ, who found working with his whole cabinet too cumbersome, let alone JFK's National Security ménage. Johnson worked with McGeorge Bundy and others to find a closer, tighter way to hear advice, a way that might choke off the leaks that so offended him. By early 1965 an informal but workable system had evolved, the Tuesday Lunch Club, sometimes called the Tuesday Cabinet.

Membership in the club remained fairly constant: Rusk, McNamara (followed by his successor as secretary of defense, Clark Clifford), McGeorge Bundy (followed by his successor, Walt W. Rostow), and Bill Moyers, White House press secretary and close LBJ confidant (followed by his successor, George Christian). General Earle Wheeler participated on an ad hoc basis until early 1966 when he joined the permanent membership.

The club met mostly on Tuesdays; the subject was Vietnam, and to the extent that policy came from these meetings, "cabinet" is not an impertinent description. Subject matter so serious required ambient surroundings, and the president picked the family lunch room—

a retreat open only to a privileged few. The room may have worked on the subconscious of those beleaguered guests; its wallpaper depicted American troops in triumph at Yorktown and other places.[16]

The minutes, which form a remarkable body of source material, were taken by two usually silent attendees, Jack Valenti and Tom Johnson.[17] But the club had a record beyond minutes; it came to have its own historian, Professor Henry Graff of Columbia University. Moyers and his assistant, Hayes Redmon, persuaded the president to ask Graff to make periodic visits to the White House, to talk to the president and other key decisionmakers, and to chronicle the Tuesday Lunch proceedings. The result was Graff's book, *The Tuesday Cabinet: Deliberation and Decision on Peace and War under Lyndon B. Johnson*, which offers an unusually candid source on Johnson's Vietnam decisions. That the president agreed to the arrangement testifies to his yearning for a place in the historical memory.

But by the time the Tuesday lunches began, the Vietnam War had greatly changed. LBJ inherited what amounted to a limited war. Kennedy had permitted incremental additions of advisers, and by November 1963 some 16,000 Americans served as trainers and advisers to South Vietnamese military leaders and units. A look at costs showed that about $500 million went to Vietnam in 1963. A broader look at the whole situation showed that North Vietnam's efforts had grown apace.[18]

As he adjusted to the Vietnam burden, LBJ kept hoping the war would somehow dwindle. "The last thing I wanted," he said, "was to become a 'wartime' President."[19] At the same time, he never wavered from his determination not to be the first American president to disavow commitment or the first to lose a war. Each day brought some further oozing into the Southeast Asian quagmire, some little sinking feeling. Laos seemed to be disappearing. The Geneva Accords were ignored by the communists; large parts of the Laotian kingdom lay under control from North Vietnam, or possibly China. Prospects for security in negotiations with Ho Chi Minh or anyone else in Hanoi were dim to nonexistent.

Each look at the war renewed LBJ's concern about the coming presidential election of 1964. Johnson wanted to be president in his own right, and he feared a broadened war would hurt his election

chances. True, the Republican standard-bearer, Senator Barry Gold-
water, advocated hard war, accused the Democrats of weakness and
fear, and offered a target of unreason that LBJ and his campaign
people could hardly miss. Still, the election prompted caution, as did
LBJ's natural affinity for congressional approval.

A lifetime's learning suggested that nothing could be done without close liaison with Capitol Hill. As LBJ grappled with the heavy
burden of trying to move JFK's legislative program through a reluctant Congress, he hoped for enough respite in Vietnam to deal with
domestic issues. If Hanoi increased the pressure south of the famed
DMZ (the so-called Demilitarized Zone along the 17th parallel) the
United States might have to send more help to its wavering ally.
More help might call for a large response—more men and more
money. If a large response was necessary, it ought to be made only
with full congressional support. Johnson steeled himself for the unhappy possibility.

In the early hours of Sunday, August 2, 1964, an urgent message
came to the president's bedroom, a message that made a large response essential. Early that morning a destroyer, the USS *Maddox*,
had been attacked in the Gulf of Tonkin by North Vietnamese warships. *Maddox* returned fire. Details were still arriving. A hastily
called meeting brought Dean Rusk, George Ball, Deputy Defense
Secretary Cyrus Vance, General Wheeler, and several intelligence
types to the White House later in the morning to decide what should
be done.

Several issues clouded an easy decision: U.S. Navy vessels were
running electronic intelligence-gathering patrols in the gulf; so were
patrol boats of the South Vietnamese Navy. These activities opened
the possibility of an accidental reaction by North Vietnamese forces.
Caution prevailed; consensus suggested no retaliation beyond a stiff
note to Hanoi.

Two days later, on August 4, came reports that the *Maddox* and
another U.S. destroyer, the *C. Turner Joy*, had been attacked in the
Gulf of Tonkin. The president wanted careful assessment of the alleged attack, and Secretary McNamara sought confirmation from
the Commander in Chief, Pacific (CINCPAC), Admiral U. S. G.
Sharp. Flurries of radio traffic, some of it intercepted from North

Vietnamese ships, offered apparently irrefutable evidence of attack. The president met with the NSC in the evening, then with key congressional leaders.[20]

To the Senate and House leadership, Johnson told what he knew, confessed that "we might be forced into further action," and asked for a congressional resolution of support "for our entire position in Southeast Asia."[21] If heavier American involvement became necessary, LBJ did not "want to go in unless Congress goes in with me."[22] Out of that meeting came the Southeast Asia Resolution, also called the Tonkin Gulf Resolution. That resolution sparks controversy yet. Did Johnson use the relatively small Tonkin crisis to secure a wide-ranging resolution that allowed undeclared war? Critics then and now point to that moment as the beginning of the public's erosion of belief in the Johnson administration's Vietnam policy.

What happened in the Gulf of Tonkin is difficult to discern. Radio traffic was confused, but there seems little doubt about the first attack. That there was a second attack even LBJ came to doubt, as have others who have studied the incident. Whether LBJ pulled a well-worn draft of a resolution from his pocket as soon as he heard of the "provocation" (a well-worn tale in itself) is doubtful. That he did want a resolution and had talked about it with staff members for some time is a matter of record. In the rush of excitement about the second attack, the president's measured reaction is understandable and in keeping with a commander in chief's responsibilities. If Hanoi's forces really were escalating confrontation so blatantly, the United States had to make a firm response. Simply doing nothing might have invited further and more dangerous depredation.

Rarely did Johnson function more effectively than in the days of the Tonkin crisis. Blending military concern with his matchless political suasion, he won wide congressional and domestic support for a difficult foreign policy. He met crisis with unexpected flair.

In later crises LBJ's reaction time shortened as the White House processes improved. When Walt Rostow became national security adviser in 1966, he insisted that General Wheeler become a regular member of the Tuesday Lunch group so that the Joint Chiefs of Staff would have a direct voice. Consequently, the group functioned more effectively. The meetings were crisp, with opposition usually limited to George Ball's lonesome complaints about wrong war, wrong place, wrong time.[23]

LBJ worked stubbornly to overcome artificial consensus with voracious questing for facts. William Bundy, assistant secretary of state for Far Eastern affairs, cherishes a strong respect for the president's demand for and retention of facts. He says that Johnson "had one of the ten best minds I have ever dealt with in any walk of life" and recalls that Johnson could "really see the practical angles [of an issue] but he could also understand the big picture perfectly well."[24] Bundy also points out that LBJ had his own methods for uncovering information: "This paper or that paper, [the president] would have read it; he would know about it. What he was looking for was the recommendation for the view that wasn't the view he had expected."[25]

After his own landslide election, Johnson felt easier in making war policy. Sifting through the opinions of the Tuesday Lunch group and of a wide-ranging group of advisers—the president might well ask any visitor to the White House a riveting question about the war—he came slowly to the belief that North Vietnam had to be pushed to accept the fact that the United States would not allow South Vietnam to collapse. Once that message reached Ho Chi Minh and others in Hanoi, LBJ believed that negotiations would begin. He based this conviction on Western logic and experience; consequently, he and his advisers could not appreciate North Vietnam's commitment to victory despite the cost in lives, treasure, and time.

Throughout most of his years in the White House, Johnson remained convinced that if he and Ho Chi Minh could sit down and "reason together" a deal could be struck. Greatly bothered that he could not "get into Ho's head," the president several times tried writing to his opponent with offers of peaceful negotiations.[26] These efforts brought no results, and LBJ continued the incremental response strategy so often criticized as too little and too scattered.

The president believed, and found no real opposition from any of his advisers except for George Ball, that the United States should raise the intensity of reaction bit by bit in order to send Hanoi a message of controlled but limitless American power: the United States could destroy all of North Vietnam's war-making capacity if necessary. This message was intended to be the main point of Operation

ROLLING THUNDER, the code name for bombing attacks on targets in North Vietnam itself, which LBJ authorized in February 1965. These attacks continued, with several well-publicized interruptions, to stimulate peace talks, until 1968. Admiral U. S. G. Sharp, who directed ROLLING THUNDER from Hawaii, described the air warfare operation as "action we hoped might prove a decisive step in the right direction."[27]

As North Vietnamese cadres continued to build support among Vietcong elements in the South, American advisers in South Vietnam called for more men and money. With great reluctance but with determination, President Johnson finally agreed to send in combat troops. On March 8, 1965, two marine battalions landed at Da Nang with orders to defend U.S. airfields. Troops continued to go to South Vietnam as North Vietnam escalated its efforts. By December of 1965 almost 200,000 American soldiers were committed.

As the war expanded, the president became increasingly involved. Johnson took personal interest in the American military leaders and had much respect for General William C. Westmoreland, who had replaced General Paul Harkins as commander of the U.S. Military Assistance Command, Vietnam (MACV), in June of 1964. Some critics ask if the president shared Clemenceau's view that war was too important to be left to the generals. Answers from key Johnson aides vary: some say, no, he had great respect for the military; others say, yes, LBJ distrusted soldiers. On the whole, the president's conduct of the war shows considerable deference to his generals' views. Experience in Congress over many years had taught him a lot about men in uniform. They might work hard, sometimes sharply, for funds, but by and large they proved to be honest and patriotic. And with LBJ, patriotism counted. McGeorge Bundy remembers Johnson as determined "never to be the Commander-in-Chief who didn't back his troops."[28]

A survey of the mounting U.S. commitment raises interesting questions about that military sine qua non, unity of command. Dean Rusk is haunted by that issue to this day. "We never achieved unity of command in Vietnam. The war in South Vietnam was under . . . Westmoreland, MACV," he recalled in 1988, "but we did not have unity of command on the ground even in South Vietnam. [The]

South Vietnamese were clearly not under our command, absolutely, and the Allied forces were handled rather gingerly by Westmoreland. In any event, even Westmoreland's command was not unified. And then the bombing of the North was handled by CINCPAC in Hawaii. . . . Very often the Tuesday luncheon sessions were dealing with these problems of divided command."[29] When pressed, Secretary Rusk responded that this failure to achieve unity of command "maybe was the fault of Lyndon Johnson as President."[30]

Bombing targets did become a personal fascination for LBJ. Stories, pictures, and recollections abound of him haunting the White House Situation Room at all hours, reading the latest reports of bombing missions, poring over maps of areas north of the DMZ, and picking targets himself. This montage suggests a president enmeshed in micromanaging the war, and it is true that to some degree he did micromanage the North Vietnam bombing campaign. McGeorge Bundy thought a personal concern sparked LBJ's attention to the bombing: "I don't think that there is the smallest doubt that a part of him that was enormously warm and human was directly engaged with every flyer's life."[31]

President Johnson shared ignorance of guerrilla warfare with most of his generals. In Vietnam, U.S. forces looked for large enemy formations to smash with massive firepower. They sought a traditional front line to see and to hold. Only rarely did North Vietnamese regulars engage U.S. or Army of the Republic of Vietnam (ARVN) forces, and when they did, they usually lost. Infiltration, ambushes, terrorist attacks against village leaders, and undermining of morale were North Vietnamese and Vietcong specialties that defied standard American rules of engagement. It took time to adjust, time for the president himself to grasp the fractured nature of a new kind of war.

History is easily ignored, even by people who know it and think they use it. Johnson used history, yet the best historical precedent for Vietnam went unremembered—the war in the Philippines. In those islands from 1898 through World War II, U.S. forces fought various guerrilla campaigns with rising success. After World War II, the Huk rebellion brought in American advisers, and although some

139

of these veterans were called on to lend their expertise in Vietnam, the main lessons had been forgotten.

In time MACV developed new tactics in conjunction with ARVN units, but the greatest security for the South Vietnamese backcountry came from strengthening the pacification programs under Robert Komer and William Colby. These efforts, building on the Diem regime's old strategic hamlet program, used local volunteers for village defense and gradually cut down the numbers of regulars committed to protection of the interior.

Patience became a presidential hallmark as the war progressed. It must have seemed to LBJ that every week brought new requests for troops, money, supplies, or diplomatic missions in search of an elusive armistice. Rarely, according to minutes of the Tuesday lunches, did Johnson's vaunted anger show. He listened attentively, probed vigorously for differing views, reserved judgment, and decided in his own time. A glance at the schedule of troop insertions shows that the president followed his own idea of incrementalism. He usually responded positively to Westmoreland's manpower requests, but not wholly—10, 15, or 25 percent of each request might be met.

That policy, not unlike British Prime Minister David Lloyd George's in World War I, kept numbers down and demanded economy of force. Such a response also made possible the gradual increase of American troops in Vietnam without a diminution of the American presence in Europe. In the Tet crisis of January–February 1968, the policy seemed vindicated. As North Vietnamese attacks flared throughout a good part of South Vietnam, U.S. and ARVN counterattacks were successful, Later, after the communist offensive collapsed, Westmoreland went on the attack and said he needed no more men. That could hardly have been surprising; he had nearly half a million men under his command.

Tet is a holiday in Vietnam, a period surrounding the lunar new year reserved for family things. It had been kept by both sides throughout the long conflict as a time of truce and was so proclaimed again in 1968. There were some rumblings from the villages through various intelligence networks of a huge enemy buildup in the weeks before Tet. Hindsight lends perception to those hints of trouble; they were correct indicators of enemy activity.

One of the tenets of the "people's war" doctrine is that there will come a time when guerrilla activity ends in a great general offensive by regular forces. This offensive will trigger a huge popular uprising that signals final victory. Tet 1968 was to be that final uprising, or so it had been planned by Hanoi.

Most of the attacks failed in a welter of blood. In the old city of Hue, a major enemy contingent held out for twenty-six days and murdered more than three thousand civilians in the process. From a military standpoint, Tet proved a communist disaster. From a propaganda and political standpoint, however, it proved to be the turning point of the war. Media coverage brought attacks on the U.S. Embassy in Saigon into every American living room; battle scenes all across Vietnam suddenly stood in stark contrast to repeated assurances of seeing "light at the end of the tunnel," of growing security, and of bringing American boys home soon. One particularly graphic photograph of a South Vietnamese general shooting a prisoner in the head shocked Americans into questions about exported morality and the wages of brutality. By the time Hue was secured, American public opinion had swung against the war and to the side of protesters appearing more frequently on college campuses across the country.[32]

Reading between the lines in Johnson's book, *The Vantage Point*, it is clear that he too sat in surprise as the multiple television sets in the White House ran broadcasts lurid with casualties, explosions, fires, and screams. At the same time, LBJ's attention was riveted on Khe Sanh, an American firebase that guarded the road into Laos not far below the DMZ. Somehow many Americans, President Johnson included, became alarmingly convinced that this remote high place bore a striking similarity to Dien Bien Phu, the great last siege in France's effort to hold Indochina. Actually there were no real similarities. Dien Bien Phu, a post nestled in a valley, could be dominated by artillery from virtually every angle and was in a position that was almost impossible to support from the air. Khe Sanh Combat Base (KSCB) had a small dirt airstrip for use by helicopters and transport aircraft; the base was within range of artillery support and also had its own resident defense company. Defended by four U.S. and one ARVN battalion, KSCB stood off two North Vietnamese regular divisions. Holding Khe Sanh became a fixation for the president. It seemed to represent an anchor in post-Tet drift.[33]

When in February of 1968 Westmoreland asked for 206,000 more men, LBJ turned a long look toward the future. McNamara, slowly losing confidence in his own assessment of Vietnam, left the administration to head the World Bank. Clark Clifford, distinguished lawyer and longtime Johnson confidant, took McNamara's place as secretary of defense. Clifford's first assignment was to take a close look at the Vietnam situation and to review it with an eye to making policy changes.

On March 26, a group of distinguished citizens, the so-called "Wise Men," joined LBJ at the White House to hear a briefing on the war. The president asked Generals Westmoreland, Wheeler, and Creighton W. Abrams to present the military situation candidly. "We don't want an inspirational talk or a gloom talk," he said. "Just give them the factual, cold, honest picture as you see it."[34] The Wise Men included Dean Acheson, George Ball, General Omar Bradley, Arthur Dean (who had negotiated the Korean War settlement), McGeorge Bundy, Henry Cabot Lodge, General Matthew Ridgway (of Korean War fame), and General Maxwell Taylor (former U.S. ambassador to Saigon).[35] A serious division of opinion among the Wise Men gave hope to both hawks and doves and left the final decision where it had always been—in LBJ's hands.

Shaken by a clear decline in confidence from so trusted a group, by the growing tumult around the country, as well as by slippage of support in Congress, Johnson prepared for a speech to the nation on March 31 and decided to halt the bombing of North Vietnam. In that speech, after offering a significant peace initiative that included the bombing halt, President Johnson announced that he would not be a candidate for reelection. He devoutly hoped that removing himself from center stage would open the way for serious negotiations between Washington and Hanoi.

The president's decision shocked the world and apparently shook Hanoi enough to bring its first serious response regarding peace. Abdication, resignation—whatever the label—the president was out. In the months remaining LBJ felt freer than ever to conduct the daily business of government, including the war. He kept all presidential candidates fully briefed on negotiations with Hanoi and hoped for an end to fighting before he left office.

In retrospect, what kind of commander in chief was Lyndon Baines Johnson?

A meddler? The record answers: rarely and only when necessary.

A carper? Rarely and usually in a hot moment.

A micromanager? Probably, in some areas.

A supporter of subordinates? Routinely and with strength.

A strategist? Not really. LBJ came to strategy by listening and putting divergent ideas into a plan he could support.

A tactician? No. He almost never tried to direct units in the field, despite rumors of his picking up the phone and calling company commanders directly.

A political commander in chief? Here is the surprise, I think, in assessing Lyndon Johnson's war leadership. LBJ ought to have been the consummate master of conjuring public and political support for the war, but his devotion to the Great Society cast him in a defensive mode about Vietnam. He hesitated to call up reserves or to raise taxes in support of the war because he feared these moves would jeopardize his domestic programs. That proved an almost fatal error in judgment.

In sum, his policies and decisions show that he commanded when he had to but always preferred consensus and that he allowed himself to suffer each casualty too personally. Most of all, the record shows that he wore his commander in chief's hat with nagging discomfort.

7

RICHARD NIXON:
A BELLIGERENT DOVE

STEPHEN E. AMBROSE

Richard Nixon was not free to act as commander in chief as he thought best. By the time he became president, it was too late to escalate in Southeast Asia into a general air, sea, and ground war. He wanted to do so, was tempted to do so, had said from 1963 to March 1968 that he would do so if he became president. But his secretaries of state and defense, his national security adviser, people he consulted with, and the common political wisdom all told him that he could not do so.

The kind of actions that students of the war have suggested as possible routes to American victory—the occupation of Hanoi and of the Ho Chi Minh Trail in Laos and Cambodia—were beyond the capability of the American armed forces in Indochina after March 1968, when President Lyndon Johnson rejected the option of reinforcing those forces. In the aftermath of the Tet offensive, Nixon accepted that decision.

Unlike Franklin D. Roosevelt, Nixon could not demand an unconditional surrender. Unlike Harry Truman and Dwight Eisenhower in Korea, he could not dig a trench across the border dividing North and South Vietnam and force the communists to stay on their own side, not so long as the Ho Chi Minh Trail remained open, providing free access to the South for the North Vietnamese Army (NVA). American mobilization was not sufficient to expand the war, and the American political situation would not allow further escalation.

But Nixon believed strongly that he could not just walk away. To do that would be cowardly, a betrayal of the people and government of South Vietnam, America's allies for fifteen years, and would

weaken American credibility and influence in the world. Yet how could he ensure the survival of the government of Vietnam (GVN) when he could only fight the tip of the enemy's spear, not the spear-thrower, much less the spear-maker?

Nixon's answer was Vietnamization. During the 1968 campaign he had said that he had a policy to end the war, presumably with a victory. As commander in chief, he adopted a plan to end American involvement in the war. He said that he would bring about "peace with honor," which, in practice, "American withdrawal with honor."

It was Richard Nixon's fate to preside over the retreat of American power. He hated it. Every instinct in him rebelled against it. For twenty years, in every crisis, at every turning point, his advice had been to take the offensive against the communists. Attack, with more firepower, now—that was his policy. Yet in 1969, when he finally came to power, he had to retreat. He knew it, he accepted the fact, and he did it. The process began at his first news conference, January 27, 1969, in answering, as president, his first questions on foreign policy. With regard to Vietnam, he said he would propose to the other side "mutual withdrawal, guaranteed withdrawal, of forces." During the political campaign just completed, Nixon had never mentioned the possibility of American withdrawal.[1]

But withdrawal did not mean surrender. When Nixon came to power, he realized that the great American air offensive, February 1965 to March 31, 1968, code named ROLLING THUNDER, had failed to break the will of the North Vietnamese, while adding greatly to the numbers in the antiwar movement at home. He knew further that the great American ground offensive, from the summer of 1966 to the Tet offensive of 1968, had failed to destroy the NVA. So he wanted to try a third option, an offensive against the Ho Chi Minh Trail in Cambodia. By interdicting these supply lines, he hoped he could sever the enemy forces in the South from North Vietnam, making it possible for him to withdraw the American troops from South Vietnam while simultaneously reinforcing his "madman" image as the man who might do anything, thereby encouraging the enemy to agree to an armistice.

In March 1969 Nixon ordered the secret bombing of the Ho Chi

Minh Trail. Secretary of State William Rogers was opposed, because of public opinion. Secretary of Defense Melvin Laird was ready to go ahead but favored "going public right away," as he thought the bombing could not be kept secret. Nixon rejected their advice, thus beginning what would become a pattern in his decision-making as commander in chief—acting alone, against advice.[2]

When he did take advice for caution, he hated himself for doing so. On April 15, 1969, national security adviser Henry Kissinger called Nixon on the telephone to inform the president that the North Koreans had shot down a navy EC-121 reconnaissance aircraft. The plane, on a routine mission off the North Korean coast, was unarmed. It carried electronic equipment and a crew of thirty-one men. The barbaric act was one of those erratic cases of gratuitous violence in which North Korea indulges from time to time, apparently in this case as a birthday present to Kim Il Sung.

Nixon's instinctive reaction was that he was being tested and that he must meet force with force. He called an NSC meeting in the cabinet room.

Nixon opened. "We're going to show them," he said.

Secretary Rogers reminded him, "That's what Lyndon Johnson said about Vietnam, and we're still there."

Secretary Laird wondered what the United States would or could do if the North Koreans responded to an aggressive retaliation by invading South Korea. At a minimum, Laird pointed out, a second ground war in Asia would require a maximum mobilization in the United States.

William Porter, American ambassador to South Korea, sent a cable warning that a strong American reaction would be taken by the South Koreans as a signal, and they might well invade North Korea.

Attorney General John Mitchell wanted to charge with guns blazing. Vice-President Spiro Agnew, equally bellicose, responded to Rogers's and Laird's advice to go slow until all the facts were in by asking, "Why do we always take the other guy's position?"[3]

Why indeed? Kissinger was, if anything, even more eager than Mitchell, Agnew, and Nixon. He was engaged in a behind-the-scenes but tense winner-take-all struggle with Rogers for possession of Nixon's heart and mind. He knew the president liked to hear tough talk, liked to indulge in mad-bomber fantasies, liked to be told he was being tested and was strong enough to meet the test. This was a test, Kissinger said. The Soviets, the North Vietnamese, and the Chinese "would all be watching" (there is no evidence that any outside power was involved in the EC-121 incident, and, in fact, the Russians, at that moment, were helping in the search for survivors).[4]

"If we strike back, even though it's risky," declared the national security adviser, "they will say, 'This guy [Nixon] is becoming irrational—we'd better settle with him.' But if we back down, they'll say, 'This guy is the same as his predecessor, and if we wait he'll come to the same end.'"[5]

Kissinger wanted an air strike against a North Korean airfield, destroying every plane on it. He spoke of the possible necessity of using nuclear weapons.[6] But Nixon hesitated. Rogers and Laird had, between them, decades of experience in government; Kissinger had three months' experience. If the president ordered a violent reaction, the campuses of the United States, already in turmoil, would explode. A second ground war in Asia was unthinkable.

Nixon chose a milder response. He announced that the reconnaissance flights would continue, to be covered by American fighter aircraft. (In this Nixon was frustrated by the bureaucracy; in response to the EC-121 incident, Laird ordered all such flights canceled for a period of weeks.) Nixon also ordered another secret bombing mission over Cambodia, on Kissinger's insistence that this would send a strong signal to North Korea.

Aside from the bombing of Cambodia, Nixon had chosen the safe, sane, sensible response to the provocation. He hated himself for doing so. As Kissinger knew so well, Nixon preferred his own vengeful and vindictive side to his reasonable, intelligent, let's-take-everything-into-account side. Talking to Kissinger later about the EC-121 incident, Nixon made a vow: "They got away with it this time, but they'll never get away with it again."[7]

Some years later, Nixon remarked that the failure to respond quickly and strongly to the North Korean attack "was the most serious misjudgment of my Presidency, including Watergate."[8]

Instead of bombing North Korea, Nixon decided to announce the beginning of the withdrawal of Americans from Vietnam as well as a program to train and equip South Vietnam's armed forces. He made the announcement from Midway Island, in June, after a meeting with GVN President Nguyen van Thieu. Nixon called the policy "Vietnamization."

Thieu was opposed; General Creighton W. Abrams was opposed; Kissinger was opposed; Johnson had resisted such a move; and Nixon hated doing it, but the American political system imposed it on the president. He could not escalate on the ground and stalemate was unacceptable; withdrawal was the only choice.

Having decided to retreat, Nixon might have gone about it with dispatch. Instead, he went about it with agonizing slowness. At Midway, he announced that he was pulling out twenty-five thousand men and that at "regular intervals" thereafter he would pull out more. The pace of withdrawal would depend on three factors: progress in the Vietnamization program to train and equip ARVN; progress in the Paris peace talks; the level of enemy activity.[9]

He had obtained no concessions from Hanoi for his action. In his memoirs, he was brutally honest in stating that he had begun "an irreversible process, the conclusion of which would be the departure of all Americans from Vietnam."[10] He had made it impossible for the United States to extract concessions in negotiations from the North Vietnamese. He had made it difficult, if not impossible, for the American military commanders in Vietnam to maintain morale among their fighting men.

The phased, slow-motion retreat was the worst mistake of his presidency. Because the war went on, tension and division filled the land, and the Nixon haters went into a frenzy. It was the continuation of the Vietnam War that prepared the ground and provided the nourishment for the Watergate seed, which without the Vietnam War would never have sprouted.

With the beginning of summer 1969, there was a lull in the fighting in South Vietnam. Whether this meant that Hanoi was exhausted or biding its time while the Americans withdrew or ready for negotiations was unclear. On July 7, Nixon held a meeting on the presidential yacht *Sequoia* to discuss the options. Present were Laird, General Earle G. Wheeler, Mitchell, General Robert Cushman (a marine officer who was deputy CIA director and former military aide to Vice-President Nixon), and Kissinger.

Everyone at the meeting agreed to respond to the lull with a reciprocal slowdown and to make a basic change in General Abrams's "mission statement." To date, Abrams had been operating under the same orders General William C. Westmoreland had received, to "defeat" the enemy and "force" its withdrawal to North Vietnam. The new statement ordered Abrams to provide "maximum assistance" to ARVN, to support pacification efforts, and to reduce the flow of supplies down the Ho Chi Minh Trail.[11]

A major effort to interdict enemy supply lines in Cambodia was already under way. The secret bombing, begun in March, expanded in June as Nixon ordered a series of attacks under the code name MENU (chosen because the individual raids were called Breakfast, Dinner, Supper, Dessert, Lunch, and so forth). Individual missions were specifically approved by Nixon. The elaborate precautions taken to keep the raids secret (from the American people and most of the American government and armed forces) continued. When Nixon asked for an assessment of the effectiveness of the raids, Laird and Abrams assured him that they "have been effective and can continue to be so with acceptable risks."[12]

But reducing the flow of supplies was not going to bring peace; at best it would bring stalemate. And Nixon was up against a time problem. He knew it better than anyone else. In September, Congress would return to Washington and the students to their campuses; Nixon recognized this would mean that "a massive new antiwar tide would sweep the country." Then Hanoi would, probably, launch a new offensive in February 1970. With congressional elections coming up in November 1970, Nixon expected, in his words, that political demands "for more troop withdrawals [would be] impossible to stop and difficult to ignore."

Through July, he discussed the problem in a series of conversations with Kissinger. He decided, as he later wrote, to "go for broke." He would "end the war one way or the other—either by negotiated agreement or by an increased use of force." Together with Kissinger, he developed "an elaborate orchestration of diplomatic, military, and publicity pressures." He decided on an ultimatum to Hanoi. He set November 1 as a deadline. That would be the first anniversary of the bombing halt.[13]

Nixon set Kissinger to work to prepare the details of a military escalation. The preparation of options took place in a section of the NSC, without Laird's participation or even knowledge (increasingly, it was characteristic of the Nixon administration that the right hand did not know what the left was doing). Kissinger's assistant, Colonel Alexander Haig, was the driving force in the planning. Haig and his staff completed a new war plan, code named DUCK HOOK. It called for massive bombing of Hanoi, Haiphong, and other key areas in North Vietnam, as well as the mining of harbors and rivers, destruction of the dike system to bring on extensive flooding, a possible invasion of North Vietnam, and an optional use of nuclear weapons against the Ho Chi Minh Trail. In short, all-out war, on the model used against Germany and Japan in 1945.[14]

On September 12, at an NSC meeting, Nixon listened appreciatively as Kissinger declared, "We need a plan to end the war, not only to withdraw troops." He wanted to make one more appeal to the new leadership in North Vietnam. If it was refused, he recommended putting DUCK HOOK into operation. The target date was November 1, when Nixon's ultimatum would run out.

Nixon was strongly tempted. But the tug in the other direction, toward continued deescalation, was also powerful. The summer had been relatively calm, the antiwar protest relatively muted, thanks to the first troop withdrawal announcement. But as Laird warned the president in early September, "I believe this may be an illusory phenomenon. The actual and potential antipathy for the war is, in my judgment, significant and increasing."[15]

Laird was right. Across the country, students were protesting against the war as they never had before. Antiwar leaders called for a national protest in a moratorium in Washington on November 15. On October 17 Kissinger, evidently considerably shaken by the moratorium, recommended against DUCK HOOK.[16] That same day, Nixon talked to a British guerrilla-warfare expert, Sir Robert Thompson, who had played a leading role in defeating a communist insurrection in Malaysia in the 1950s.

"What would you think if we decided to escalate?" Nixon asked.

Thompson was opposed. He thought it would cause a worldwide furor without enhancing South Vietnam's long-term survival chances. Vietnamization, the improvement of ARVN, was the right course, in Thompson's opinion. The analogy was Korea, where the improvement of the Republic of Korea forces, not a massive offensive against North Korea or a political settlement, had ensured the survival of South Korea.

Vietnamization meant a continuation of American involvement in the war beyond Nixon's proclaimed target date to end the war by 1970 or earlier. He asked Thompson if he thought it important for the United States "to see it through."

"Absolutely," Thompson replied. "In my opinion the future of Western civilization is at stake in the way you handle yourselves in Vietnam."

That was bombast, pure and simple, but Nixon agreed with Thompson's apocalyptic view. He also accepted Thompson's judgment, and Kissinger's recommendation, about the DUCK HOOK plan. He felt that "the Moratorium had undercut the credibility of the ultimatum." DUCK HOOK was dead.[17]

Put cynically, after having proclaimed that he would not let policy be made in the streets, Nixon let policy be made in the streets. Put positively, he had repressed his instinct to smash the enemy in favor of a more moderate course with better long-term prospects. Put objectively, he had recognized that even though he was commander in chief of the world's most powerful armed forces, there were definite limits on his power.

Almost twenty years later, in April of 1988, Nixon said on "Meet the Press" that his decision against DUCK HOOK was the worst of his presidency. He said that if he had implemented the offensive, he could have had peace in 1969. He did not explain why he thought so or how that could have happened.

Instead of getting tough in the field, he got tough with the rhetoric. In an attempt to undercut the moratorium, he delivered his "Silent Majority" speech. His peroration was a paraphrase of what Sir Robert Thompson had told him two weeks earlier, and as sweeping and silly: "Any hope the world has for the survival of peace and freedom will be determined by whether the American people have the moral stamina and the courage to meet the challenge [in Vietnam]."[18]

"Very few speeches actually influence the course of history," Nixon wrote in his memoirs. "The November 3 speech was one of them."[19]

That was nonsense. Had Nixon announced DUCK HOOK, or had he announced a complete withdrawal by the end of the year, along with a unilateral cease-fire, the speech might have changed the course of history, but by announcing that he was going to continue doing what he had been doing for nine months, all Nixon did was to divide the nation more deeply than ever. It was true that in the process he showed, at least temporarily, that support for his policies was greater than most people imagined, but as James Reston wrote in the *New York Times* the next day, "It was a speech that seemed to be designed not to persuade the opposition but to overwhelm it, and the chances are that this will merely divide and polarize the debaters in the United States, without bringing the enemy into serious negotiations."[20]

On December 15, Nixon announced a further reduction of 50,000 troops in Vietnam, the withdrawal to be completed by April of 1970. This would mean a total reduction of 115,550 men since he took office.[21] Of course the pace was much too slow to satisfy the doves, and of course there was no end in sight to the war, and of course in his November 3 speech Nixon had done the opposite of his pledge to "bring us together," and of course he had not had much of a choice about withdrawal from the moment Johnson decided not to reinforce Westmoreland's victory in Tet.

Nevertheless, Nixon's deescalation of the war, his troop withdrawal program, was a historic event of the first magnitude. He had reversed a policy that had its roots in the Spanish-American War of 1898 and the subsequent conquest of the Philippines. The United States was no longer on the offensive in Asia. Johnson's March 31, 1968, speech, followed by Nixon's November 1, 1969, decision to forgo DUCK HOOK, along with the Nixon Doctrine, meant that the United States was committed to a new strategy in the struggle against communism in Asia.

At the beginning of the decade that was now coming to an end, Dwight Eisenhower had continued his commitment to the Diem regime in Saigon, as he sent in more advisers and more equipment and more money. Kennedy had increased, dramatically, the numbers of fighting men and the quantity of equipment, even as he blatantly interfered in the inner workings of the GVN. Johnson had escalated by leaps and bounds, from 16,000 (when he took office) to 100,000 to 250,000 to 500,000 to 550,000.

Nixon, at the end of the decade, reversed the process. For all the criticism that can be brought against his Vietnam policy—and there is much to criticize, and this author has not hesitated, and will not hesitate, to engage in such criticism—it must be recognized that Nixon's deescalation of the war in Vietnam was one of his historic achievements. Quite possibly no one else could have pulled it off; quite obviously none of his predecessors had been able to do so.

Nixon being Nixon, much of his policy in Vietnam was convoluted. He was doing what the doves wanted, albeit not so rapidly as they wished, and rejected what the hawks wanted, the DUCK HOOK plan. Yet it was the hawks to whom he appealed for support and the doves whose anger he exacerbated.

On February 12, 1969, the long-feared North Vietnamese offensive began, but to the surprise of the Americans, it came in Laos, not Vietnam. On February 16, at an NSC meeting, Nixon ordered a B-52 strike to support the government forces, in response to a request from Laotian premier Souvanna Phouma. The United States was already heavily involved in the fighting in Laos, not only in bombing the Ho Chi Minh Trail in southern Laos but in the ground war as well, with hundreds of cross-border operations by army and marine units. The fact was that Laos, like Cambodia, was an integral part of the war in South Vietnam, even though all the parties involved, including the United States, tried to maintain the fiction of neutrality.

At the end of April 1970, Nixon responded by ordering an incursion into Cambodia. It was a counterattack, not an offensive; its objective was to find and destroy communist supplies, not the NVA. There was nevertheless the most tremendous uproar, culminating in the Kent State shootings on May 4. Nixon, on the defensive, held a news conference to explain his policies. He said that the Cambodian incursion was necessary to protect the remaining American troops in Vietnam and called it "a decisive move." He said it was a warning to the enemy that if "he escalates while we are trying to de-escalate, we will move decisively and not step-by-step." He specifically threatened that if the NVA were to move massive forces across the DMZ, against the marines in that area, "I would certainly not allow those men to be massacred without using more force and more effective force."

As against those generalized threats, he made a specific pledge, one that went a long way toward defusing the domestic situation: "The great majority of all American units will be out by the second week of June, and all Americans of all kinds, including advisers, will be out of Cambodia by the end of June."[22]

To his critics on the right, Nixon had just let policy be made in the streets. There was no way the troops could clear out those sanctuaries, find all the hidden material, and uncover COSVN (the Central Office for South Vietnam) in so short a time. The storm of protest was sure to blow itself out, for it certainly could not get any worse; having endured it so far, for Nixon to buckle now seemed senseless to the hawks.

To his critics on the left, Nixon had for once heeded common sense. Unless the United States was prepared to occupy Cambodia indefinitely, something not even the most extreme hawk was advocating, nothing decisive could be accomplished there. Nixon's offensive had accomplished what it was going to accomplish—the uncovering and destruction of some six months' worth of supplies. It had set the communists back and had bought time. Meanwhile the domestic turmoil simply had to be brought to an end. Nixon's pledge, and his general demeanor, made a major contribution to that goal.

Whatever one thought of his actions, everyone could agree that the president had just put in an alarmingly inconsistent week.

Of all the irritations and problems Nixon had to face in early 1971, the worst by far was Vietnam. And in Vietnam, aside from the obvious fact that if the war was still going on in November 1972, it could well cost him his job, Nixon's most worrisome problem was the rapid deterioration of military morale. He was commander in chief of an army that had lost the will to fight, an army in which discipline was in danger of disappearing altogether, an army that was being rocked to its very foundations.

It was his own fault. He was the one who kept sending half-trained, at best, eighteen-year-olds halfway around the world to engage in a war he had long since decided he could not win, to participate in rearguard action designed to protect a corrupt and nonrepresentative government long enough to secure his own reelection. These were hardly causes likely to make a patriot's heart beat faster.

The evidence of the army's deterioration was overwhelming. By the spring of 1971, of the quarter-million American GIs in Vietnam, some forty thousand were heroin addicts. There was a higher risk of a soldier going to Vietnam becoming hooked on heroin than becoming a war casualty. Marijuana use threatened to become universal. An entire generation of America's fighting men was being corrupted.

Nixon's response to a report on the drug abuse in Vietnam was to order H. R. Haldeman to "get our story out fast by the inspired leak route (talk to [William] Safire). Submit a report."[23] The trouble was, the administration had no story on this one; the facts were the facts. A helicopter pilot reported that almost entire American units, including officers, were "doing heroin." He said, "The majority of people were high all the time. For ten dollars you could get a vial of pure heroin the size of a cigarette butt, and you can get liquid opium, speed, acid, anything you wanted. You could trade a box of Tide for a carton of prepacked, pre-rolled marijuana cigarettes soaked in opium."[24]

Then there was "fragging"—fragmentation-grenade attacks by enlisted men against unpopular officers. More than two hundred incidents had been reported in 1970, and the rate was increasing in early 1971. Racial tension was at an all-time high as America's most integrated army divided itself into "bloods" and "honkies." Rednecks from the Deep South hated the California and New York liberals, and vice versa. The president who had vowed to "bring us

157

together" was watching in apparent helplessness as even his own army tore itself apart.

Not that Nixon didn't try to deal with the crisis. He appointed a commission to look into the problem of drug addiction among young Americans generally and servicemen specifically. He pledged to undertake a "national offensive" against drugs. He described himself as unalterably opposed to legalizing marijuana. He said he would halt drug traffic at the foreign sources, prosecute sellers, initiate a "massive" educational effort in the United States, and provide treatment facilities for addicts, especially servicemen.[25] The follow-up failed to match the fanfare. The problem continued, indeed grew worse.

At the end of May, Nixon went to West Point to speak at the Military Academy's graduation ceremonies. He was brutally realistic: "It is no secret," he told his newly commissioned officers, "that the discipline, integrity, patriotism and self-sacrifice, which are the very life blood of an effective armed force and which the corps represents, can no longer be taken for granted in the Army in which you will serve." They would be leading troops who were guilty of drug abuse and insubordination. It was up to them, Nixon said, to reaffirm "the military ethic . . . and to give it new life and meaning." He did not tell them how to accomplish that goal.[26]

On March 30, 1972, the NVA launched the first phase of an offensive against South Vietnam. Using tanks and artillery in numbers never before seen in the war, the communist forces crossed the DMZ and headed toward Quang Tri. The area had once been defended by U.S. Marines; now it was held by ARVN units that, after some initial resistance, cracked.

A catastrophe loomed. It did no good to say that the offensive, after the two-year lull in the fighting in South Vietnam, had long since been anticipated. Nixon had to react. Any hesitation and he might well face personal as well as national disaster. If the North Vietnamese won the war through force of arms, Nixon's three-year-old policy of Vietnamization would be exposed as a fraud, he would be humiliated and lose the election, and the United States would be disgraced.

Nixon did react, instinctively and immediately. Brushing aside bureaucratic opposition and counsels of moderation, he ordered an all-out counterattack by sea and air power. He sent in B-52s, and more fighter-bombers, more aircraft carriers, more cruisers; he took off all budgetary restraints on air sorties; he ordered tactical air strikes up to the 18th parallel in North Vietnam; he ordered naval attacks twenty-five miles up the coast of North Vietnam.

In short, he counterattacked with almost everything he had available. What he did not do was launch a counteroffensive. He did not send in troops; he did not even slow the pace of ground forces withdrawal; he did not invade North Vietnam; he did not bomb Hanoi or Haiphong. His relative restraint was all the more remarkable because his anger was boundless. He thought the communists had played with him for years, using negotiations as smoke screen to prepare for a massive invasion. He was furious with the Soviets, whose tanks and artillery made the offensive possible. He felt that everything he had worked to achieve was threatened.

But his anger was more understandable than it was justified. In 1970 and 1971 he had been the one to launch offensives in Cambodia and in Laos. Even after they failed, his negotiating stance with Hanoi remained the same: give back the POWs, pull back your forces to North Vietnam, abandon your gains in Cambodia and Laos, and some months later the United States will complete its withdrawal (although he was never explicit on whether this withdrawal would include American air and sea power). Meanwhile Thieu would still be in power in Saigon (the promise that he would step down one month before elections was meaningless, as all his appointees would remain in charge and would be the ones to conduct the election). Nixon, in other words, was demanding that Hanoi surrender its war aims, even as he withdrew American ground forces. How could he have expected the NVA not to attack when its leaders judged the moment to be right?

With regard to the Soviets, Nixon's complaints that they made the offensive possible were certainly true, but he ignored other relevant points. The United States was supplying more material to Saigon than the Soviets were to Hanoi. Soviet control of the actions of the men in Hanoi was never as complete as Nixon assumed it was. The Soviets had not sped the shipment of arms in the winter of 1971–1972, nor had they ordered the offensive. The NVA had accumulated its arsenal thanks to the two-year lull on the battlefield and decided on its own when and how to strike.

Nor did Nixon pay sufficient attention to what the Soviets did not do. While they gave Hanoi MIG aircraft and surface-to-air missiles (SAMs) to defend their airspace, the Russians did not give the NVA fighter-bombers with which to attack the American air bases in Thailand nor submarines with which to attack the American aircraft carriers in the Gulf of Tonkin. Like Nixon, they exercised some degree of restraint.

On April 7, the NVA moved into the second phase of its offensive, attacking from Cambodia to the northwest of Saigon, toward An Loc. By then, the American counterattack was under way, as B-52s struck 145 miles north of the DMZ (the first use of B-52s in North Vietnam since early 1968), inflicting heavy casualties. Still the NVA came on; still ARVN failed to do its duty. Nixon had Kissinger's assistant, Al Haig, prepare a contingency plan; if all else failed, it called for bombing all military targets throughout North Vietnam and mining North Vietnamese ports. ARVN was unable to push back the NVA. Nixon railed at the Pentagon. Why couldn't more be done? He wanted more B-52s sent north to hit strategic and diplomatic targets, as well as tactical targets in the south.

Laird dissented. He feared that the relatively slow and not very maneuverable eight-jet bombers would be easy targets for Hanoi's SAMs. He also feared the congressional uproar that would follow. Rogers feared that such an escalation would endanger the summit.

Nixon insisted. He ordered B-52 raids against the oil depots around Hanoi and Haiphong; he even announced them in advance. On April 14, the president said that 150 B-52s, each carrying thirty tons of bombs (ten times the capacity of the F-4 Phantom fighter-bombers), would hit North Vietnam the following day. It was obvious that such raids would have no effect on the battles around An Loc and Quang Tri; a Pentagon spokesman explained that the purposes were to slow the flow of supplies south, to demonstrate to President

Thieu that he could count on Nixon, and to create a bargaining chip.[27]

The next day, April 15, the bombers moved in. They struck inside and outside Hanoi and Haiphong. They caused extensive damage, but the NVA claimed that eleven American planes had been shot down. Still, Nixon was pleased. He told Haldeman, "Well, we really left them our calling card this weekend."[28]

One weekend of bombing was not going to change the course of the war. Nixon wanted a sustained campaign. But he also wanted to go to Moscow for a summit; so did Kissinger, who urged caution. He reminded the president that General Abrams wanted to use B-52s inside South Vietnam to break up the enemy attacks at the point of contact, not hundreds of miles behind the lines where the effect of the raids would not be felt on the battlefield for months. And he warned Nixon that he could not bomb and have the summit too, that the Soviets would have to cancel, blaming Nixon and the bombing. Then Nixon would really catch it from the doves, who would go after him over the bombing and over the cancellation of the summit.

Nixon acknowledged that "it was hard to see how I could go to the summit and be clinking glasses with Brezhnev while Soviet tanks were rumbling through [South Vietnam]." But he wanted to bomb so badly. But he wanted to go to Moscow so badly. He was in an agony of indecision.

He decided to postpone a decision on Hanoi-Haiphong and the summit until the following week. Meanwhile he ordered plans prepared and told Kissinger to get ready to cancel the summit. If he decided on all-out action, he wanted to preempt the Soviets by canceling first.[29]

Whatever he decided about Hanoi-Haiphong, he was determined to escalate the air war to teach the enemy a lesson. On May 4 he ordered fifty additional fighter-bombers to Southeast Asia and ordered the fleet brought up to six aircraft carriers on active duty station. This meant that in the past month he had increased the B-52 force in the war from 8 to 140, the number of fighter-bombers from 400 to 900, the number of carriers from 3 to 6, and the air and navy personnel from 47,000 to 77,000. Meanwhile, he had reduced the number of ground troops from 95,000 to 68,100. None of those figures included the ARVN air force, by 1972 the fourth-largest in the world.

But the enemy could escalate too. On the day Nixon sent in the extra carriers and the fifty fighter-bombers, the Vietcong announced the establishment of a "provisional revolutionary administration" in Quang Tri City. It was the first time in the war the communists had succeeded in setting up a government on a provincial level in South Vietnam.[30]

Nixon continued to waver. He checked with John Connally, former secretary of the navy under John Kennedy. Connally told him to show his guts and leadership. "Caution be damned," Connally said.[31] That was what Nixon wanted to hear. Once he knew Connally's views, he asked Connally to join him, Haig, Haldeman, and Kissinger in his office in the old Executive Office Building for a council of war.

They reviewed the options, including the possibility of declaring a blockade. They decided a blockade would be too risky, as it carried the danger of having to confront the Soviet Navy. Mining was better. Nixon pumped himself up. "As far as I'm concerned," he declared, "the only real mistakes I've made were the times when I didn't follow my own instincts." He wished he had bombed North Korea in 1969 after the EC-121 was shot down. He wished he had bombed the hell out of North Vietnam in 1970, when he went into Cambodia. "If we'd done that then, the damned war would be over now. . . . The summit isn't worth a damn if the price for it is losing in Vietnam. My instinct tells me that the country can take losing the summit, but it can't take losing the war."[32]

Nixon met with the NSC. Laird opposed escalation. So did Rogers. The CIA warned that mining Haiphong would not be decisive because the enemy had alternative supply routes available. The joint chiefs said they were more interested in fighting the battle in South Vietnam than engaging in strategic projects of dubious immediate benefits in North Vietnam.

Nixon defended his decision. "The real question is whether the Americans give a damn anymore," he said. He warned that if he followed the lead of *Time* magazine, the *Washington Post*, the *New York Times*, and the television networks and just pulled out, "the U.S.

would cease to be a military and diplomatic power. If that happened, then the U.S. would look inward towards itself and would remove itself from the world." But if the United States stayed strong and willing to act, "then the world will remain half-Communist rather than becoming entirely Communist."[33]

With nearly ten thousand atomic weapons, plus all its additional firepower, plus its unrivaled economic strength, it is difficult to see how the United States would have ceased to be a great power if it failed to mine Haiphong harbor, but evidently no one at the NSC protested against Nixon's statement.

The following morning Nixon, quite full of himself, went after the Pentagon. He regarded the additional bombing proposals the military had put forward as "timid" at best. He sent a memorandum to Kissinger (who had somehow become his executive officer for implementing military decisions). He told Kissinger he was determined to "go for broke. . . . Our greatest failure now would be to do too little too late. . . . I intend to stop at nothing to bring the enemy to his knees. . . . I want the military to get off its backside. . . . We have the power to destroy [the enemy's] war-making capacity. The only question is whether we have the *will* to use that power. What distinguishes me from Johnson is that I have the *will* in spades. . . . For once, I want the military . . . to come up with some ideas on their own which will recommend *action* which is very *strong, threatening*, and *effective*."[34]

He never meant any of that; he was just puffing himself up. He had already ruled out any truly decisive action, such as reintroducing American ground troops or invading North Vietnam or bombing the dikes or using nuclear weapons. He was making war by temper tantrum; his rage had no sustaining power to it. Mining Haiphong and bombing Hanoi were not decisive acts; they were irritants, major irritants to be sure, but hardly enough to turn back an enemy so determined as the North Vietnamese.

What Nixon had done was to demonstrate his determination not to be humiliated. He was hurting Hanoi, not destroying it: he had, in effect, conceded Hanoi's right to keep troops in South Vietnam. What he had not done was agree to abandon Thieu, and he made it clear he never would do that. He would even risk the summit, détente, his whole new era of peace, to preserve the government of South Vietnam. He had given Hanoi and Moscow much to think about; he had not changed the course of the war.

A combination of the bombing and a somewhat improved performance from ARVN halted the NVA's Easter offensive. Kissinger then entered into a deal with the North Vietnamese; they would return the American POWs and allow the Thieu government to remain in power in Saigon, in return for American agreement that they could keep 160,000 NVA troops in South Vietnam (where they had, in effect, annexed the two northernmost provinces) and the Vietcong could hold to their gains.

This was not exactly peace, and it certainly wasn't victory but it was the best deal the Americans could get after nine years of war. It did give the South Vietnamese a chance to retain some part of their independence and a part of their territory.

Nevertheless, Thieu would not accept Kissinger's deal. So, following the election of 1972, Nixon inaugurated the Christmas bombing of Hanoi. This was not so much a military action, however, as a diplomatic one; in effect, Nixon was telling Thieu he could rely on the Americans to come to his aid if the North Vietnamese violated the cease-fire. Thieu went along, reluctantly, and Nixon's role as commander in chief in wartime came to an end.

Nixon's shortcomings as commander in chief are obvious. He was unable to persuade the country to unite for an all-out effort. More often than not he was hesitant and indecisive. He escalated the rhetoric while reducing the action. Before making a decision, he consulted with political advisers, especially Kissinger and Connally, rather than military advisers. He was unclear about his objective; he set himself the impossible goal of fighting a war while retreating from it without attempting to win it but refusing to admit that his country had lost it.

The reason for his shortcomings are equally obvious. Not even a George Washington or an Abraham Lincoln could have united the country for an all-out effort in Southeast Asia. None of Nixon's options were good, nor did his decisions reflect his best thinking; he always had to look over his shoulder at the ever-growing dove movement, especially in the Congress. His political and military advisers had no clear-cut advice to give.

He believed that his one chance at victory was operation DUCK HOOK. Whether it would have worked we do not know. Clearly it would have sent the doves into an even greater frenzy. Just as clearly, Sir Robert Thompson was right in saying that a successful DUCK HOOK would have left the United States with the same problem—maintaining an unpopular government in Saigon—plus a new, overwhelming one: maintaining that same government in command in North Vietnam.

Consider this analogy. The Soviet Union spent a full decade in Afghanistan. The Red Army did launch its own version of DUCK HOOK, with well-known results.

EPILOGUE:
THE WAR PRESIDENTS

ROGER A. BEAUMONT

In the examining of the manifold themes and patterns, both subtle and bold, that run through these chapters, John Erickson's conceptual triad for analyzing military institutions—technology, doctrine, and style[1]—seems especially useful, since the war presidencies, however varied in degree and kind, have generated a sort of military institution. Although, like any analytical construct, Erickson's paradigm is an abstraction, it helps to focus attention on both event and process.

Military historians, let alone those in other subdivisions of Clio's broad realm, rarely specifically describe those *technologies* that give structure to political and military power and those that enhance its exercise, or the effects that such systems have on process. Detailed descriptions of the actual workings of power—how things get done—are also scarce. Interpretive histories sometimes rely on allusion and inference when approaching the mechanics of the complex systems that lie behind decisions and policies, and even sequential and detailed documents may reveal little about process or technology. Thus, these chapters, in terms of Erickson's triad, tend to bear most heavily on the legs of "doctrine" and "style" and to assume that rational actors and systems have been at work.

The use of technology by wartime presidents stands out most prominently in Lewis Gould's chapter on McKinley. The process of power has often consisted of gathering information and applying doctrine (used in the broadest sense of enfolding politics, ideology, mindset, and military doctrine) through technical communication systems and organizational structure. Application of doctrine carries the stamp of the individual style of a particular president. The influence of distance, time lag, and filtering through the levels within a communication system are factors that lie outside of presidential control.

James K. Polk was the first war president to be linked to distant military operations by telegraph, and later Lincoln, McKinley, and Lyndon Johnson each spent many hours in the White House communications facility. From Polk's time to McKinley's, the growth of American power was a function of the extension of telegraph and cable lines, as access to and control of communication networks became an increasingly vital factor in international power. With Britain dominating transoceanic cable systems before World War I, nations fought patent battles over radio techniques. The volatile Zimmermann note affair, which contributed to American entry into the Great War, dramatized that struggle, and the U.S. Navy's decoding of foreign delegates' diplomatic messages during the Washington Naval Conference of 1920 provided American leaders with a wealth of information. Thereafter, America's "rise to globalism" and the rise of the imperial presidency were measured in the growing dominance of the United States in what the French have deemed *télématique*. To George III and his ministers, who waited months for their communications "loops" to bear news and yield returns to messages and orders, the content of the cable traffic of Washington with Corregidor in 1941–1942, of Truman and the joint chiefs with Douglas MacArthur in 1950–1951, and of Johnson and Robert McNamara with General Westmoreland in 1964–1968 would have seemed hardly less miraculous than more modern systems that instantly convey detailed information at great distances. The vast increase in the ability of national leaders (including presidents) to "read each other's mail" during World War II was reflected later in Truman's dismissal of MacArthur on the basis of diplomatic intercepts[2] and in the creation of the National Security Agency soon afterward, which created many options for the "imperial presidency."

By the end of World War I, telegraphy, both over-the-wire and wireless, and telephones had been supplemented by limited-range radiotelephones. Refinements in encoding and encryptions were made throughout the interwar period, as well as the development of scrambler devices of the type used to secure the trans-Atlantic conversations of Roosevelt and Churchill—which were not, it turned out, secure during the early part of the war. Although the use of such secure lines expanded, until the facsimile transmission (FAX) revolution of the late 1980s, most traffic between Washington and the field tended to be TWX/TELEX messages or cables. (It was pointed out to the author by a State Department official during the mid-1970s that secure-line technology, during the Vietnam War, had flattened out many of the subtleties of speech that convey nuances of meaning.)

Paralleling such evolutions of technology was the establishment, from the early 1950s onward, of what became known in the early 1960s as "Wimex"—the World-Wide Military Command and Control System. A vast nexus of complex computer-sensor communications subnetworks was put in place, designed for managing nuclear-age crises, preventing surprise attacks, and, in the worst case, managing battles themselves. The symbolic power of the "red phone" became a part of presidential politics and of the inventory of American anxieties centering on the much expanded role of the president as commander in chief, and it provided the somber and never-absent leitmotif for the exercise of presidential authority from Truman onward.

The change from the relatively clubby atmosphere in Franklin Roosevelt's White House was reflected in the incremental beleaguerment of the presidency from the late 1940s onward, which appeared to be mainly a consequence of the Cold War, the refinement of technologies centralizing power in the presidency, and the mounting frequency of assassination attempts since the 1930s—such as those against Roosevelt, Truman, Kennedy, Ford, and Reagan.

Among the most powerful changes affecting the presidency, however, were technological forces, such as the working out of rapid evacuation plans, the secret underground command post at Thunder Mountain, and the development of NEACP—"Kneecap"—the National Emergency Airborne Command Post. The growing role of the president as active peacetime commander in chief had led to revolutionary restructuring in the National Security Act of 1947. In the middle 1950s, the deepening concerns regarding nuclear-war battle management were reflected in the creation by executive order of the National Command Authority, which realigned the succession of presidential authority through the vice-president to secretary of defense to military commanders, as opposed to the old line through the Congress and Supreme Court.

The pressure of technology was also visible in the omnipresence in the presidential retinue of officers bearing briefcases containing key codes and the STOP—the Single Integrated Operational Plan—the nuclear war battle management plan. By the early 1990s, the arrival of new presidential aircraft allowed the president to be in near-instananeous personal contact with vast networks of sensors, commanders, and forces, while being able to travel in comfort to much of the world in few hours—a long way from the railroads that were the primary mode of presidential travel for more than a century and a mainstay of "whistle-stop" campaigning that faded away barely a generation ago.

Beyond the evolution in communications technology, many other technological advances have affected the scope of presidential power. In 1898, for example, McKinley's main instrument of power, the U.S. Navy, was the fifth largest in the world while by 1916, Wilson's fleet topped the list. In that half-generation, the size, armor, gun range, rate of fire, accuracy, armoring, and speed of capital ships all tripled. During the next two generations, similar developments followed in aviation, artillery, mechanization of ground forces, chemical warfare, rocketry, radar, jet propulsion, nuclear weapons, computers, and satellite reconnaissance and communications, yielding missiles and precision-guided munitions. By the mid-twentieth century, the reach of the American presidents' power far exceeded the wildest visions of the late-nineteenth-century fantasists.

Boundaries between technology, doctrine, and style are, of course, not lines but smears. How much each shapes the other, and especially the interplay of doctrine and technology, sets the proverbial chicken-egg dilemma into a hall of mirrors. Thus the role of personal motive, reflex, and attitude are hard to trace in such cases as Wilson's and Roosevelt's focus on naval power, Herbert Hoover's withdrawal of marines from Latin America, Truman's decision to use atomic weapons and to intervene in Korea, Johnson's embroilment in Vietnam, and George Bush's Persian Gulf commitment in 1991.

Whatever the capacities and deficiencies of the technical systems that American war presidents have relied upon in shaping policy and conveying their will, a great many other elements have helped shape their doctrine. One element—mass communications—has been far less compliant than the networks of power within the government. In the late nineteenth century, the steam-driven printing press, the Linotype machine, telephones, and rotogravure broadened the Fourth Estate's influence. Newsreels appeared during Theodore Roosevelt's administration, radios in the 1920s, and sound film in the early 1930s. FDR was the first, and perhaps most masterful, U.S. president to use radio to speak to the nation directly in his "Fireside Chats." As Norman Graebner stresses in chapter 1, television in the late 1940s changed both presidential image and essence. From World War II onward, the coming of fast, long-range air travel changed not only political campaigning but also the access of presidents and their lieutenants to far-flung forces in distant theaters of military operations, as dramatized by Truman's Wake Island meeting with General MacArthur in October 1950.

Erickson's elements of style and doctrine, alone or interacting, are far more difficult to plot with exactitude. Subconscious impulses aside, principals may not recall through the effects of fatigue, anger, or stress the blizzard of events that they must cope with, without rest and reflection. Leaders or their partisans usually present their decisions and actions in the best light, and their foes, the most harsh. More importantly, the underlying design and purpose of presidential actions is difficult to trace and assign a value to, however comfortable Freud was in analyzing Wilson from afar.[3] We know much of what the presidents have said and done but far less of what they thought. Informal processes of power, the interaction of the presidents with advisers and executors, are seen through a glass darkly, if at all, or are filtered through the lenses of personal perception. Raw material—such as Truman's memos for the record and the Nixon tapes—that provides sharp perspective on style and motive is rare indeed.

Another major change in underlying structure, doctrine, and

style, from World War II onward, has been the growth of secrecy in the exercise of presidential power. That is not to suggest, however, that the executive branch had no intelligence capacity before World War II. Allen Pinkerton, Lafayette Baker, the Office of Naval Intelligence, Wilson's agents in Mexico, and the U.S. Army's Black Room decoding team all stand as refutation of that. The rise of the FBI in the 1930s and substantial tutelage from the British during World War II swelled the scale and complexity of the matrix, setting up a structural tension between public policy and covert action, a tension reflected in the CIA's involvement in the U-2 incident, the Bay of Pigs, Watergate, Operation EAGLE CLAW (the abortive raid to free Americans held hostage in Iran in 1980), and the Reagan administration's Iran-Contra affair.

Consideration of the overlap between style and doctrine moves closer to a centroid of these essays, inasmuch as they are all, to varying degrees, tours de force, refreshing and challenging in their kicking over the traces of cliché and stereotype. Lewis Gould's search for motive amid weak documentation foreshadows the efforts of his colleagues, and his description of McKinley's prodding of General Shafter during the Cuban campaign reflects the balancing between central authority and delegation that constitutes a central dilemma for a wartime president. It is not surprising that some observers drew strong parallels between the events of 1898 and 1991 as the Gulf War loomed.

Robert Ferrell's tracing of Woodrow Wilson's behavior as commander in chief to certain attitudes toward war stands well away from other views of Wilson as a purposeful or stubborn visionary who deliberately distanced himself from the role of active commander in chief to play the role of an honest broker of a balanced peace who focused primarily on diplomacy and postwar goals. Wilson's boyhood in the war-devastated South does not count for much in this appraisal; neither is the gigantic naval construction program that he suspended during the war, nor the National Defense Act of 1916, nor his reliance on force in Mexico and the Caribbean. Whatever Wilson's motivation, in seeking to puncture his image as a virtuoso of governmental orchestration, Ferrell underscores the artificiality of the sharp distinction between civilian and military in both American folk values and political analyses, which might also be ascribed to America's long isolation during the nineteenth century. Pointing out how Wilson grappled with that artificial dichotomy and how executive and congressional purpose went out of phase, as it so often has, are points worth making. Wilson's difficulties foreshadowed not those of his immediate successors, but of all presidents after Franklin Roosevelt, who, as Cold War leaders, faced difficulties similar to Wilson's in balancing domestic political leadership with the function of commander in chief.

Warren Kimball's examination of Roosevelt as "Dr. Win-the-War" traces the interplay of doctrines and FDR's style in balancing domestic and alliance politics with grand strategy. While Roosevelt, the most dynamic of modern war presidents, acted within his constitutional charge, he crowded its limits, as did Nixon in bombing Cambodia in 1973 and Bush in invoking the Feed and Forage Act of 1861 to sustain U.S. forces in Saudi Arabia in 1991. From the mid-1930s onward, Roosevelt made it clear that he meant to have his way as commander in chief. He twice thwarted General Hugh Drum's aspiration to be chief of staff, reached down the promotion lists to bring forward George Marshall and Husband Kimmel, slid around the neutrality acts after the Munich Crisis, proclaimed his prerogative to determine high command structure on the eve of war in Europe, instigated the quasiwar in the Atlantic, permitted the covert raising of the American Volunteer Group (the "Flying Tigers"), and established the Office of Strategic Services and the Manhattan Engineer District. Roosevelt's wartime interventions in *res militariae*, other than those noted by Kimball, were sometimes tactical, such as his urging the commando model on the army and marines and diverting B-29 Superfortress bombers from Europe to China, and sometimes strategic, as was his ordering of MacArthur to Australia and hampering of French anti-Japanese efforts in Indochina.

Aristocratic in breeding and demeanor, Roosevelt sometimes veered toward an imperious if not an imperial style, and he vigorously advanced the boundary stakes of presidential power, from the later paragraphs of his inaugural speech in 1933 and the Court-packing fight to his slugging match with Congress in 1942, when some right-wing Republicans sought to displace him as commander in chief and bring MacArthur back as generalissimo. Whatever the legal niceties, Roosevelt understood the aphorism "he has the power who uses it." Although Roosevelt's style as war chief did much to project an image of centralized power, the actual mechanisms fell far short of expansion of the presidential infrastructure under his successors.

The experience of Harry Truman, well adumbrated by D. Clayton James, reflected an interplay of personal style and rapidly changing technology and doctrine. Truman was the first nuclear-age and mass-televised president. During his administration doctrine intermeshed with dogma and ideology as the Cold War crystallized. And, stylistically, Truman was the most feisty chief executive since Andrew Jackson. Delving beyond Truman's salient actions and decisions—dropping the atomic bomb, intervening in Korea, and sacking MacArthur—James's essay outlines how the role of commander in chief became dramatically more complex and demanding as the United States moved from least militarized of the great powers in peacetime in 1939 to the mightiest by 1955.

One might well argue that all of Roosevelt's successors have been war presidents, especially in view of the burgeoning of covert and special operations. Under Truman, for example, the CIA and the National Security Agency were created. A case along the lines of Ferrell's argument regarding Wilson's motives could also be made in respect to Truman. He was frustrated in seeking an appointment to West Point and served as a National Guard captain in France. As chair of the Truman Committee of the U.S. Senate during World War II, he was immersed in the complexities of military procurement, while monitoring corruption and vendor rivalry. As senator, Truman also observed the machinations of service champions, such as Georgia Congressman Carl Vinson, which led him to make the strongest move of any modern president toward service unification and structural linking. Although the National Security Act of 1947 fell short of his intentions, it was the first step up the long ladder of studies and changes, the latest rung of which was set by the Goldwater-Nichols Act of 1986.

In examining the tandem cases of Lyndon Johnson and Richard Nixon, who expanded and terminated American involvement in the

Vietnam War, Frank Vandiver and Stephen Ambrose present vivid variations on the technology-doctrine-style triad in which ironies and paradoxes, and parallelisms and divergences abound. As he moved to war, Johnson had it all—a huge plurality in the 1964 election; his party in control of Congress; vast military and economic superiority over a small, poor dictatorship; the best educated and most war-experienced elites in American history as advisers; generally supportive media; and overwhelming support in public opinion polls. In contrast, Nixon's plight when he took office in 1969 was Promethean. Bound by an implicit promise to end the war soon, he gained a bare election margin; the Democrats controlled Congress; polls showed that most Americans opposed the war; the media, most of the intelligentsia, and many students were hostile and often adversary; and the North Vietnam regime was then viewed in a favorable light by many people.

Both Vandiver and Ambrose labor valiantly within the cramped space of the essay format to explain how that vast inversion took place and how their subjects were weighed in the balances and found wanting. The slightly perplexed tone of their respective conclusions remind one of Athenian drama. The central character is not without strengths and abilities and is wracked by uncertainties. Time seems out of joint, and underlying is the theme of hubris, downfall born of an overweening sense of power and pride. Indeed, this theme was often brought into play by critics of Johnson during the war.

In examining the dimension of style, a Euripidean chorus could be rung in to point out the deviousness that marked both the Johnsonian and Nixonian styles. But if that was a fatal flaw, why did it not lay low the master of that craft, Franklin Roosevelt? Or was it that FDR walked the ledge more artfully than those who tried to follow the maestro through the turns? FDR said that he hated war and would not send American boys to fight on foreign soil. When he ultimately did, it was not on his own, but with a declaration of war in hand and a roused nation at this back. Johnson's promise in the 1964 campaign not to send American boys "ten thousand miles from home to do what Asian boys ought to be doing for themselves"[4] seems not too far off rhetorically, but it proved a world away in substance. Nixon's "secret" bombing of Cambodia added to the mounting tension in Congress that crested in the late summer of 1974. Thus General Bruce Palmer's observation regarding Johnson rings true in regard to the ultimate political fate of both Johnson and Nixon: "a galling defeat of the very soul. That the defeat was largely self-inflicted made it no less real or crippling."[5]

Were, then, Johnson's and Nixon's individual acts, and the others by implication, merely a case of swimming with or against a much deeper tide? Was there a dire web of fate in Vietnam, as many who served there sensed, that could not be unraveled or cut? Was the United States, swaggering arrogantly through the ruins of dead and faltering empires since 1945, fated for a sobering setback? A question asked at the time and often since is that why, with so many intelligent people involved in weaving the tangled web, was there no coherent strategy or mechanism to forge it?[6]

The historian is tempted to elaborate on Ambrose's observation and ask why, if both Johnson and Nixon were historically aware, did they not bring into their inner councils those with a close grasp of the matter at hand? Why did Johnson prefer Bill Moyers and Clark Clifford to David Halberstam or Edward Lansdale? Why, for Nixon, was it Henry Kissinger and John Connally and not Creighton Abrams or Bull Simons? An especially ominous pattern in the exercise of presidential power is the pervasive practice, focused on by Vandiver and Ambrose, but evident in all the war presidents, of relying on cronies. One can argue, paradoxically, that the struggle that Johnson, Nixon, and many others engaged in was not so unworthy as many came to see it, but that they went at it in ways that failed to draw effectively on the capacity of Americans in arms and the nation as a whole. For Johnson, master of the Senate in the 1950s, the French experience in Indochina and Algeria was close at hand—complete with rioting students, activist film stars, and military alienation. Yet French examples were airily dismissed—and not by Johnson alone.

Standing back from the individual cases, one can ask what patterns appear, beyond the technological trends noted earlier. Psychohistorians have already targeted some of the war presidents; Wilson, Johnson, and Nixon.[7] The interaction with aides and advisers, closer to sociology and anthropology, is a major theme in analyses of the president as commander in chief, as seen, for example, in Graham Allison's study of the Cuban Missile Crisis,[8] and in the memoirs of presidential aides.[9] While less behavioral in focus, each case treated in these chapters is flavored with the special drama of people under stress, politically beleaguered, facing war, and risking the national weal and their own historical reputation.

Beyond the academic domains of historical explanation, causation, and interpretation lies the question of what other patterns stand forth or lie embedded in the war presidencies, a special challenge to those who shape policy and make decisions in the "real world" of war and crisis. Are there lessons, guideposts, or warning signs to be discerned amid that complex and often bewildering record? Has technology been increasingly outstripping human ability to monitor and orchestrate the complex dynamics of power? How do the risks of resorting to military force weigh against possible advantage?

Historians, journalists, memoirists, and biographers have not been hesitant to judge the presidents, wartime and otherwise, in the matching of doctrine to strategic formulation, in the shaping and articulating of strategy, or in the resorting to military or other forms of suasion in the pursuit of goals. A crude ranking of performance, in the manner of rating heavyweight boxers or baseball players, or, in military history, the "Great Captains," beyond running the risk of seeming sensationalist or presumptuous, tends to overlook the lack of unambiguous criteria and the extent to which paradoxes abound. War is neither an academic exercise nor a sporting event. Presidents have never been wartime presidents only, and one cannot measure what they did against any sure pattern of what they might have done. An essential question arising from these cases is to what extent U.S. war presidents found war to be less of continuation of policy in the Clausewitzian sense than a failure of policy, as General Hans von Seeckt observed. And is it a corollary to that dilemma, or a pattern as opposed to coincidence, that all but one of the major modern American war presidents died or left office during or just after the conflicts they initiated?

To the extent that historical analysis offers any sense of trends, patterns, or syndromes, considering the dramatic shifting of the matrices of international power under way in the last decade of the twentieth century, the many questions and issues raised by these essays suggest the appropriateness of emulating our colleagues in the sciences, social and otherwise, who often conclude their findings with the observation that more research and analysis needs to be done.

NOTES

FOREWORD

1. Alexander DeConde, *The Quasi-War: The Politics and Diplomacy of the Undeclared War with France, 1797–1801* (New York: Scribner, 1966), 91, 96.

2. James D. Richardson, ed., *A Compilation of the Messages and Papers of the Presidents*, 20 vols. (New York, n.d.), 1:314–15.

3. Dudley W. Knox, ed., *Naval Documents Related to the United States Wars with the Barbary Powers: Naval Operations Including Diplomatic Background from 1785 through 1807*, 6 vols. (Washington, D.C.: Government Printing Office, 1939–1944), 2:51–52.

4. Dennis W. Brogan, *American Themes* (New York: Harper, 1949), 47.

5. McKinley's message to Congress, December 5, 1890, in Richardson, ed., *Compilation of the Messages and Papers of the Presidents*, 13:6321.

6. *Spanish Diplomatic Correspondence and Documents, 1896–1900: Presented to the Cortes by the Minister of State* (Washington, D.C.: Goverment Printing Office, 1905), 364.

7. Samuel I. Rosenman, *The Public Papers and Addresses of Franklin D. Roosevelt*, 13 vols. (New York: Random House, 1950), 12:39. See also Raymond G. O'Connor, *Diplomacy for Victory: FDR and Unconditional Surrender* (New York: Norton, 1971).

8. *Pravda*, June 27, 1950, quoted in Carl Berger, *The Korea Knot: A Military-Political History* (Philadelphia: University of Pennsylvania Press, 1957), 101.

9. See also Raymond G. O'Connor, *Force and Diplomacy: Essays Military and Diplomatic* (Miami, Fla.: University of Miami Press, 1972), and *War, Diplomacy, and History: Papers and Reviews* (Washington, D.C.: University Press of America, 1979).

INTRODUCTION

1. Two works present short introductions: Warren W. Hassler, Jr., *The President as Commander in Chief* (Reading, Mass.: Addison-Wesley, 1971),

touches on constitutional and leadership issues from Washington to Nixon; Harold M. Hyman, *Quiet Past and Stormy Present? War Powers in American History* (Washington, D.C.: American Historical Association, 1986), contains a helpful sixty-page discussion but only a brief bibliography. Perhaps the most thought-provoking book on the subject, and pivotal to any study of the modern commanders in chief, is Arthur M. Schlesinger, Jr., *The Imperial Presidency* (Boston: Houghton Mifflin, 1973). Among the most durable and widely cited of all presidential studies is Ernest R. May, ed., *The Ultimate Decision: The President as Commander in Chief* (New York: George Braziller, 1960), which contains short analytical chapters on Madison, Polk, Lincoln, McKinley, Wilson, FDR, Truman, and Eisenhower. The present volume is intended to update May's work and offer fresh analyses of the modern presidents. One place to begin is from the perspective of World War II, and George F. Milton, *The Use of Presidential Power, 1789–1943* (Boston: Little, Brown, 1944), provides insights from a contemporary observer of the masterful Franklin Roosevelt. Long recognized as one of the deans of presidential scholarship, Edward S. Corwin wrote, among other books, *The President: Office and Powers, 1787–1957*, 4th ed. (New York: New York University Press, 1957), which includes many valuable points. Another worthwhile study is Edgar E. Robinson et al., *Powers of the President in Foreign Affairs* (San Francisco: Commonwealth Club, 1966), which includes six essays by four historians, stressing Truman, Eisenhower, Kennedy, and Lyndon Johnson. An overview from the Vietnam years is Merlo J. Pusey, *The Way We Go to War* (Boston: Houghton Mifflin, 1969). Incorporating information from the social sciences is R. Gordon Hoxie, *Command Decision and the Presidency: A Study of National Security Policy and Organization* (New York: Reader's Digest Press, 1977). Skeptical of powerful presidents and their belligerent actions, Richard J. Barnet's *The Rockets' Red Glare: When America Goes to War—The Presidents and the People* (New York: Simon and Schuster, 1990) is written in an acerbic style. Richard Neustadt's *Presidential Power and the Modern Presidents: The Politics of Leadership from Roosevelt to Reagan* (New York: Wiley, 1960; rev. ed., New York: Free Press, 1990) is an engaging and thoughtful work and deserves high ranking as one of the best books on the presidency. Other studies include Louis Henkin, *Constitutionalism, Democracy, and Foreign Affairs* (New York: Columbia University Press, 1991), and Michael J. Glennon, *Constitutional Democracy* (Princeton, N.J.: Princeton University Press, 1991).

2. Louis Smith, *American Democracy and Military Power: A Study of Civil Control of the Military Power in the United States* (Chicago: University of Chicago Press, 1951), 62.

3. An excellent introduction to the conflict is Wiley Sword, *President Washington's Indian War: The Struggle for the Old Northwest* (Norman: University of Oklahoma Press, 1985).

4. Alexander DeConde, *The Quasi-War* (New York: Scribner, 1966); Craig L. Symonds, *Navalists and Antinavalists: The Naval Policy Debate in the United States, 1785–1827* (Newark: University of Delaware Press, 1980); Leonard F. Guthridge and Jay D. Smith, *The Commodores* (New York: Harper & Row, 1969), 60–62, 65–66, 109–111, and passim.

5. Marcus Cunliffe, "Madison," in May, ed., *Ultimate Decision*, 21–53; J. C. A. Stagg, *Mr. Madison's War: Politics, Diplomacy, and Warfare in the Early Republic, 1783–1830* (Princeton, N.J.: Princeton University Press, 1983), 141–44, 164–67, and passim; Donald R. Hickey, *The War of 1812* (Urbana: University of Illinois Press, 1989), 106–107, 143–144, 196, 202, and passim. See also Irving Brant, *James Madison: Commander in Chief* (Indianapolis, Ind.: Bobbs-Merrill, 1961), and Robert A. Rutland, *The Presidency of James Madison* (Lawrence: University Press of Kansas, 1990).

6. Leonard D. White, "Polk," in May, ed., *Ultimate Decision*, 55–75; John S. D. Eisenhower, "Polk and His Generals," in *Essays on the Mexican War*, ed. Douglas W. Richmond (College Station: Texas A&M University Press, 1986), 34–65; Otis A. Singletary, *The Mexican War* (Chicago: University of Chicago Press, 1960), 24–27, 104–105, 148–49; K. Jack Bauer, *The Mexican War, 1846–1848* (New York: Macmillan, 1974), 71, 73, 86, 232–37, 259–60, 335–36; T. Harry Williams, *Americans at War* (Baton Rouge: Louisiana State University Press, 1960), 39–41. See also Charles A. McCoy, *Polk and the Presidency* (Austin: University of Texas Press, 1960), and Paul H. Bergeron, *The Presidency of James K. Polk* (Lawrence: University Press of Kansas, 1987).

7. See the excellent broad study by D. P. Crook, *The North, the South, and the Powers, 1861–1865* (New York: Wiley, 1974). See also Stuart Anderson, "1861: Blockade vs. Closing the Confederate Ports," *Military Affairs* 41 (December 1977): 190–94.

8. Frank L. Owsley, *King Cotton Diplomacy: Foreign Relations of the Confederate States of America* (Chicago: University of Chicago Press, 1959); Emory M. Thomas, *The Confederate Nation, 1861–1865* (New York: Harper & Row, 1979), 80–85, 176–78; Crook, *The North, the South, and the Powers*, passim.

9. The Lincoln literature is vast, but James G. Randall, *Constitutional Problems under Lincoln* (Urbana: University of Illinois Press, 1951; rev. ed., 1964), provides a starting point, especially his discussions on "War Powers" (chapter 2) and "The Legal Nature of the Civil War" (chapter 3). Still thought-provoking is the study by Clinton L. Rossiter, *Constitutional Dictatorship: Crisis Government in the Modern Democracies* (Princeton, N.J.: Princeton University Press, 1948), esp. 224–29. See also Hassler, *The President as Commander in Chief*, 59–64; T. Harry Williams, *Lincoln and His Generals* (New York: Alfred A. Knopf, 1952); Harold M. Hyman and William M. Wiecek, *Equal Justice under Law: Constitutional Development 1835–1875* (New York: Harper & Row, 1982), 214–20, 232–42, 261–66; and Mark E. Neely, Jr., *The Fate of Liberty: Abraham Lincoln and Civil Liberties* (New York: Oxford University Press, 1990), passim.

10. Lincoln quoted in Roy P. Basler, ed., *Collected Works of Abraham Lincoln* (New Brunswick, N.J.: Rutgers University Press, 1953), 5:421. See also Schlesinger, *The Imperial Presidency*, 58–67; and Ludwell H. Johnson III, "Abraham Lincoln and the Development of Presidential War-Making Powers: Prize Cases (1863) Revisited," *Civil War History* 35 (September 1989): 208–24, quoted on p. 224.

11. Among several studies of Davis and the Confederacy see Emory M.

Thomas, *The Confederacy as a Revolutionary Experience* (Englewood Cliffs, N.J.: Prentice-Hall, 1971), esp. 64–71; Rembert W. Patrick, *Jefferson Davis and His Cabinet* (Baton Rouge: Louisiana State University Press, 1944), esp. 43–45; Frank E. Vandiver, *Their Tattered Flags: The Epic of the Confederacy* (New York: Harper's Magazine Press, 1970), 32–36, 129–32, 268–72; Paul D. Escott, *After Secession: Jefferson Davis and the Failure of Confederate Nationalism* (Baton Rouge: Louisiana State University Press, 1978), 54–60, 62–69, 177–78, 208–211, 273–74.

12. Thought-provoking support for Davis is found in Ludwell H. Johnson III, "Jefferson Davis and Abraham Lincoln as War Presidents," *Civil War History* 27 (March 1981): 49–63. A balanced evaluation is in Steven E. Woodworth, *Jefferson Davis and His Generals: The Failure of Confederate Command in the West* (Lawrence: University Press of Kansas, 1990), esp. 305–16. Strongly critical of Davis are Bell I. Wiley, *The Road to Appomattox* (New York: Atheneum, 1968), 14–42, and David M. Potter, "Jefferson Davis and the Political Factors in Confederate Defeat," in *Why the North Won the Civil War*, ed. David Donald (Baton Rouge: Louisiana State University Press, 1960), 91–114. See also William C. Davis, *Jefferson Davis: The Man and His Hour* (New York: HarperCollins, 1991).

13. On Secretary Alger, see especially David F. Trask, *The War with Spain in 1898* (New York: Macmillan, 1981), 145–49, 153–54, 165, and Russell F. Weigley, *History of the United States Army* (New York: Macmillan, 1967), 305–306, 311–12. For a contrasting view see Graham A. Cosmas, "Russell A. Alger," in *Dictionary of American Military Biography*, ed. Roger J. Spiller, 3 vols. (Westport, Conn.: Greenwood Press, 1984), 1:12–15. See also Cosmas, "Henry C. Corbin," ibid., 1:208–12.

14. See, for example, Robert Dalleck, *The American Style of Foreign Policy: Cultural Politics and Foreign Affairs* (New York: Knopf, 1983), 62–70. Wilson was well educated (holding a law degree as well as a Ph.D. in political science and history) and established a solid record in domestic legislation, but Dalleck concludes that Wilson was a "parochial American with limited interest in and knowledge of foreign affairs," ibid., 63. See also Arthur S. Link, *Wilson: Confusions and Crises, 1915–1916* (Princeton, N.J.: Princeton University Press, 1964), passim.

15. Harvey A. DeWeerd, *President Wilson Fights His War: World War I and the American Intervention* (New York: Macmillan, 1968), 10–11; Edward M. Coffman, *The War to End All Wars: The American Military Experience in World War I* (New York: Oxford University Press, 1968), 16–17; and John P. Finnegan, *Against the Spector of a Dragon: The Campaign for American Preparedness, 1914–1917* (Westport, Conn.: Greenwood Press, 1974). See also Smith, *American Democracy and Military Power*, 68.

16. In addition to Ferrell's note 1, chapter 3, see the critical remarks by John M. Palmer in *Washington, Lincoln, Wilson: Three War Statesmen* (Garden City, N.Y.: Doubleday, Doran, 1930), 308, 342–43, 349, 351–52. Supportive of the president is Eric F. Goldman, "Woodrow Wilson: The Test of War," in *Woodrow Wilson and the World of Today*, ed. Arthur P. Dudden (Philadelphia: University of Pennsylvania Press, 1957), 47–66, and Arthur S. Link

and John W. Chambers II, "Woodrow Wilson as Commander in Chief," *Revue Internationale D'Histoire Militaire* 69 (1990): 317–75.

17. On Bliss and Scott see Coffman, *War to End All Wars*, 9, 22–25, 34, 36, 49–50, 52, 143, 168; on Scott's role on the Supreme War Council, see David F. Trask, *The United States in the Supreme War Council* (Middletown, Conn.: Wesleyan University Press, 1961), passim. Regarding Pershing see Frank E. Vandiver, *Black Jack: The Life and Times of John J. Pershing*, 2 vols. (College Station: Texas A&M University Press, 1977), and Donald W. Smythe, *Pershing: General of the Armies* (Bloomington: Indiana University Press, 1986). For Graves, see Betty Miller Unterberger, "William S. Graves," in *Dictionary of American Military Biography*, Spiller, ed., 1:400–403. Coffman covers March in *The Hilt of the Sword: The Career of Peyton C. March* (Madison: University of Wisconsin Press, 1966).

18. Betty Miller Unterberger, *America's Siberian Expedition, 1918–1920: A Study in National Policy* (Durham, N.C.: Duke University Press, 1956); Unterberger, "Woodrow Wilson and the Russian Revolution," in *Woodrow Wilson and a Revolutionary World, 1913–1921*, ed. Arthur S. Link (Chapel Hill: University of North Carolina Press, 1982), 49–104; Unterberger, *The United States, Revolutionary Russia, and the Rise of Czechoslovakia* (Chapel Hill: University of North Carolina Press, 1989); Eugene P. Triani, "Woodrow Wilson and the Decision to Intervene in Russia; A Reconsideration," *Journal of Modern History* 48 (September 1976): 440–61.

19. Henry Stimson and McGeorge Bundy, *On Active Service in Peace and War* (New York: Harper, 1947), 495. A Republican, Stimson had also held the portfolios of secretary of war under President William Taft and secretary of state under President Herbert Hoover. His significant career has been analyzed by Richard N. Current, *Secretary Stimson: A Study in Statecraft* (New Brunswick, N.J.: Rutgers University Press, 1954); Elting E. Morison, *Turmoil and Tradition: A Study of the Life of Henry L. Stimson* (Boston: Houghton Mifflin, 1960); Robert H. Ferrell, *Henry L. Stimson*, vol. 11, *The American Secretaries of State and Their Diplomacy*, ed. Robert H. Ferrell and Samuel Flagg Bemis (New York: Cooper Square, 1963); and Godfrey Hodgson, *The Colonel: The Life and Wars of Henry Stimson, 1867–1950* (New York: Knopf, 1990). On Knox, see George H. Lobdell, "Frank Knox," in *American Secretaries of the Navy*, ed. Paolo Coletta (Annapolis, Md.: Naval Institute Press, 1980).

20. J. Samuel Walker, "The Decision to Use the Bomb," *Diplomatic History* 14 (Winter 1990): 97–114; Paul Fussell, *Thank God for the Atom Bomb and Other Essays* (New York: Summit Books, 1988), 13–37.

21. The historical literature on the Cold War fills many shelves. See, for instance, John L. Gaddis, *The United States and the Origins of the Cold War, 1941–1947* (New York: Columbia University Press, 1972); Walter LaFeber, *America, Russia, and the Cold War, 1945–1984* (New York: Knopf, 1985); Stephen E. Ambrose, *Rise to Globalism: American Foreign Policy since 1938* (New York: Penguin, 1989); John L. Gaddis, *Strategies of Containment: A Critical Appraisal of Postwar American National Security Policy* (New York: Oxford University Press, 1982). See also the analytical summary by Cecil V.

Crabb, Jr., *The Doctrines of American Foreign Policy* (Baton Rouge: Louisiana State University Press, 1982), 107–52.

22. Weigley, *History of the United States Army*, 599–600.

23. Ibid., 485–504, esp. 486, 493, 501–503; Paul Y. Hammond, *Organizing for Defense: The American Military Establishment in the Twentieth Century* (Princeton, N.J.: Princeton University Press, 1961), 227–47.

24. Glen D. Paige, *The Korean Decision, June 24–30, 1950* (New York: Free Press, 1968); Richard F. Haynes, *The Awesome Power: Harry S. Truman as Commander in Chief* (Baton Rouge: Louisiana State University Press, 1973); Robert J. Donovan, *Tumultuous Years: The Presidency of Harry S. Truman* (New York: Norton, 1982); Burton I. Kaufman, *The Korean War: Challenges in Crisis, Credibility, and Command* (New York: Knopf, 1986); Raymond G. O'Connor, "Harry S. Truman: New Dimensions of Power," in Robinson et al., *Powers of the President in Foreign Affairs*, 17–76.

25. Stephen E. Ambrose, *Eisenhower: Soldier, General of the Army, President Elect, 1890–1952* (New York: Simon and Schuster, 1983); Ambrose, *Eisenhower: The President* (New York: Simon and Schuster, 1984), esp. 30–32, 51–52, 97–107; Kaufman, *Korean War*, 292–95, 300–301, 304–305, 307–308, 313–14, 319–20, 328–29.

26. Several presidents have sent U.S. forces into dangerous situations or combat without congressional declarations. In additon to President Washington's Indian War, the U.S. government conducted numerous wars against American Indian tribes. Without congressional authorization, McKinley dispatched an expeditionary force to China during the Boxer Rebellion and prosecuted the guerrilla war in the Philippines. Wilson ordered two invasions of Mexico—at Vera Cruz in 1914 and in northern Mexico in 1916–1917—each taking significant percentages of U.S. military ground forces at that time. Between 1900 and 1933 several presidents sent marine units into a number of Latin American nations, including Cuba, Honduras, Nicaragua, Haiti, and Santo Domingo. Truman's predecessor, Franklin Roosevelt, had by December 1941 made a series of political, economic, and military decisions that simultaneously brought the United States to the verge of war with Japan in the Pacific and placed the nation in a de facto state of war with German naval forces in the Atlantic. By October 1941, German submarines had already torpedoed an American destroyer on convoy duty. In response, Roosevelt's "shoot-on-sight" orders to U.S. warships in the Atlantic were tantamount to a presidential declaration of war against Germany. (See Robert Dalleck, *Franklin D. Roosevelt and American Foreign Policy, 1932–1945* [New York: Oxford University Press, 1979], esp. 269–313, and Patrick Abbazia, *Mr. Roosevelt's Navy: The Private War of the U.S. Atlantic Fleet, 1939–1942* [Annapolis, Md.: Naval Institute Press, 1975].) President Kennedy authorized a naval quarantine of Cuba during the 1962 missile crisis that almost led to war with the Soviet Union, and Kennedy deployed 16,000 advisers to Indochina from 1961 to 1963. Ronald Reagan sent U.S. military forces into Grenada (1984) and Lebanon (1983–1984). George Bush's Panama incursion (1989) paled next to the massive array of power placed in the Persian Gulf (1990–1991).

27. Edward Keynes, *Undeclared War: Twilight Zone of Constitutional*

Power (University Park: Pennsylvania State University Press, 1982), 171, 173; Ann Van Wynen Thomas and A. J. Thomas, Jr., *The War-Making Powers of the President: Constitutional and International Law Aspects* (Dallas, Tex.: Southern Methodist University Press, 1982), 128–46; Francis D. Wormuth, Edwin B. Firmage, and Francis P. Butler, *To Chain the Dog of War: The War Power of Congress in History and Law* (Dallas, Tex.: Southern Methodist University Press, 1986), 186–87, 215–16, 249–50, 262–63. See also Schlesinger, *The Imperial Presidency*, and Barnet, *The Rockets' Red Glare*.

28. Herbert S. Parmet, *JFK: The Presidency of John F. Kennedy* (New York: Dial Press, 1983), esp. 136–38, 141, 148–49, 150–55, 327–29, 332–37. See also the argument proposed by Henry Fairlie, *The Kennedy Promise: The Politics of Expectation* (New York: Doubleday, 1973).

29. Edgar E. Robinson, "Lyndon B. Johnson: Extensions of Power," in Robinson, *Powers of the President*, 199–242; Larry Berman, *Planning a Tragedy: The Americanization of the War in Vietnam* (New York: Norton, 1982); Berman, *Lyndon Johnson's War: The Road to Stalemate in Vietnam* (New York: Norton, 1989); Harry G. Summers, Jr., *On Strategy: A Critical Analysis of the Vietnam War* (Novato, Calif.: Presidio Press, 1982).

30. David Halberstam, *The Best and the Brightest* (New York: Random House, 1972). See also Thomas J. Schoenbaum, *Waging Peace and War: Dean Rusk in the Truman, Kennedy and Johnson Years* (New York: Simon and Schuster, 1988).

31. On McNamara, see, for example, George C. Herring, "Robert S. McNamara," in *Dictionary of American Military Biography*, Spiller, ed., 2:699–702; William W. Kaufman, *The McNamara Strategy* (New York: Harper & Row, 1964); Carl W. Borklund, *Men of the Pentagon: From Forrestal to McNamara* (New York: Praeger, 1966); James M. Roherty, *Decisions of Robert S. McNamara* (Coral Gables, Fla.: University of Miami Press, 1970); Henry L. Trewhitt, *McNamara* (New York: Harper & Row, 1971); Clark A. Murdock, *Defense Policy Formation: A Comparative Analysis of the McNamara Era* (Albany: State University of New York Press, 1974); Gregory Palmer, *The McNamara Strategy and the Vietnam War* (Westport, Conn.: Greenwood Press, 1978); and Andrew Krepinevich, *The Army and Vietnam* (Baltimore, Md.: Johns Hopkins University Press, 1986). An incisive critique is Douglas Kinnard, *The Secretary of Defense* (Lexington: University of Kentucky Press, 1980), 72–112. James E. Hewes, Jr., describes what he calls The McNamara Revolution in *From Root to McNamara: Army Organization and Administration, 1900–1963* (Washington, D.C.: U.S. Army Center of Military History/Government Printing Office, 1975), 299–315, 348–55.

32. To command American field forces in Vietnam, Johnson picked Westmoreland, a West Point graduate of the class of 1936. A veteran of the European campaigns of World War II and leader of a crack airborne unit in Korea, Westmoreland went on to become a dynamic superintendent at the Military Academy (1960–1963). By most accounts, Westmoreland's experience and inclinations all pointed to his strengths as a first-rate officer whose forté was conventional linear warfare. E. B. Furguson, *Westmoreland: The Inevitable General* (Boston: Little, Brown, 1968); William C. Westmoreland,

A Soldier Reports (New York: Doubleday, 1976); Westmoreland, "Vietnam in Perspective," *Military Review* 59 (January 1979): 34–43; Dave R. Palmer, *Summons of the Trumpet: U.S.-Vietnam in Perspective* (San Rafael, Calif.: Presidio Press, 1978), passim; Blair Clark, "Westmoreland Appraised: Questions and Answers," *Harper's* 241 (November 1970): 96–101; Bruce Palmer, Jr., *The 25-Year War: America's Military Role in Vietnam* (Lexington: University of Kentucky Press, 1984).

It is open to question whether any senior American officer of the 1960s would have fought the war for President Johnson any differently. Westmoreland's successor, Creighton W. Abrams, had been deputy commander in Vietnam for more than a year before taking the top job from July 1968 to June 1972. After the Nixon administration announced a disengagement policy, by necessity Abrams had to take a more flexible approach to the war than Westmoreland's. Van M. Davidson, Jr., "Creighton W. Abrams," in *Dictionary of American Military Biography*, Spiller, ed., 1:5–8; Palmer, *25-Year War*, 63–64, 72–81, 94, 108, 110–12, 115, 122, 125; interview with Abrams, *U.S. News and World Report* 63 (December 4, 1967): 62–65.

33. Douglas Pike, *Viet Cong: The Organization and Techniques of the National Liberation Front of South Vietnam* (Cambridge: Massachusetts Institute of Technology Press, 1966); Pike, *PAVN: People's Army of Vietnam* (Novato, Calif.: Presidio Press, 1986); Douglas S. Blaufarb, *The Counterinsurgency Era: U.S. Doctrine and Performance, 1950 to Present* (New York: Free Press, 1977); John M. Gates, "The Philippines and Vietnam: Another False Analogy," *Asian Studies* 10 (April 1972): 64–76; Gates, "Indians and Insurrectos: The U.S. Army's Experience with Insurgency," *Parameters* 13 (March 1983): 59–68; Larry E. Cable, *Conflict of Myths: The Development of American Counterinsurgency Doctrine and the Vietnam War* (New York: New York University Press, 1986); Rick Atkinson, *The Long Gray Line: The American Journey of West Point's Class of 1966* (Boston: Houghton Mifflin, 1989); Krepinevich, *Army and Vietnam*, 37–53.

34. Ronald H. Spector, *Advice and Support: The Early Years, 1941–1960* (Washington, D.C.: Government Printing Office, 1983); Jeffrey J. Clark, *Advice and Support: The Final Years, 1965–1973* (Washington, D.C.: Government Printing Office, 1988). See also the revealing study by James L. Collins, Jr., *The Development and Training of the South Vietnamese Army, 1950–1972* (Washington, D.C.: Government Printing Office, 1975).

35. Tad Szulc, *The Illusion of Peace: Foreign Policy in the Nixon Years* (New York: Viking, 1978); Allan E. Goodman, *The Lost Peace: America's Search for a Negotiated Settlement of the Vietnam War* (Stanford, Calif.: Hoover Institution, 1978); Stephen E. Ambrose, *Nixon: Triumph of a Politician* (New York: Simon and Schuster, 1989); Kinnard, *The Secretary of Defense*, 113–52; Mark Clodfelter, *The Limits of Airpower: The American Bombing of North Vietnam* (New York: Free Press, 1989).

36. Schlesinger, *Imperial Presidency*, viii–ix; Charles C. Tansill, "War Powers of the President of the United States with Special Reference to the Beginning of Hostilities," *Political Science Quarterly* 45 (March 1930): 11; Charles Fairman, "The President as Commander in Chief," *Journal of Politics* 11 (February 1949), 157. See also Hoxie, *Command Decision and the*

Presidency, 33, 49, 312, 383, and passim. Military analyst Harry Summers, at least, has argued for the necessity of a congressional declaration of war. Harry G. Summers, Jr., *On Strategy: A Critical Analysis of the Vietnam War*, 14–17, 20–25.

37. Thomas E. Cronin, "Presidential Power Revisited and Reappraised," *Western Political Quarterly* 32 (December 1979): 392; J. William Fulbright, quoted in Louis Fisher, "War Powers: A Need for Legislative Reassertion," in *The Presidency Reappraised*, ed. Rexford G. Tugwell and Thomas E. Cronin (New York: Praeger, 1974), 57; J. William Fulbright, *The Arrogance of Power* (New York: Random House, 1967); Thomas E. Cronin, *The State of the Presidency*, 2d ed. (Boston: Little, Brown, 1975), 196.

38. The literature on the War Powers Resolution is substantial and growing. See Cronin, *The State of the Presidency*, 197–98; Fisher, "War Powers," 65–67; Robert Scigliano, "The War Powers Resolution and the War Powers," in *The Presidency in the Constitutional Order*, ed. Joseph M. Bessette and Jeffrey Tullis (Baton Rouge: Louisiana State University Press, 1981), 115–53; Cecil V. Crabb, Jr., and Kevin V. Mulcahy, *Presidents and Foreign Policy Making: From FDR to Reagan* (Baton Rouge: Louisiana State University Press, 1986), 31–35; Hoxie, *Command Decision and the Presidency*, x–xi, 31–34; Thomas and Thomas, *War-Making Powers of the President*, 128–46; Wormuth, Firmage, and Butler, *To Chain the Dog of War*, 186–87, 215–16, 249–50, 252–54, 262–63; W. Taylor Reveley III, *War Powers of the President and Congress* (Charlottesville: University of Virginia Press, 1981), 225–62.

39. See Judith Miller and Laurie Mylroie, *Saddam Hussein and the Crisis in the Gulf* (New York: Times Books, 1990), for an overview. U.S. officials had recognized the potential danger Iraq posed to Kuwait, but the emir had refused to negotiate an agreement for an American military base on Kuwaiti soil.

40. Norman Friedman, *Desert Victory: The War for Kuwait* (Annapolis, Md.: Naval Institute Press, 1991), 40–41, 48, 66.

41. "Chronology" (of the Persian Gulf War), in *Military Review* 71 (September 1991): 65. See also Arthur H. Blair, *At War in the Gulf: A Chronology* (College Station: Texas A&M University Press, 1992).

42. "Chronology," *Military Review*, 66.

43. Ibid., 65–68; Friedman, *Desert Victory*, 50, 52–53, 56.

44. Jean Edward Smith, *George Bush's War* (New York: Holt, 1992), passim; Friedman, *Desert Victory*, 97–98, 114–15; "Chronology," *Military Review*, 66–67. See also the valuable discussion of the crisis and its resolution in Harry G. Summers, Jr., *On Strategy II: A Critical Analysis of the Gulf War* (New York: Dell Books, 1992).

45. Friedman, *Desert Victory*, 109–12; "Chronology," *Military Review*, 68.

46. "Chronology," *Military Review*, 69.

47. Ibid.; Michael J. Glennon, "The Gulf War and the Constitution," *Foreign Affairs* 70 (Spring 1991): 84–101, esp. 84–89, 96–97, 100. In regard to the War Powers Resolution, Glennon contends that the resolution is defective and that "the law's near-complete irrelevance to the events leading up

to the war in the gulf speaks volumes about those defects" (ibid., 98). For the district court ruling, see *Dellums v. Bush*, 752 F. Supp. (D.D.C., 1990), 1141–52.

48. "Chronology," *Military Review*, 71–72.

49. Friedman, *Desert Victory*, 169–96, 214–35.

50. See, for example, George C. Wilson, "Bush and the Gulf: Uncomfortable Parallels to Vietnam," *Washington Post National Weekly Edition* (December 10–16, 1990): 9; Fredric Smoler, "What Does History Have to Say about the Persian Gulf?" *American Heritage* 41 (November 1990): 100–107. Summers presents an interesting comparison and contrast of various Vietnam-related aspects of the war in *On Strategy II*, 1–3, 7–10, 13–15, 27–33, 44–57, 66–69, 104–111, 122–26, 154–56, 167–69, 204–207, 223–25, 239–40, 242–43.

51. For a brief description of the Iraqi army see Friedman, *Desert Victory*, 19–24, 126–27, 270–71.

52. Alvin Z. Rubinstein, "New World Order or Hollow Victory?" *Foreign Affairs* 70 (Fall 1991): 53–65.

CHAPTER 1. THE PRESIDENT AS COMMANDER IN CHIEF

1. For an extensive treatment of this argument see Leonard R. Sorenson, "The Federalist Papers on the Constitutionality of Executive Prerogative," *Presidential Studies Quarterly* 19 (Spring 1989): 267–82.

2. Spooner's remarks in the Senate, January 23, 1906, *Congressional Record*, 59th Cong., 1st sess., 1906, 40, pt. 2:1418.

3. Max Farrand, ed., *The Records of the Federal Convention of 1787*, 4 vols. (New Haven, Conn.: Yale University Press, 1911), 1:21.

4. Ibid., 1:64–65.

5. Ibid., 1:65–66, 73–74.

6. Ibid., 1:66–67, 70.

7. Ibid., 1:236, 244.

8. Ibid., 1:292.

9. Ibid., 2:157, 182, 185.

10. Ibid., 2:279.

11. Ibid., 2:318.

12. Ibid., 2:319.

13. Ibid., 2:318.

14. Ibid., 2:318–19.

15. Ibid., 2:319.

16. Ibid., 2:326, 330–31, 341.

17. Ibid., 2:384–88.

18. Ibid., 2:575.

19. Alexander Hamilton, John Jay, and James Madison, *The Federalist*, ed. Edward Mead Earle (New York: Modern Library, 1937), 261–62, 264.

20. Ibid., 148.

21. Ibid., 481–82.

22. Ibid., 448.

23. Madison quoted in Walter LaFeber, "The Constitution and United States Foreign Policy: An Interpretation," *Journal of American History* 74 (December 1987): 697.

24. Farrand, *Records of the Federal Convention*, 2:465.

25. Calhoun's statement of May 12, 1846, *Congressional Globe*, 29th Cong., 1st sess. 1846:797.

26. Lincoln to Herndon, February 15, 1848, in *The Collected Works of Abraham Lincoln*, ed. Roy P. Basler (New Brunswick, N.J.: Rutgers University Press, 1953), 1:451.

27. James G. Randall and David Donald, *The Civil War and Reconstruction* (Boston: Heath, 1961), 173–75, 275–79.

28. *Foreign Relations of the United States, 1950*, 7 (Washington, D.C.: Government Printing Office, 1976), 158.

29. Ibid., 202, 263.

30. Kefauver's statement in the Senate, June 27, 1950, *Congressional Record*, 81st Cong., 2d sess., 90, pt. 7:9233; Bridges, June 26, 1950, ibid., 9154.

31. Taft's remarks, June 28, 1950, ibid., 9322–23. Taft complained that if Congress permitted the president to intervene in Korea without its approval, there was nothing to stop him from going to war "in Malaya or Indonesia or Iran or South America."

32. Tom Connally, *My Name is Tom Connally* (New York: Crowell, 1954), 346.

33. Vandenberg to Truman, July 3, 1950, in *The Private Papers of Senator Vandenberg*, ed. Arthur H. Vandenberg, Jr., and Joe Alex Morris (Boston: Houghton Mifflin, 1952), 543.

34. Richard F. Haynes, *The Awesome Power: Harry S. Truman as Commander-in-Chief* (Baton Rouge: Louisiana State University Press, 1973), 131–82.

35. Douglas's speech in the Senate, July 5, 1950, *Congressional Record*, 81st Cong., 2d sess. 96, pt. 7:9649. Connally agreed that a declaration of war was unnecessary "because we were fighting to preserve the status quo in Korea." Connally, *My Name is Tom Connally*, 351.

36. *The Military Situation in the Far East*, Hearings before the Committee on Armed Services and the Committee on Foreign Relations. U.S. Senate, May–June 1951, 82d Cong., 1st sess., 1951, pt. 2:1965, pt. 3:2813.

37. Dean Acheson, *Present at the Creation: My Years in the State Department* (New York: Norton, 1969), 408; *The Military Situation in the Far East*, pt. 1:10.

38. The Department of State *Bulletin* 23 (July 31, 1950), 173–78; Robert J. Donovan, *Tumultuous Years: The Presidency of Harry S. Truman, 1949–1953* (New York: Norton, 1982), 224.

39. Truman's press conference, January 11, 1951, *Public Papers of the Presidents of the United States: Harry S. Truman, 1951* (Washington, D.C.: Government Printing Office, 1965), 19. At a press conference on March 1, 1951, Truman commented on Congress's right to debate foreign policy: "I don't mind their talking about anything they want to. This is a free country.

They can make any number of speeches they want . . . but that does not mean that it helps the relations with the rest of the world" (ibid., 176).

40. *Foreign Relations, 1950*, 7:169–70, 174–75, 444, 712; Harry S. Truman, *Years of Trial and Hope* (Garden City, N.Y.: Doubleday, 1956), 345; Donovan, *Tumultuous Years*, 211–12; Acheson, *Present at the Creation*, 409–10.

41. Taft quoted in Donovan, *Tumultuous Years*, 295.

42. Norman A. Graebner, *The New Isolationism* (New York: Ronald Press, 1956), 54; Robert A. Taft, *A Foreign Policy for Americans* (Garden City, N.Y.: Doubleday, 1951), 60–61.

43. Jenner's remarks in the Senate, January 8, 1951, *Congressional Record*, 82d Cong., 1st sess., 97, pt. 1:96; Dirksen's speech, March 29, 1951, ibid., 97, pt. 3:2980. Republicans then condemned the administration for involving the United States in the Korean War without a formal declaration.

44. Taft's speech, March 29, 1951, ibid., 2994.

45. On the collision between the president and the general, see John W. Spanier, *The Truman-MacArthur Controversy and the Korean War* (Cambridge, Mass.: Harvard University Press, 1959), passim; and D. Clayton James, *The Years of MacArthur: Triumph and Disaster, 1945–1964* (Boston: Houghton Mifflin, 1985), 500–17, 540–42, 581–84, 590–91, 597–602.

46. It was President Johnson's false allegations of communist aggression in the Dominican Republic that established the foundation for the doubts of Senator J. William Fulbright and others that the central issue in Vietnam was international communist aggression. See Lee Riley Powell, *J. William Fulbright and America's Lost Crusade: Fulbright, the Cold War and the Vietnam War* (Little Rock, Ark.: Rose Publishing, 1984), 93, 116, 142–43, 155, 160–77.

47. For a pervading critique of the Vietnam War see Hans J. Morgenthau, "U.S. Misadventure in Vietnam," *Current History* 54 (January 1968): 29–34.

48. *War Powers Legislation*, Hearings before the Committee on Foreign Relations, United States Senate, 92nd Cong., 1st Sess., March-October, 1971, 580. James Reston in *New York Times*, January 27, 1985, E21.

49. Newton H. Minow et al., *Presidential Television: A Twentieth Century Fund Report* (New York: Basic Books, 1973).

50. The Department of State *Bulletin* 54 (March 28, 1966): 484.

51. *New York Times*, August 19, 1967.

52. Quoted in D. L. Robinson, "Presidential Autocracy and the Rule of Law," *Worldview* 16 (March 1973): 11.

53. James Reston in *Daily Progress* (Charlottesville, Va.), March 19, 1973.

54. *New York Times*, October 22, 1972.

55. Editorial, *Washington Post*, January 7, 1973.

56. *New York Times*, May 13, 1973; *Washington Post*, May 13, 1973.

57. *Newsweek*, May 21, 1973: 37–38.

58. Ibid., July 9, 1973: 26–27. For this executive-legislative struggle see Cecil V. Crabb, Jr., and P. M. Holt, *Invitation to Struggle: Congress, the President, and Foreign Policy* (Washington, D.C.: Congressional Quarterly Press,

1980); Thomas M. Frank and Edward Leisband, *Foreign Policy by Congress* (New York: Oxford University Press, 1979).

59. On the background of the War Powers Resolution see Alton Frye, *A Responsible Congress: The Politics of National Security* (New York: McGraw-Hill, 1975); Robert F. Turner, *The War Powers Resolution: Its Implementation in Theory and Practice* (Philadelphia: Foreign Policy Research Institute, 1983).

CHAPTER 2. WILLIAM MCKINLEY

1. John Hay to Theodore Roosevelt, July 27, 1898, Theodore Roosevelt Papers, Manuscript Division, Library of Congress.

2. For the most recent restatement of McKinley's alleged message from God about taking the Philippines, see Stanley Karnow, *In Our Image: America's Empire in the Philippines* (New York: Random House, 1989), 127–28. The problems with the credibility of the incident are discussed in Lewis L. Gould, *The Presidency of William McKinley* (Lawrence: University Press of Kansas, 1980), 140–42. The historical writings about McKinley may be reviewed in Lewis L. Gould and Craig H. Roell, eds., *William McKinley: A Bibliography* (Westport, Conn.: Meckler Publishing, 1988).

3. Margaret Leech, *In the Days of McKinley* (New York: Harper & Brothers, 1959); H. Wayne Morgan, *William McKinley and His America* (Syracuse, N.Y.: Syracuse University Press, 1963); David Healy, "McKinley as Commander-in-Chief," in *Threshold to American Internationalism: Essays in the Foreign Policies of William McKinley*, ed. Paolo Coletta (New York: Exposition Press, 1970), 77–119; and David F. Trask, *The War with Spain in 1898* (New York: Macmillan, 1981). More critical of McKinley's leadership are Ernest R. May, "McKinley (1898)," in *The Ultimate Decision: The President as Commander in Chief*, ed. Ernest R. May (New York: George Braziller, 1960), 93–107, and John Dobson, *Reticent Expansionism: The Foreign Policy of William McKinley* (Pittsburgh, Pa.: Duquesne University Press, 1988).

4. William E. Curtis, "President McKinley and the War," *Chautauquan* 28 (October 1898): 49.

5. Charles S. Olcott, *The Life of William McKinley*, 2 vols. (Boston: Houghton Mifflin, 1916), 2:346; Root's italics.

6. *Souvenir of the Visit of President McKinley and Members of the Cabinet to Boston, February 1899* (Boston: Home Market Club, 1899), 47; Charles Emory Smith to Elihu Root, August 12, 1903, Henry C. Corbin Papers, Manuscript Division, Library of Congress; A. B. Nettleton, "The Man at the Helm," *American Monthly Review of Reviews* 18 (October 1898): 405–14; D. Randolph Keim, "The Presidents's War," *Frank Leslie's Popular Monthly* 50 (June 1900): 107–22.

7. *Public Opinion* 22 (1897): 135, quotes the editor. Russell A. Alger, *The Spanish-American War* (New York: Harper & Brothers, 1901), offers the secretary's defense of his wartime performance.

8. Nettleton, "The Man at the Helm," 412; Smith to Root, August 12, 1903, Corbin Papers. For Corbin's reliability, see Graham A. Cosmas, *An*

Army for Empire: The United States Army in the Spanish-American War (Columbia: University of Missouri Press, 1971), passim. The standard biography of Miles—Virginia W. Johnson, *The Unregimented General: A Biography of Nelson A. Miles* (Boston: Houghton Mifflin, 1962)—focuses on the Indian Wars and slights the Spanish War. Robert Wooster is writing a new biography of Miles.

9. Keim, "The President's War," 120, 121; Waldon Fawcett, "The War Room at the White House," *World's Work* 3 (March 1902): 1841–43. See also Ida M. Tarbell, "President McKinley in War Times," *McClure's Magazine* 11 (July 1898): 209–24.

10. Richard T. Loomis, "The White House Telephone and Crisis Management," *United States Naval Institute Proceedings* 95 (December 1969): 64–65.

11. Olcott, *McKinley*, 2:55–56. For an astute discussion of McKinley and his management of the press, see Robert C. Hilderbrand, *Power and the People: Executive Management of Public Opinion in Foreign Affairs, 1897–1921* (Chapel Hill: University of North Carolina Press, 1981).

12. Trask, *The War with Spain in 1898*, 168–69, 172 (quotation); Hermann Hagedorn, *Leonard Wood*, 2 vols. (New York: Harper & Brothers, 1931), 1:141.

13. Diary entry of May 15, 1898, George B. Cortelyou Papers, Box 52, Manuscript Division, Library of Congress; John D. Long to George Dewey, April 24, 1898, in John Davis Long, *The New American Navy*, 2 vols. (New York: Outlook Co., 1903), 1:181–82. The legend about Roosevelt sending Dewey to the Philippines unilaterally seems irrepressible, though scholars have long known of its inaccuracy. See Trask, *The War with Spain*, 80–81, 92–93, for informed, sensible comments.

14. McKinley to Russell A. Alger, May 19, 1898, in *Correspondence Relating to the War with Spain and Conditions Growing Out of the Same, including the Insurrection in the Philippine Islands and the China Relief Expedition between Adjutant-General of the Army and Military Commanders in the United States, Cuba, Puerto Rico, China, and the Philippine Islands from April 15, 1898 to July 30, 1902*, 2 vols. (Washington, D.C.: Government Printing Office, 1902), 2:676–78, hereafter *Correspondence Relating to the War*; May, *Ultimate Decision*, 97.

15. Gould, *The Presidency of William McKinley*, 101–106.

16. On the army's lack of readiness, see the important book by Graham A. Cosmas, *An Army for Empire*, 69–100. John J. Leffler, "The Paradox of Patriotism: Texans in the Spanish-American War," *Hayes Historical Journal* 8 (Spring 1989): 24–48, explores some of the cultural dimensions behind the way in which the United States mobilized in 1898.

17. Trask, *The War with Spain*, 156–57.

18. Ibid., 159; Gould, *The Presidency of William McKinley*, 104–106.

19. "Charges of Incompetence in the Army," *Literary Digest* 16 (1898): 722.

20. Theodore Roosevelt to Henry Cabot Lodge, June 10, 1898, in *The Letters of Theodore Roosevelt*, ed. Elting E. Morison et al., 8 vols. (Cambridge, Mass.: Harvard University Press, 1951–1954), 2:837.

21. Henry C. Corbin to William R. Shafter, May 30, 1898 (sent on May 31), *Correspondence Relating to the War*, 1:18–19. A pro-Shafter treatment of that general's responsibilities is Paul H. Carlson's *"Pecos Bill": A Military Biography of William R. Shafter* (College Station: Texas A&M University Press, 1989), chapter 11.

22. Corbin to Shafter, June 1, 1898, Alger to Shafter, June 7, 1898, *Correspondence Relating to the War*, 1:21, 30.

23. Shafter to Alger, July 1, 1898, July 3, 1898, Shafter to Corbin, July 1, 1898, July 2, 1898, *Correspondence Relating to the War*, 1:70, 72. For thorough discussions of these events, see Trask, *The War with Spain*, 238–56, and Graham A. Cosmas, "San Juan Hill and El Caney, 1–2 July 1898," in *America's First Battles, 1776–1965*, ed. Charles E. Heller and William A. Stofft (Lawrence: University Press of Kansas, 1986), 109–48.

24. Alger to Shafter, July 3, 1898, Corbin to Shafter, July 3, 1898, *Correspondence Relating to the War*, 1:74–75, 76.

25. Corbin to Shafter, July 4, 1898, *Correspondence Relating to the War*, 1:82.

26. Draft of Corbin to Shafter, July 9, 1898, with McKinley's changes, Box 68, Cortelyou Papers; Corbin to Shafter, July 9, 1898, *Correspondence*, 1:119; Olcott, *McKinley*, 2:50; Trask, *The War with Spain*, 301.

27. Alfred T. Mahan, quoted in Trask, *The War with Spain*, 306.

28. Charles G. Dawes, *A Journal of the McKinley Years*, ed. Bascom Timmons (Chicago: R. R. Donnelly & Sons, 1950), 164.

29. Autobiography, Box 213, John Bassett Moore Papers, Manuscript Division, Library of Congress; Paul Cambon to Theophile Delcasse, July 8, 1898, Ministère des Affaires Etrangères, *Documents diplomatiques francais, 1871–1914, vol. 14: 4 janvier–30 decembre 1898* (Paris: Costes, 1957), 372.

30. Olcott, *McKinley*, 2:165; see also John Offner, "The United States and France: Ending the Spanish-American War," *Diplomatic History* 7 (Winter 1983): 1–21.

31. Henry Cabot Lodge to William R. Day, July 29, 1898, William R. Day Papers, Box 10, Manuscript Division, Library of Congress.

32. McKinley memorandum, July 26, 1898, William McKinley Papers, Manuscript Division, Library of Congress; James Wilson to William Boyd Allison, August 3, 1898, William Boyd Allison Papers, Box 329, Iowa State Department of History and Archives, Des Moines; Olcott, *McKinley*, 2:63.

33. Diary entries, July 30, 31, 1898, Box 52, Cortelyou Papers.

34. Shafter to Corbin, August 2, 1898, Alger to Shafter, August 2, 1898, *Correspondence Relating to the War*, 1:194, 196.

35. Shafter to Corbin, August 3, 1898, Alger to Shafter, August 4, 1898, *Correspondence*, 1:200, 204.

36. Shafter to Corbin, August 3, 1898, *Correspondence*, 1:202: Roosevelt to Shafter, August 3, 1898, in Morison, ed., *Letters of Theodore Roosevelt*, 2:864–65. See, for example, *New York Times*, August 4, 1898.

37. McKinley to Shafter, August 5, 1898, draft in Box 56, diary entry, August 4, 1898, Box 52, Cortelyou Papers.

38. Cambon to Delcasse, August 10, 1898, *Documents diplomatiques francais*, 444–45.

39. Gould, *The Presidency of William McKinley*, 123–27.

40. Draft of letter, McKinley to Commission for the Evacuation of Cuba, December 5, 1898, with Cortelyou's note of McKinley's remark, Box 70, Cortelyou Papers.

41. David Yancy Thomas, *A History of Military Government in Newly Acquired Territories of the United States* (New York: Columbia University Press, 1904), 320.

42. William McKinley to the Secretary of War, December 21, 1898, *Correspondence Relating to the War*, 2: 858–59; "McKinley Really Acts as Head of the Army," unidentified clipping dated 1899, Corbin Papers.

43. Thomas, *A History of Military Government*, 320; George R. Devitt, *A Supplement to a Compilation of the Messages and Papers of the Presidents, 1789–1902* (Washington, D.C.: Bureau of National Literature and Art, 1903), 95; *Congressional Record*, 56th Cong., 2d sess., 34, pt. 4, March 1, 1901: 3346; Carl Marcy, *Presidential Commissions* (New York: Columbia University Press, 1945), 60.

44. Arthur M. Schlesinger, Jr., *The Imperial Presidency* (Boston: Houghton Mifflin, 1973), 88–89; "Developments in China," *Literary Digest* 21 (1900): 13.

45. Perry Belmont, "The President's War Power and an Imperial Tariff," *North American Review* 170 (March 1900): 433–45; Healy, "McKinley as Commander-in-Chief," 115. For topics related to the theme of this essay, see Lewis L. Gould, "William McKinley and the Expansion of Presidential Power," *Ohio History* 87 (January 1978): 5–20, and David F. Trask, "President McKinley as Strategist in 1898," in *Proceedings of the Citadel Conference on War and Diplomacy*, ed. David H. White and John Gordon (Charleston, S.C.: Citadel Development Foundation, 1979), 111–16.

CHAPTER 3. WOODROW WILSON

1. A reader perhaps needs warning that my point of view agrees with that of some students and differs from others. See, for instance, Edward M. Coffman, *The War to End All Wars: The American Military Experience in World War I* (New York: Oxford University Press, 1968), 20, who writes that "since Woodrow Wilson had little interest in military matters, his secretary of war assumed great responsibilities in the spring of 1917." Harvey A. De-Weerd, *President Wilson Fights His War: World War I and the American Intervention* (New York: Macmillan, 1968), 251, concludes, "Wilson was able to go through a year and a half of war without ever acting as 'Commander-in-Chief.'" Ernest R. May, ed., *The Ultimate Decision: The President as Commander in Chief* (New York: George Braziller, 1960), 131, relates how Wilson "evaded his duty as commander in chief in order to do his larger duty as President of the United States." A significant, contrasting, pro-Wilson viewpoint is David F. Trask, "Woodrow Wilson and the Reconciliation of Force and Diplomacy, 1917–1918," *Naval War College Review* 27 (January/February 1975): 23–31. See also the excellent analysis by Betty Miller Unterberger, *The United States, Revolutionary Russia, and the Rise of Czechoslo-*

vakia (Chapel Hill: University of North Carolina Press, 1989), which agrees with Trask. Unterberger sees a large role for Wilson in dealing with the military demand to declare war against Austria-Hungary after Caporetto, his relationship with the Supreme War Council, his decisions in regard to the eastern front (sending American troops to Murmansk and Vladivostok), support of his generals in winning the war on the western front, interest in problems involved with modern and coalition warfare—especially when the United States in April 1917 declared war only against Germany and not all the Central Powers. It may be, of course, that the "sides" in this academic disagreement are attempting to deal with different things. My side considers the phrase "commander in chief" in a more narrowly military sense than does the other. For general works on the United States at war see Grosvenor B. Clarkson, *Industrial America in the World War: The Strategy behind the Line, 1917–1918* (Boston: Houghton Mifflin, 1923); Bernard M. Baruch, *American Industry in the War* (New York: Prentice-Hall, 1941); David F. Trask, *The United States in the Supreme War Council: American War Aims and Inter-Allied Strategy, 1917–1918* (Middletown, Conn.: Wesleyan University Press, 1961); Daniel R. Beaver, *Newton D. Baker and the American War Effort: 1917–1919* (Lincoln: University of Nebraska Press, 1966); and Robert D. Cuff, *The War Industries Board: Business-Government Relations during World War I* (Baltimore, Md.: Johns Hopkins University Press, 1973). It is perhaps worth mentioning that Wilson's Democratic successor, Franklin D. Roosevelt, was highly critical of his administration. Making allowance for what might have been casual overstatement, it is interesting that FDR told Secretary of the Interior Harold L. Ickes that "Wilson literally didn't know what was going on in the Government." FDR said that Wilson left everything to the chairman of the War Industries Board, Bernard Baruch, his secretary of the Treasury, William G. McAdoo, "and a few others." And again: "The President said that there were two kinds of Presidents, one like himself who kept track of everything and the other like Woodrow Wilson, who did not know what was going on but who let his Cabinet run the show." See *The Secret Diary of Harold L. Ickes: The Lowering Clouds, 1939–1941* (New York: Simon and Schuster, 1954), 201, 232.

2. Arthur S. Link, *Wilson: The Road to the White House* (Princeton, N.J.: Princeton University Press, 1947), 2.

3. Here my learned colleague Betty Unterberger disagrees. Wilson, she writes (letter to the author, June 4, 1990), "grasped the true nature of modern war more quickly than did most Americans." He sensed the horrors of modern technological warfare and certainly understood the relevance of modern technology in war much more clearly than did his great contemporary, Theodore Roosevelt. See John Milton Cooper, Jr., *The Warrior and the Priest: Woodrow Wilson and Theodore Roosevelt* (Cambridge, Mass.: Harvard University Press, 1983), 310, 325–26, and Arthur S. Link et al., eds., *The Papers of Woodrow Wilson* (Princeton, N.J.: Princeton University Press, 1966–), vol. 40 (1982):69–70.

4. Robert H. Ferrell, *Woodrow Wilson and World War I: 1917–1921* (New York: Harper & Row, 1985), 103–104.

5. In the 1930s, President Franklin D. Roosevelt appointed Denman a

federal appeals judge, and he held that post until his death, long after his moment in the limelight.

6. Goethals seems to have learned of Denman's description of him as an "s.o.b." and got up a magnanimous letter of resignation, which George Rublee took to the president's private secretary, Joseph P. Tumulty. Rublee oral history, pp. 155–56, Oral History Collection, Columbia University, New York.

7. Ferrell, *Woodrow Wilson and World War I*, 102.

8. Alfred D. Chandler, Jr., and Stephen Salsbury, *Pierre S. Du Pont and the Making of the Modern Corporation* (New York: Harper & Row, 1971), 359–430.

9. There was a side of Baker, not often seen, that was cold and hard. Bishop Charles H. Brent, leader in the Episcopal Church who spent time in France supervising the chaplains of the AEF and who talked to Baker about chaplains, found him not merely ignorant but resistant. When the secretary told the bishop that the latter should feel free to write him personally about the chaplain problem, Brent told his diary he assuredly would not do it, that Baker was too cold a fish for such an exchange, that the secretary thought the war would be won by force and politics. Brent diary, September 23, 1918, Brent MSS, Library of Congress.

10. Frederick Palmer, *Newton D. Baker: America at War*, 2 vols. (New York: Dodd, Mead, 1931), 1:11.

11. Ibid., 1:159.

12. Coffman, *The War to End All Wars*, 21.

13. Elting E. Morison, "Newton D. Baker," *Dictionary of American Biography, Supplement Two* (New York: Scribner's, 1958), 17–19.

14. C. H. Cramer, *Newton D. Baker: A Biography* (Cleveland, Ohio: World, 1961), 138. See also Beaver, *Newton D. Baker and the American War Effort.*

15. House diary, March 27, 1917, Edward M. House MSS, Library of Congress.

16. Letter of December 30, 1929, James G. Harbord MSS, Library of Congress.

17. Stanley Washburn oral history, pp. 112–13, Oral History Collection, Columbia University; Franklin Lane to George W. Lane, February 16, 1917, in Anne W. Lane and Louise H. Wall, eds., *The Letters of Franklin K. Lane: Personal and Political* (Boston: Houghton Mifflin, 1922), 238.

18. For Scott and the Indians see Angie Debo, *A History of the Indians of the United States* (Norman: University of Oklahoma Press, 1970), 237.

19. Mrs. Hugh Scott to Baker, May 27, 1918, Baker MSS, Library of Congress.

20. The influence of Bliss upon the Peace Conference is not easy to measure, and it may well be that the general was of considerable importance. President Wilson praised Bliss, for which see Arthur S. Link et al., eds., *The Papers of Woodrow Wilson*, vol. 53 (1986):320 ("he considered him a real statesman, all of his judgments being mature"); 54 (1986):34 (the president "spoke of Bliss in the highest terms"). See also the books by David F. Trask: *The United States in the Supreme War Council* and *General Tasker Howard*

Bliss and the "Sessions of the World," 1919 (Philadelphia, Pa.: American Philosophical Society, 1966). But there is testimony against Bliss's effectiveness. When the president nominated him as a peace commissioner, Colonel House thought well of the choice: "General Bliss is the best appointment, Lansing and White [Secretary of State Robert Lansing and the retired diplomat Henry White] are weak and will be of but little help" (House diary, December 1, 1918, House MSS, Library of Congress). But opinions changed. During the conference Charles Seymour wrote his wife that "I finally take back what I said some months ago about Bliss. He is a man of very interesting ideas and I think in the main very good ones. But he lacks the force to put them over, or perhaps I should say the peculiar power of influencing the President; and the President is all-powerful. The General also lacks the power of organization. Hence his influence here has been practically negligible." Harold B. Whiteman, ed., *Charles Seymour: Letters from the Paris Peace Conference* (New Haven, Conn.: Yale University Press, 1965), 207. The journalist Stephen Bonsal assisted House at the conference and wrote in an undated portion of his diary for August 1919 that "Bliss, of course, was a great mistake. . . . Bliss was constantly making amateurish political suggestions which so bored the President that he could hardly bring himself to listen to Bliss when he spoke on matters within his competence." In an entry for September 19, Bonsal credited the general with remarking about the president: "I do not like the man and I have no confidence in him. There is something feminine, feline, cattish, about him which I abhor." But Wilson himself had said of Bliss, in Bonsal's hearing: "I sent Bliss over here to advise me on military problems, but whenever he opens his mouth he talks to me about the Jugo-Slavs—of whom he has but a superficial knowledge, if any." The above unpublished portions of the Bonsal diary are in the Bonsal MSS, Library of Congress.

21. Letter of December 24, 1917, Bryce MSS, microfilm, Bodleian Library, Oxford University. Lord Bryce formerly served as Great Britain's ambassador to the United States.

22. Memorandum by Colonel J. S. Fair, April 1, 1919, Fair MSS, Box 507, Record Group 165, National Archives; James E. Hewes, *From Root to McNamara: Army Organization and Administration, 1900–1963* (Washington, D.C.: Government Printing Office, 1975), 23.

23. House diary, December 18, 1917, January 18, 1918, House MSS, Library of Congress; Ferrell, *Woodrow Wilson and World War I*, 105.

24. The colonel's diary for January 17, 1918, deserves quotation in extenso (House diary, House MSS, Library of Congress):

Last night when Garfield's coal order was given out, bedlam broke loose. Press Associations, newspaper editors etc. etc. made my life miserable. This has continued all day. There is nothing that the administration has done that I regret so much. It may be necessary, but it certainly was not necessary to do it in such a casual and abrupt way. It is one of the things I have feared the President would sometime do. He seems to have done it. I have never heard such a storm of protest. What I am afraid of is that it will weaken confidence in his administrative ability and bring Congress about his ears. I look to see an insistent demand that some change be made in the organization responsible for the conduct of the war. This question has disturbed me since my return from Europe. Men of every shade of political opinion condemn the organization as it now exists. The President and Secretary Baker seem to be the only ones that think the organization is as it should be. Men like [Robert S.] Lovett, Nelson Perkins, Baruch, Cyrus McCormick, Bainbridge Colby and other staunch supporters of the Administration have but one story to tell. They look to me to influence the President. I have hesitated to mention the matter to him for the reason that I tried at the beginning of the war to get him to accept what I thought to be the right sort of organization—an organization which everybody now thinks is essential. I do not like to intrude my advice upon him again. He knows quite well what I think, and he knows that I do not believe that he has an effective war organization, and I have been content to let it go at that. The fact that he does not consult me about these matters indicates that he knows we disagree, but he has believed he could work it out along the lines which he has pursued. . . . However, matters have gotten so bad now since this coal order of Garfield's that I have concluded, in justice to the President, that I should give a helping hand whether he asks for it or not. I have therefore arranged for Secretary Baker to come over Sunday to be with me a large part of the day. If I can get him into a proper frame of mind to see the necessity for a radical and thorough reorganization of affairs, I will take it up with the President. The President will not want it but, at the moment, it looks as if he will have no choice, for if he does not do it himself, Congress may force it upon him.

25. Reed Smoot diary, January 29, 1918, courtesy of Jan Shipps; Colville Barclay to Balfour, January 30, FO 371/3486, 370–74, Public Record Office, London; David Lawrence to Wilson, January 28, Baker MSS, Library of Congress.
26. Quoted in Arthur S. Link, *Woodrow Wilson: A Brief Biography* (Cleveland, Ohio: World, 1963), 23.
27. See Edward M. Coffman, *The Hilt of the Sword: The Career of Peyton C. March* (Madison: University of Wisconsin Press, 1966).

CHAPTER 4. FRANKLIN ROOSEVELT

My thanks to Mark A. Stoler of the University of Vermont and Fred E. Pollock, a research associate at Rutgers University, Newark, for taking the time to read this essay and make most helpful suggestions.

1. Historian Arthur Funk tells of George Baughman (later on the staff at Florida State University but a young bureaucrat during World War II) having such an experience. Roosevelt told Secretary of State Cordell Hull that he would rather be addressed as commander in chief than as president (Eric Larrabee, *Commander in Chief* [New York: Harper & Row, 1987], 13).

2. The "elusive" politician phrase is from A. E. Campbell, "Franklin Roosevelt and Unconditional Surrender," in *Diplomacy and Intelligence during the Second World War*, ed. Richard Langhorne, (Cambridge, England: Cambridge University Press, 1985), 223. It is but one of many such characterizations. This argument for Roosevelt's consistency is a major theme of my study, *The Juggler: Franklin Roosevelt as Wartime Statesman* (Princeton, N.J.: Princeton University Press, 1991).

3. Drs. New Deal and Win-the-War appear in Samuel I. Rosenman, ed., *The Public Papers and Addresses of Franklin D. Roosevelt*, 13 vols. (New York: Harper & Brothers, 1938–1950), *1943*, press conference of December 28, 1943, p. 573; Hull is quoted by James MacGregor Burns, *Roosevelt: The Soldier of Freedom* (New York: Harcourt Brace Jovanovich/Harvest Book, 1970), 157.

4. Burns, *Roosevelt*, 424.

5. Ibid., 424. John W. Jeffries, "The 'New' Deal: FDR and American Liberalism, 1937–1945," *Political Science Quarterly* 105 (Fall 1990): 397–418. Others, like Barry Karl, *The Uneasy State* (Chicago: University of Chicago Press, 1983), would disagree with this view.

6. Whatever FDR thought of business leaders in the thirties he used the war to train and civilize them, or so he thought. Granted, most of these retrained business leaders also happened to be Democrats, but being a Democrat had, for FDR, the same effect as immersion for a Baptist. The person was born-again until proven otherwise. In any event, FDR had aped his cousin Theodore's New Nationalism by trying to coopt at least some of the "malefactors of great wealth." See Bruce Catton, *The War Lords of Washington* (New York: Harcourt Brace & Co., 1948), and John Morton Blum, *V was for Victory* (New York: Harcourt Brace Jovanovich/Harvest Book, 1976), esp. chapter 4.

On FDR and the internationalization of the New Deal see Karl, *The Uneasy State*; Charles S. Maier, "The Politics of Productivity: Foundations of American International Economic Foreign Policy after World War II," *International Organization* 31 (Autumn 1977): 607–33; Lloyd C. Gardner, *Economic Aspects of New Deal Diplomacy* (Madison: University of Wisconsin Press, 1964); and Warren F. Kimball, *Swords or Ploughshares? The Morgenthau Plan for Defeated Nazi Germany* (Philadelphia: Lippincott, 1976).

7. Larrabee, *Commander in Chief*, has neat, useful summaries of that selection process. Roosevelt's initial reaction to Admiral King was unfavorable—with references to his fondness for drink. But two secretaries of the navy supported the admiral, and when the Pearl Harbor attack necessitated a change in navy leadership, King was the obvious choice for CNO. Whatever King's background, the president trusted and relied on him throughout the war. See ibid., 153–205.

8. See, for example, John Gunther, *Roosevelt in Retrospect* (New York: Harper & Brothers, 1950), 324–32, who pictures Roosevelt as "never" interfering with his military chiefs and becoming increasingly disinterested in military matters. Kent Roberts Greenfield gives additional examples in *American Strategy in World War II* (Baltimore, Md.: Johns Hopkins Press, 1963), 50–51.

9. See, for example, the public and private comments of Senator Arthur Vandenberg who had earlier labeled Roosevelt "the Ace Power Politician of the World" (Vandenberg, *The Private Papers of Senator Vandenberg*, ed. Arthur H. Vandenberg, Jr. [Boston: Houghton Mifflin, 1952], 9).

10. All those listed, except for Emerson, worked on the *U.S. Army in World War II* series for the Office of the Chief of Military History. Two led the way in refuting the notion that Roosevelt routinely followed the advice and initiatives of his military leaders: Greenfield in "Franklin D. Roosevelt: Commander-in-Chief," an essay in his *American Strategy in World War II*, and William Emerson in his article "Franklin Roosevelt as Commander-in-Chief in World War II," *Military Affairs* 22 (Winter 1958-1959): 183-92, also published in a revised form in *The Ultimate Decision: The President as Commander in Chief*, ed. Ernest R. May (New York: George Braziller, 1960), 135-77. Greenfield dismisses the importance of political factors in Roosevelt's decisions to intervene in military matters, the one major exception being the North African campaign. Emerson, on the other hand, asserts that "the political motive was uppermost in Roosevelt's mind" (p. 206). Greenfield lists twenty overrules and twelve significant initiatives by FDR on military matters. Perhaps the key move was the creation of the Executive Office of the President in July 1939, an indication of just how much FDR wanted to hold the reins. Greenfield's speculation that Roosevelt may have believed, throughout the war, "that the role of America was from first to last to serve as 'the arsenal of Democracy' " is worth considering. As he points out, the president repeatedly cut back on his chiefs of staff recommendations for a massive American commitment to the invasion of northern France (see Greenfield, p. 74). Both Emerson and Greenfield use Roosevelt's control over national mobilization policy as an example of his effectiveness as commander in chief. For further evidence see Albert A. Blum, "Birth and Death of the M-Day Plan," in *American Civil-Military Decisions*, ed. Harold Stein (Birmingham: University of Alabama Press, 1963), 61-94.

11. Larrabee, *Commander in Chief*, 1.

12. As Stephen Ambrose has pointed out, the decision not to race for Berlin was based on both political and military reasons, although the atmosphere of the decision was that Eisenhower's review of the military options gave Roosevelt justification to take the political decision he favored. See Ambrose, *Eisenhower and Berlin, 1945: The Decision to Halt at the Elbe* (New York: Norton, 1967).

13. See Kimball, *The Juggler*, esp. "Naked Reverse Right: Roosevelt, Churchill, and Eastern Europe, from TOLSTOY to Yalta—and a Little Beyond," 159-83. At the Quebec Conference in September 1944, Churchill raised the issue of Soviet expansion in Europe but did not persist after Roosevelt opposed sending a cautionary message to Stalin; U.S. Department of State, *Foreign Relations of the United States* (hereafter cited as *FRUS*), (Washington, D.C.: Government Printing Office, 1861-), *Conference at Quebec, 1944*, 490-91.

14. Churchill to Eisenhower, March 28, 1953, as quoted in *Churchill & Roosevelt: The Complete Correspondence*, ed. Warren F. Kimball, 3 vols. (Princeton, N.J.: Princeton University Press, 1984), 1:5.

15. *FRUS*, 1942, 3:594.

16. Ibid.; Kimball, *Churchill & Roosevelt*, 1:C-92 and R-152, particularly the early draft; Robert Sherwood, *Roosevelt and Hopkins*, rev. ed. (New York: Grosset & Dunlap/Universal Library, 1950), 577. The entire matter is discussed in Mark A. Stoler, *The Politics of the Second Front* (Westport, Conn.: Greenwood Press, 1977), and Lloyd C. Gardner, *Architects of Illusion: Men and Ideas in American Foreign Policy 1941–1949* (Chicago: Quadrangle, 1970), 26–54.

17. A reading of the preparedness reports available to Marshall suggests he had to conclude that 1943 would be the earliest possible date for a cross-Channel invasion in force. But to admit that would give impetus to just what eventually happened—a rush to get American troops engaged against the enemy even earlier. Harry Hopkins thought that Marshall believed "the force of circumstances" would bring on a second front in 1942 (Sherwood, *Roosevelt and Hopkins*, 569). The forty-division request from Molotov is also in Sherwood, 562. See also Richard W. Steele, *The First Offensive: Roosevelt, Marshall, and the Making of American Strategy* (Bloomington: Indiana University Press, 1973); Forrest C. Pogue, *George C. Marshall: Organizer of Victory* (New York: Viking, 1973); Mark A. Stoler, *George C. Marshall: Soldier-Statesman of the American Century* (Boston: Twayne, 1989); and Thomas Parrish, *Roosevelt and Marshall: Partners in Politics and War* (New York: William Morrow, 1989).

The code names for all these variations are confusing, and they confused the British and Americans so much that Churchill finally cabled Roosevelt with a suggested clarification of SLEDGEHAMMER, ROUNDUP, and GYMNAST (Kimball, *Churchill and Roosevelt*, 1:C-106 and R-163).

18. The Hopkins memo is quoted in Sherwood, *Roosevelt and Hopkins*, 518–19. Gardner, in "Franklin D. Roosevelt: The Perils of Second Front Diplomacy," *Architects of Illusion*, 35, argues that Roosevelt's reference to a Big Four system in the postwar world was essentially an artifice, because "FDR had no real faith in the concept, other than as a way of establishing rapport with his Allies." My position is set forth more fully in *The Juggler*, especially the chapter " 'The Family Circle': Roosevelt's Vision of the Postwar World." See also Raymond G. O'Connor, *Diplomacy for Victory* (New York: Norton, 1971), 42–47; Gaddis Smith, *American Diplomacy during the Second World War, 1941–1945*, 2d ed. (New York: Knopf, 1985), 44–47; Christopher Thorne, *Allies of a Kind* (New York: Oxford University Press, 1978), 131–32; and Herbert Feis, *Churchill, Roosevelt, Stalin* (Princeton, N.J.: Princeton University Press, 1957), 58–67. Steven M. Miner, *Between Churchill and Stalin* (Chapel Hill: University of North Carolina Press, 1988), 236–51, discusses Molotov's visit to London and the negotiation of the Anglo-Soviet Friendship Treaty.

The ever-present fear in Washington and London of separate Soviet-German peace negotiations is discussed in Vojtech Mastny, *Russia's Road to the Cold War* (New York: Columbia University Press, 1979), esp. chapter 3. See also Kimball, *Churchill & Roosevelt* 2:C-334 and passim.

19. The importance of the Soviet contribution was always in the mind of U.S. planners as demonstrated by Mark A. Stoler, "From Continentalism to

Globalism: General Stanley D. Embick, the Joint Strategic Survey Committee, and the Military View of American National Policy during the Second World War," *Diplomatic History* 6 (Summer 1982): 303–21. One such appraisal by U.S. Army planners is reproduced in Sherwood, *Roosevelt and Hopkins*, 417.

20. Sherwood, *Roosevelt and Hopkins*, 588–615; Stoler, *Politics of the Second Front*, 3–63; and Larrabee, *Commander in Chief*, 127–37, are but three of the many who discuss the U.S. military's objections to the North African strategy. The "suction pump" analogy is quoted from Forrest C. Pogue, *George C. Marshall: Organizer of Victory, 1943–1945* (New York: Viking, 1973), 22. Stimson's characterization of British fears is quoted in Stoler, *Politics of the Second Front*, 110.

21. The advantages and practicalities of a 1943 invasion are argued by John Grigg, *1943: The Victory That Never Was* (New York: Hill & Wang, 1980), and Walter S. Dunn, *Second Front Now—1943* (Tuscaloosa: University of Alabama Press, 1980). Fear of public pressure for shifting American concentration to the Pacific is discussed by Mark A. Stoler, "The 'Pacific-First' Alternative in American World War II Strategy," *The International History Review* 2 (July 1980): 432–52; and Richard W. Steele, "American Popular Opinion and the War against Germany: The Issue of Negotiated Peace, 1942," *Journal of American History* 65 (December 1978): 704–23; and Steele, *The First Offensive*, 81–93. Those fears are apparent from a reading of the Harry Hopkins Papers, Franklin D. Roosevelt Library (Hyde Park, New York), and Sherwood, *Roosevelt and Hopkins*, for example, p. 594. Of course Roosevelt had to ensure that inaction in the Pacific did not bring about the same pressures, hence his approval for the Guadalcanal campaign in 1942. FDR's concern about finding a place to fight is from his memorandum to Harriman, June 20, 1942, quoted in Rudy Abramson, *Spanning the Century: The Life of W. Averell Harriman, 1891–1986* (New York: Morrow, 1992), 330.

22. Arthur L. Funk, *The Politics of TORCH: The Allied Landings and the Algiers Putsch 1942* (Lawrence: University of Kansas Press, 1974), points out that when Roosevelt supported Marshall's objections to any American landings inside the more restricted waters of the Mediterranean, the president took the more cautious military path for political reasons. Landings at Bizerte, east of the Strait of Gibraltar, might have brought quicker victory in North Africa, but failure could have given justification to those who supported greater efforts in the Pacific—and that was something Roosevelt did not want to risk.

23. One of FDR's admirers and defenders, Theodore Draper, flatly states that "Franklin D. Roosevelt did not give the Soviet Union control of Eastern Europe; the Red Army did" (Draper, *A Present of Things Past* [New York: Hill & Wang, 1990], 251).

24. That those claims of probable losses were later exaggerated in order to justify dropping the bomb is not the point. When Roosevelt made the final agreements with Stalin, agreements that seemed to ensure Soviet support or at least neutrality in Chiang Kai-shek's struggle against the Chinese Communists, the atomic bomb was still untested. There is no evidence to

suggest anything but an honest military assessment by Marshall and other military advisers when they weighed the value of Soviet participation in the war against Japan. See Pogue, *Organizer of Victory*, 528–35.

The historiography of the later question of why Truman dropped the bomb is well surveyed by J. Samuel Walker in "The Decision to Use the Bomb," *Diplomatic History* 14 (Winter 1990): 97–114.

25. Pogue, *Organizer of Victory*, 533–34. Marshall was concerned about making sure that the Soviets attacked at the right time.

26. The latest entry into the lists is Robert Nisbet, *Roosevelt and Stalin: The Failed Courtship* (Washington, D.C.: Regnery Gateway, 1988).

27 I have elaborated on this extensively in *The Juggler*, particularly the chapters titled " 'The Family Circle': Roosevelt's Vision of the Postwar World," and " 'Baffled Virtue . . . Injured Innocence'—Roosevelt and Regionalism: The Good Neighbor as Role Model."

28. See Kimball, *The Juggler*, especially the chapters on the Good Neighbor Policy and "The Family Circle." On Greenland and creative geography see Nancy Fogelson, "Greenland: Strategic Base on a Northern Defense Line," *Journal of Military History* 53 (January 1989): 51–63, and Alan K. Henrikson, "The Map as an 'Idea': The Role of Cartographic Imagery during the Second World War," *American Cartographer* 2 (1975): 19–53.

29. See Warren F. Kimball, "Crisis Diplomacy, June–December 1941," in *Soviet-U.S. Relations, 1933–1942*, ed. G. N. Sevost'ianov and W. F. Kimball, (Moscow: Progress Publishers, 1989), 53–71. An expanded version is in Kimball, *The Juggler*.

30. This is not to suggest that these two battles were *the* turning points of the war. Rather, they serve as convenient markers indicating the limits of German and Japanese expansion.

31. Russell F. Weigley, in his masterful study of "The Campaigns of France and Germany, 1944–1945," *Eisenhower's Lieutenants* (Bloomington: Indiana University Press, 1981), mentions the president only three times— each in passing.

32. Arthur Bryant, *Triumph in the West* (Garden City, N.Y.: Doubleday, 1959), 93–94.

33. For Orde Wingate see Kimball, *Churchill & Roosevelt*, 3:43–45, and Ronald H. Spector, *Eagle against the Sun* (London: Penguin, 1985), 347–48. Spector briefly describes Merrill's Marauders, a commando outfit, on pp. 355–60, as does Barbara Tuchman, *Stilwell and the American Experience in China, 1911–1945* (New York: Macmillan, 1971), 432–33.

34. On Mountbatten see Philip Zielgler, *Mountbatten* (London: Fontana/ Collins, 1986). Some of "Dickie" Mountbatten's plans and exploits are discussed in Kimball, *Churchill & Roosevelt*: In vol. 1:C-62, Churchill called "Dickie's show at St. Nazaire [to sink a dry dock], though small in scale, bracing;" in vol. 1:C-177, there is a reference to operation PLOUGH, a scheme to drop commandos by glider and parachute during winter into Romania, Norway, and northern Italy where, using specially designed snowmobiles, they would sabotage oil and hydroelectric plants.

FDR had mentioned, early in the war, plans for commando forces that could liberate islands held by small Japanese garrisons. Churchill, eager to ensure that American activities in the Pacific would not threaten the Europe-first strategy, gave enthusiastic support to such a flashy, small-scale endeavor. But the president soon moved on to bigger things (Kimball, *Churchill & Roosevelt*, 1:322, 383, 439).

Sending India-based bombers to attack a Shanghai electric plant was proposed to Roosevelt by Chinese diplomat T. V. Soong and reported by Gunther, *Roosevelt in Retrospect*, 325. The suggestion was actually made at a meeting of the Pacific War Council; see Minutes of the 11th Pacific War Council meeting, June 17, 1942, and H. H. Arnold to the president, June 15, 1942, both in Map Room Papers, Box 168, Franklin D. Roosevelt Library, Hyde Park, New York.

35. Marshall was occasionally surprised when Leahy became an advocate for something, but overall Leahy acted as an expediter and often as the president's errand boy rather than a policy adviser. Shortly after the end of the war, Leahy's job transmogrified into the position of chair of the Joint Chiefs of Staff. See Stoler, *Marshall*, 92.

36. Studies of Franco-American wartime relations include Raoul Aglion, *Roosevelt and De Gaulle* (New York: Macmillan/Free Press, 1988), and Julian G. Hurstfield, *America and the French Nation, 1939–1945* (Chapel Hill: University of North Carolina Press, 1986).

37. Stoler, *Marshall*, 73–74.

38. The "cuff-links" gang was composed of people who had worked with him in his first national election campaign, when he ran for vice-president of the United States in 1920. Each received a pair of gold cuff links with their initials on one link and FDR's on the other (Sherwood, *Roosevelt and Hopkins*, 946; see also Geoffrey C. Ward, *A First-Class Temperament: The Emergence of Franklin Roosevelt* [New York: Harper & Row, 1989], 558).

39. John Morton Blum, *From the Morgenthau Diaries*, 3 vols. (Boston: Houghton Mifflin, 1959–1967), describes the Roosevelt-Morgenthau relationship in warm terms, but contemporaries recall some bitter arguments. See Warren F. Kimball, *The Most Unsordid Act: Lend-Lease, 1939–1941* (Baltimore, Md.: Johns Hopkins University Press, 1969), 5, and Henry Morgenthau III, *Mostly Morgenthaus: A Family History* (New York: Ticknor & Fields, 1991). Roosevelt's treatment of Hopkins is revealed in Sherwood, *Roosevelt and Hopkins*, and George McJimsey, *Harry Hopkins* (Cambridge, Mass.: Harvard University Press, 1987). Roosevelt's inclination to "callous, even cruel" humor toward loyal friends is depicted by Ward, *A First-Class Temperament*, 293, 546.

40. Thomas Parrish, *Roosevelt and Marshall: Partners in Politics and War* (New York: William Morrow, 1989), 91.

41. Reading Larrabee, *Commander in Chief*, one gets the idea that the dumbest thing FDR did was to recall MacArthur, but see p. 350 and Gunther's comment. Larrabee writes of FDR with the same uncritical, worshipful tone that he mocks Willoughby and Whitney for using in their memoirs about MacArthur (pp. 333–34). Larrabee claims FDR "tamed" MacArthur (p. 307), but if so, it was more the mesmerizing of snake by charmer than the subduing of lion by trainer.

MacArthur's appointment was also a way for Roosevelt to defang the Pacific-first advocates, since the general's reputation made it seem as if the president was emphasizing the Pacific campaign. See Warren F. Kimball, "Roosevelt and the Southwest Pacific: 'Merely a Facade'?" in *The Making of Australian Foreign Policy: The Contribution of Dr. H. V. Evatt*, ed. David Day (St. Lucia, Australia: Queensland University Press, forthcoming).

42. Marshall convinced Congress of his complete honesty, and Roosevelt's opponents frequently assumed his testimony would be unfavorable to the administration. Such was never the case, although it sometimes took some political maneuvering to make that happen (see Pogue, *Organizer of Victory*, Stoler, *Marshall*, and Parrish, *Roosevelt and Marshall*). During hearings before passage of the Lend-Lease Act, Hamilton Fish and others who sought to challenge Roosevelt's overall policy of aid to Britain tried to get Marshall to testify as a witness for the minority (the Republicans).He refused on the grounds that he was already scheduled to be an administration witness. Marshall then requested to be heard in executive session, effectively preventing the public from learning how he answered the question Fish always asked—was Germany a military threat to the United States? (see Kimball, *The Most Unsordid Act*, 153–64).

43. Maurice Matloff, *Strategic Planning for Coalition Warfare, 1943–1944* (Washington, D.C.: Office of the Chief of Military History, 1953), 338.

44. Mark A. Stoler, "Civil-Military Relations during World War II," *Parameters* 21 (Autumn 1991): 60–73. The Usher's Diary is in the Roosevelt Papers at the Franklin D. Roosevelt Library, Hyde Park, New York.

45. Stoler, *Marshall*, 107; Larrabee, *Commander in Chief*, 11.

46. Mark A. Stoler, "From Continentalism to Globalism: General Stanley D. Embick, the Joint Strategic Survey Committee, and the Military View of American National Policy during the Second World War," *Diplomatic History* 6 (Summer 1982): 303–21.

47. This and other generalizations about Marshall are taken from Stoler, *Marshall*, Pogue, *Organizer of Victory*, Parrish, *Roosevelt and Marshall*, and Larrabee, *Commander in Chief*. All agree on both Marshall's integrity and his understanding of how to work with Roosevelt.

48. Eliot Janeway, *The Struggle for Survival* (New Haven, Conn.: Yale University Press, 1951); Richard M. Leighton and Robert W. Coakley, *Global Logistics and Strategy, 1940–1943* (Washington, D.C.: Office of the Chief of Military History, 1955).

49. See Kimball, *The Juggler*, "In Search of Monsters to Destroy."

50. Charles C. Tansill, in *The Back Door to War* (Chicago: Henry Regnery, 1952), condemned Roosevelt for bringing the United States into an unnecessary war with Japan in order to fight the Germans. Bruce Russett, distressed by the effect on American postwar policy of entry into World War II, argues that the national security of the United States was not threatened by either Japan or Germany and that intervention was not justified (*No Clear and Present Danger* [New York: Harper & Row, 1972]).

51. Kent Roberts Greenfield, ed., *Command Decisions* (Washington, D.C.: Office of the Chief of Military History, 1960), iv.

52. Stetson Conn, "The Decision to Evacuate the Japanese from the Pacific Coast," in *Command Decisions*, Greenfield, ed., 125–49.

53. The title of commander in chief of British and imperial armed forces belonged formally to the king, George VI. However, Churchill took on the post of defense minister, which effectively put him in charge of the military.

54. See the studies done by the Soviet Studies Center at Fort Leavenworth, Kansas, particularly the various published works of David Glantz. He has scrutinized both Soviet and German battle reports and argues convincingly (and not surprisingly) that the military often exaggerated external influences—the Germans wrote of Soviet hordes and Hitler's meddling; the Soviets, writing of the same battle, would picture themselves as badly outgunned by forces of equal size. See the excellent historiographical essay by Glantz, "American Perspectives on Eastern Front Operations in World War II," in *Soviet-U.S. Relations, 1933–1942*, Sevost'ianov and Kimball, eds., 140–59.

55. See, for example, S. M. Shtemenko, *The Soviet General Staff at War, 1941–1945*, 2 vols. (Moscow: Progress Publishers, 1981–1986), and G. Zhukov, *Reminiscences and Reflections*, 2 vols. (Moscow: Progress Publishers, 1985). There are signs that Soviet historians are reassessing their military history during World War II, but in their eagerness to adopt the new orthodoxy, they run the risk of distorting history by downplaying Stalin's role in victories, while exaggerating his contribution to reversals. This is the finding of the U.S. subcommittee of the U.S.-Soviet Project on the History of World War II, initially sponsored by the American Council of Learned Societies (reports filed with International Research & Exchanges Board). A published example is Dimitri Volkogonov, *Stalin: Triumph and Tragedy*, trans. Harold Shukman (New York: Grove Weidenfeld, 1991).

56. Janeway, *Struggle for Survival*; Emerson, "Roosevelt as Commander-in-Chief," *Military Affairs*, 183–92; Greenfield, *American Strategy in World War II*, 62.

57. Robert Ross Smith, "Luzon versus Formosa," in *Command Decisions*, Greenfield, ed., 474.

58. See Martin Blumenson, *Mark Clark* (New York: Congden and Weed, 1984), and Sidney T. Matthews, "General Clark's Decision to Drive on Rome," in *Command Decisions*, Greenfield, ed., 351–63.

59. Stoler, *Marshall*, 74.

60. Edward S. Corwin, *Presidential Power and the Constitution: Essays by Edward S. Corwin*, ed. Richard Loss (Ithaca, N.Y.: Cornell University Press, 1976), 113, 114–15. For a penetrating discussion of these constitutional issues, see Walter Lafeber, "American Empire, American Raj," in *World War II and the Shaping of Modern America*, ed. Warren F. Kimball (New York: St. Martin's Press, 1992).

CHAPTER 5. HARRY S. TRUMAN

1. Barton J. Bernstein, ed., *The Atomic Bomb: The Critical Issues* (Boston: Little, Brown, 1976), xiv.

2. Harry S. Truman, *Memoirs*, 2 vols., 2d ed. (New York: New American Library, 1965), 1:462.

3. Henry L. Stimson, "The Decision to Use the Atomic Bomb," *Harper's Magazine* 194 (February 1947): 56.

4. See Gregg Herken, *The Winning Weapon: The Atomic Bomb in the Cold War, 1945–1950* (New York: Alfred A. Knopf, 1980); Martin J. Sherwin, *A World Destroyed: The Atomic Bomb and the Grand Alliance* (New York: Alfred A. Knopf, 1975); Gar Alperovitz, *Atomic Diplomacy: Hiroshima and Potsdam* (New York: Simon and Schuster, 1965).

5. Gregg Herken, "Atomic and Hydrogen Bombs," in *The Harry S. Truman Encyclopedia*, ed. Richard S. Kirkendall (Boston: G. K. Hall, 1989), 15–16.

6. U.S. Department of State, *Foreign Relations of the United States: Conference of Berlin (Potsdam), 1945*, (FRUS) 2 vols. (Washington, D.C.: U.S. Department of State, 1955), 1:897.

7. Marlene J. Mayo, "American Wartime Planning for Occupied Japan: The Role of the Experts," in *Americans as Proconsuls: United States Military Government in Germany and Japan, 1944–1952*, ed. Robert Wolfe, (Carbondale: Southern Illinois University Press, 1984), 44.

8. U.S. Joint Chiefs of Staff (JCS), Directive to General of the Army Douglas MacArthur, September 6, 1945, Record Group 5, MacArthur Memorial Archives, Norfolk, Virginia.

9. Truman, *Memoirs*, 1:455.

10. JCS, Directive to MacArthur, September 6, 1945.

11. Truman, *Memoirs*, 2:524.

12. Dean G. Acheson, *Present at the Creation: My Years in the State Department* (New York: W. W. Norton, 1969), 405.

13. Marshall was army chief of staff, 1939–1945; special envoy to China, 1945–1947; Secretary of State, 1947–1949; and Secretary of Defense, 1950–1951. Leahy was chair of the Joint Chiefs of Staff and presidential chief of staff, 1942–1949.

14. U.S. Department of State, *FRUS, 1950*, vol. 7, *Korea* (Washington, D.C.: Government Printing Office, 1976), 346, 503–4.

15. Truman, *Memoirs*, 2:525.

16. Alexander L. George, "American Policy-Making and the North Korean Aggression," in *Korea: Cold War and Limited War*, ed. Allen Guttman, 2d ed. (Lexington, Mass.: D. C. Heath, 1972), 106.

17. See Bruce Cumings, *The Origins of the Korean War: Liberation and the Emergence of Separate Regimes, 1945–1947* (Princeton, N.J.: Princeton University Press, 1981); William W. Stueck, Jr., *The Road to Confrontation: American Policy toward China and Korea, 1947–1950* (Chapel Hill: University of North Carolina Press, 1981); Charles M. Dobbs, *The Unwanted Symbol: American Foreign Policy, the Cold War, and Korea, 1945–1950* (Kent, Ohio: Kent State University Press, 1981).

18. Ernest R. May, *"Lessons" of the Past: The Use and Misuse of History in American Foreign Policy* (London: Oxford University Press, 1973), 83.

19. Truman, *Memoirs*, 2:501.

20. Testimony of Secretary of Defense George C. Marshall, May 7, 1951,

in U.S. Senate, Committees on Armed Services and Foreign Relations, *Military Situation in the Far East: Hearings* . . . , 5 parts in 2 vols. (Washington, D.C.: Government Printing Office, 1951), pt. 1, p. 325.

21. The four commands that Ridgway took over from MacArthur were the United Nations Command, U.S. Far East Command, U.S. Army Forces in the Far East, and Allied Occupation of Japan.

22. MacArthur to JCS, December 30, 1950, Matthew B. Ridgway Papers, U.S. Army Military History Institute, Carlisle Barracks, Pennsylvania.

23. Harry S. Truman, *Off the Record: The Private Papers of Harry S. Truman*, ed. Robert H. Ferrell (New York: Harper & Row, 1980), 196, 199, 210–11.

24. Jack D. Foner, *Blacks and the Military in American History: A New Perspective* (New York: Praeger, 1974), 183; *Washington Post*, March 6, 1990.

25. Barton J. Bernstein, "The Ambiguous Legacy: Civil Rights," in *Politics and Policies of the Truman Administration*, ed. Barton J. Bernstein, 2d ed. (New York: New Viewpoints, 1974), 297.

26. Foner, *Blacks and the Military in American History*, 190; Clay Blair, *The Forgotten War: America in Korea, 1950–1953* (New York: Times Books, 1987), 684.

27. *New York Times*, May 28, 1951.

28. JCS, Directive to MacArthur, September 15, 1950, in James F. Schnabel and Robert J. Watson, *The History of the Joint Chiefs of Staff: The Joint Chiefs of Staff and National Policy*, vol. 3, *The Korean War*, pt. 1 (Wilmington, Del.: Michael Glazier, 1979), 230.

29. Marshall to MacArthur, September 29, 1950, Record Group 6, MacArthur Memorial Archives.

30. MacArthur to Marshall, September 30, 1950, Record Group 6, MacArthur Memorial Archives.

31. United Nations General Assembly, Resolution on Korea, October 7, 1950, in *Documents on American Foreign Relations*, ed. Raymond Dennett et al., vol. 12 (Princeton, N.J.: Princeton University Press, 1953), 459–61.

32. Richard E. Neustadt, *Presidential Power: The Politics of Leadership* (New York: John Wiley, 1960), 127.

33. *New York Times*, January 8, 1951.

34. Lawrence S. Kaplan, "The Korean War and U.S. Foreign Relations: The Case of NATO," in *The Korean War: A 25-Year Perspective*, ed. Francis H. Heller, (Lawrence: Regents Press of Kansas, 1977), 68.

35. Other works that provided important background data for this essay were Robert J. Donovan, *Conflict and Crisis: The Presidency of Harry S. Truman, 1945–1948* (New York: W. W. Norton, 1977); Donovan, *Tumultuous Years: The Presidency of Harry S. Truman, 1949–1953* (New York: W. W. Norton, 1982); Margaret Truman, *Harry S. Truman* (New York: William Morrow, 1973); Robert H. Ferrell, *Harry S. Truman and the Modern Presidency* (Boston: Little, Brown, 1983); Ferrell, *George C. Marshall* (New York: Cooper Square, 1966); Richard F. Haynes, *The Awesome Power: Harry S. Truman as Commander in Chief* (Baton Rouge: Louisiana State University Press, 1973); Forrest C. Pogue, *George C. Marshall*, 4 vols. (New York: Viking Press, 1963–1987); Ernest R. May, ed., *The Ultimate Decision: The President*

as Commander in Chief (New York: George Braziller, 1960); and Warren W. Hassler, Jr., *The President as Commander in Chief* (Reading, Mass.: Addison-Wesley, 1971).

CHAPTER 6. LYNDON JOHNSON

1. McGeorge Bundy, interview with Frank E. Vandiver, December 8, 1988, p. 3, in Papers of Frank E. Vandiver, College Station, Texas. (All other transcripts of interviews with Frank E. Vandiver cited are in the same location.)
2. Dean Rusk, interview with Frank E. Vandiver, November 12, 1988, p. 10.
3. Lyndon B. Johnson, *The Vantage Point: Perspectives on the Presidency, 1963–1969* (New York: Holt, Rinehart and Winston, 1971), 566.
4. Mrs. Lyndon B. Johnson, interview with Frank E. Vandiver, August 23, 1989, p. 14. See also Claudia T. (Lady Bird) Johnson, *A White House Diary* (New York: Holt, Rinehart and Winston, 1970), and George C. Herring, *"Cold Blood": LBJ's Conduct of Limited War in Vietnam*, U.S. Air Force Academy Harmon Memorial Lecture no. 33 (Washington, D.C.: Government Printing Office, 1990).
5. Memorandum to the president from the vice-president, May 23, 1961, p. 1, in "Vice President's Visit to Southeast Asia, May 9–24, 1961" folder, Vice-Presidential Security File, Box 1, Lyndon Baines Johnson Library (hereafter, LBJ Library), Austin, Texas.
6. Ibid., p. 2.
7. Johnson, *Vantage Point*, 43.
8. Ibid.
9. John A. McCone Oral History, August 19, 1970, LBJ Library, Austin, Texas; quote on p. 29.
10. Johnson, *Vantage Point*, 44.
11. McGeorge Bundy, interview with Frank E. Vandiver, December 8, 1988, p. 2.
12. Lyndon B. Johnson, *The Choices We Face* (New York: Bantam Books, 1969), 24.
13. Johnson, *Vantage Point*, 43.
14. Ibid., 20.
15. Dean Rusk, with Richard Rusk, *As I Saw It* (New York: Norton, 1990).
16. Henry Graff, *The Tuesday Cabinet: Deliberation and Decision on Peace and War under Lyndon B. Johnson* (Englewood Cliffs, N.J.: Prentice Hall, 1970), 5.
17. See also the notes of Jack Valenti and Tom Johnson, LBJ Library, Austin, Texas.
18. Guenter Lewy, *America in Vietnam* (New York: Oxford University Press, 1978), 24. See also George C. Herring, *America's Longest War: The United States and Vietnam, 1950–1975* (New York: Knopf, 1986).
19. Johnson, *Choices We Face*, 28.

20. Edward J. Marolda and Oscar P. Fitzgerald, *The United States Navy and the Vietnam Conflict*, vol. 2: *From Military Assistance to Combat, 1959–1965* (Washington, D.C.: Department of the Navy, 1986), 393–462.

21. Johnson, *Vantage Point*, 115.

22. Ibid.

23. See George Ball, *The Past Has Another Pattern* (New York: W. W. Norton, 1982).

24. William Bundy, interview with Frank E. Vandiver, December 7, 1988, p. 17.

25. Ibid., p. 9.

26. Lady Bird Johnson, interview with Frank E. Vandiver, August 23, 1989, p. 18.

27. U. S. G. Sharp, *Strategy for Defeat: Vietnam in Retrospect* (Novato, Calif.: Presidio Press, 1978), 63.

28. McGeorge Bundy, interview with Frank E. Vandiver, February 7, 1990, p. 9.

29. Dean Rusk, interview with Frank E. Vandiver, November 12, 1988, pp. 5–6.

30. Ibid., p. 5.

31. McGeorge Bundy, interview with Frank E. Vandiver, February 7, 1990, p. 9.

32. Peter Braestrup, *Big Story: How the American Press and Television Reported and Interpreted the Crisis of Tet 1968*, 2 vols. (Boulder, Colo.: Westview Press, 1977); Stanley Karnow, *Vietnam; A History* (New York: Viking, 1983); Don Oberdorfer, *Tet: The Turning Point of the Vietnam War* (New York: Doubleday, 1971).

33. Moyers S. Shore II, *The Battle for Khe Sanh* (Washington, D.C.: U.S. Marine Corps Historical Branch, 1969), 8.

34. Johnson, *Vantage Point*, 416.

35. Ibid.

CHAPTER 7. RICHARD NIXON

1. *Public Papers of the Presidents of the United States: Richard Nixon* (1969), (Washington, D.C.: Government Printing Office, 1971), 15–17 (hereafter cited as *Nixon, Public Papers* [year]).

2. Richard Nixon, *The Memoirs of Richard Nixon* (New York: Grosset & Dunlap, 1978), 380–81; Seymour M. Hersh, *The Price of Power: Kissinger in the Nixon White House* (New York: Summit Books, 1983), 72–73; Henry Kissinger, *White House Years* (Boston: Little, Brown, 1979), 245.

3. Nixon, *Memoirs*, 382–83; Hersh, *Price of Power*, 72–73.

4. Raymond Garthoff, *Detente and Confrontation: American–Soviet Relations from Nixon to Reagan* (Washington, D.C.: Brookings Institution, 1985), 75.

5. Nixon, *Memoirs*, 384.

6. H. R. Haldeman, *The Ends of Power* (New York: New York Times Books, 1978), 85.

7. Nixon, *Memoirs*, 385.

8. Nguyen Tien Hung and Jerrold Schecter, *The Palace File* (New York: Harper & Row, 1986), 31.

9. *Nixon, Public Papers* (1969), 443.

10. Nixon, *Memoirs*, 392.

11. Kissinger, *White House Years*, 276.

12. Ibid., 247-49.

13. Nixon, *Memoirs*, 393.

14. Hersh, *Price of Power*, 120.

15. Kissinger, *White House Years*, 284-85; Laird to Nixon, September 4, 1969, Nixon Presidential Materials Project, Alexandria, Virginia (hereafter cited as NPMP).

16. Kissinger, *White House Years*, 285.

17. Nixon, *Memoirs*, 405.

18. *Nixon, Public Papers* (1969), 901-9.

19. Nixon, *Memoirs*, 409.

20. *New York Times*, November 4, 1969.

21. *Nixon, Public Papers* (1969), 1027.

22. *Nixon, Public Papers* (1970), 413-19.

23. News Summary, May 28, 1971, NPMP. Safire was one of Nixon's top speech writers.

24. Stanley Karnow, *Vietnam: A History* (New York: Viking, 1984), 631.

25. *Nixon, Public Papers* (1971), 605-10.

26. *New York Times*, May 30, 1971.

27. Ibid., April 15, 1972.

28. Ibid., April 16, 1972; Nixon, *Memoirs*, 590.

29. Nixon, *Memoirs*, 601; Kissinger, *White House Years*, 1176.

30. *New York Times*, May 5 and 6, 1972.

31. Kissinger, *White House Years*, 1177; Nixon, *Memoirs*, 601-2.

32. Nixon, *Memoirs*, 602.

33. Kissinger, *White House Years*, 1179.

34. Nixon, *Memoirs*, 606-7.

EPILOGUE

1. John Erickson, "The Soviet Military System: Doctrine, Technology and 'Style'," in *Soviet Military Power and Performance*, ed. John Erickson and E. J. Feuchtwanger (Hamden, Conn.: Archon, 1979), 18-43.

2. Joseph C. Goulden, *The Untold Story of the Korean War* (New York: New York Times Books, 1982), 476-78.

3. Sigmund Freud and William C. Bullitt, *Thomas Woodrow Wilson; Twenty-eighth President of the United States; A Psychological Study* (Boston: Houghton-Mifflin, 1967).

4. Stephen Ambrose, *The Rise to Globalism: American Foreign Policy since 1938*, 5th ed. (New York: Penguin, 1988), 211.

5. Bruce Palmer, Jr., *The 25-Year War: America's Military Role in Vietnam* (Lexington: University of Kentucky Press, 1984), 262.

6. See, for example, Robert Komer, *Bureaucracy Does Its Thing: Institutional Constraints on U.S.-G.V.N. Performance in Vietnam* (Santa Monica, Calif.: Rand Corporation, 1972).

7. E.g., Doris Kearns Goodwin, *Lyndon Johnson and the American Dream* (New York: Harper & Row, 1976); and Fawn Brodie, *Richard Nixon: The Shaping of His Character* (New York: Norton, 1981).

8. Graham Allison, *Essence of Decision: Explaining the Cuban Missile Crisis* (Boston: Little, Brown, 1971).

9. E.g., see Edward M. House, *The Intimate Papers of Colonel House Arrayed as a Narrative...* 4 vols. (Boston: Houghton-Mifflin, 1925–1928); Rexford Tugwell, *The Brains Trust* (New York: Viking, 1968); Robert E. Sherwood, *Roosevelt and Hopkins: An Intimate History* (New York: Harper, 1948); Sherman Adams, *First-Hand Report: The Story of the Eisenhower Administration* (New York: Harper, 1966); Bernard Baruch, *Baruch*, 2 vols. (New York: Henry Holt, 1957 and 1960); James F. Byrnes, *All in One Lifetime* (New York: Harper, 1958); Arthur Schlesinger, Jr., *A Thousand Days: John F. Kennedy in the White House* (Boston: Houghton-Mifflin, 1965); Bill Moyers and Richard Stout, *Presidents and Politics* (Alexandria, Va.: P.B.S. Videos, 1983); John Ehrlichman, *Witness to Power: The Nixon Years* (New York: Simon and Schuster, 1982); and Donald T. Regan, *For the Record* (San Diego, Calif.: Harcourt, Brace, Jovanovich, 1988).

ABOUT THE EDITOR AND CONTRIBUTORS

STEPHEN E. AMBROSE is Boyd Professor of History at the University of New Orleans. He formerly taught at Louisiana State University and at the Johns Hopkins University, where he was an associate editor of the Eisenhower Papers. He has lectured or been visiting professor at several colleges and universities, including the U.S. Military Academy, the Naval War College, Kansas State University, and the University of Kansas. Ambrose's published works range broadly across American military and political history and include such books as *Halleck, Lincoln's Chief of Staff* (1962), *Upton and the Army* (1964), *Duty, Honor, Country: A History of West Point* (1966), *Eisenhower and Berlin* (1967), *Supreme Commander: The War Years of Dwight D. Eisenhower* (1970), and *Crazy Horse and Custer* (1975). Ambrose has also published two major biographies of American presidents, *Eisenhower* (2 vols., 1983–1985), and *Nixon* (2 vols., 1987–1989). His reviews, essays, and chapters have appeared in numerous magazines, newspapers, historical journals, and edited books.

ROGER A. BEAUMONT is professor of history at Texas A&M University. He taught previously at University of Wisconsin-Milwaukee and Marquette University. He served a term on the U.S. Army Historical Advisory Committee, was Secretary of the Navy Fellow at the U.S. Naval Academy, and has given invited lectures at the U.S. Army Command and General Staff College and the U.S. Marine Corps Command and General Staff College. He is the author of *Military Elites* (1974), *Sword of the Raj: The British Army in India,*

1747–1947 (1977), and *Special Operations and Elite Units, 1939–1988* (1988). He is also the author of many monographs, book chapters, articles in historical journals and magazines, as well as essays in defense publications.

JOSEPH G. DAWSON III is associate professor of history and director of the Military Studies Institute at Texas A&M University. He is the author of *Army Generals and Reconstruction: Louisiana, 1862–1877* (1982) and associate editor of *The Dictionary of American Military Biography* (3 vols., 1984). He compiled *The Late 19th Century U.S. Army, 1865–1898* (1990).

ROBERT H. FERRELL is Distinguished Professor, Emeritus, at Indiana University. He has been visiting professor at a number of universities and colleges, including University of Notre Dame, University of Connecticut, the Naval War College, and the U.S. Military Academy. Among his many published works are *Peace in Their Time: The Origins of the Kellogg-Briand Pact* (1952), *American Diplomacy in the Great Depression: Hoover-Stimson Foreign Policy* (1957), *George C. Marshall* (vol. 15 of *American Secretaries of State and Their Diplomacy*, 1966), *Harry S. Truman and the Modern American Presidency* (1983), and *Woodrow Wilson and World War I* (1986). In addition, he has edited several books and contributed to many historical journals.

LEWIS L. GOULD is Eugene C. Barker Centennial Professor in American History at the University of Texas, where he has been a faculty member since 1967. He has published widely on America's Gilded Age and the progressive era. His books include *Wyoming: A Political History, 1868–1896* (1968; rev. ed., 1989), *Progressives and Prohibitionists: Texas Democrats in the Wilson Era* (1973), *Reform and Regulation: American Politics, 1900–1916* (1978; rev. ed., 1986), *The Presidency of William McKinley* (1980), *The Spanish-American War and President McKinley* (1982), *Lady Bird Johnson and the Environment* (1988), and *The Presidency of Theodore Roosevelt* (1990). He has contributed many articles and reviews to historical journals and numerous chapters or essays in edited books.

NORMAN A. GRAEBNER is Randolph P. Compton Professor of History and Public Affairs, Emeritus, at the University of Virginia. He served as Edward R. Stettinius Professor in Modern American History at the University of Virginia from 1967 to 1982. During his active teaching career he also held appointments at Iowa State University and the University of Illinois. He was a visiting professor or an invited lecturer at several universities, including Louisiana State University, Pennsylvania State University, Stanford University, and the U.S. Military Academy, as well as Oxford University and Cambridge University in Great Britain. Among his many books are *Empire on the Pacific* (1955), *The New Isolationism* (1956), *Ideas and Diplomacy* (1964), *The Age of Global Power* (1979), *America as a World Power: A Realist Appraisal from Wilson To Reagan* (1984), and *Foundations of American Foreign Policy: A Realist Appraisal from Franklin to McKinley* (1985). He has also edited several works, including *The Enduring Lincoln* (1959) and *An Uncertain Tradition: American Secretaries of State in the Twentieth Century* (1961). His other writings include more that one hundred scholarly articles and book chapters.

D. CLAYTON JAMES holds the John Biggs Chair of Military History at the Virginia Military Institute. He was a professor for many years at Mississippi State University. He has also taught at the Army War College and the U.S. Army Command and General Staff College. He is most well known for his comprehensive biography, *The Years of MacArthur* (3 vols., 1970–1985). He is also the author of *Antebellum Natchez* (1968), *A Time for Giants: Politics of the American High Command in World War II* (1987), and *Refighting the Last War: Command and Crisis in Korea* (1992). His articles have been published in several historical journals, and he has contributed chapters to several edited works.

WARREN F. KIMBALL is professor of history at Rutgers University at Newark, New Jersey. He previously taught at the U.S. Naval Academy, Georgetown University, and the University of Georgia and has held visiting lectureships in Spain, Great Britain, and Australia. His published works include *The Juggler: Franklin Roosevelt as*

Wartime Statesman (1990), *Churchill and Roosevelt: The Complete Correspondence, 1939–1945* (3 vols., 1984), *Swords or Ploughshares? The Morgenthau Plan for Defeated Nazi Germany* (1976), and *The Most Unsordid Act: Lend-Lease, 1939–1941* (1969). His other published work has appeared in historical journals, edited books, and encyclopedias.

RAYMOND G. O'CONNOR taught for many years at the University of Miami, where he filled the posts of professor of history and chair of the department of history; he retired in 1980 with emeritus status. He previously held faculty positions at Stanford University, the University of Kansas, and Temple University. He also taught at the Naval War College. He is coauthor of *American Defense Policy in Perspective* (1965) and *Presidential Powers in Foreign Affairs* (1966). He edited *The Japanese Navy in World War II* (1969). He is the author of *Perilous Equilibrium: U.S. Navy and the London Naval Conference of 1930* (1962), *Diplomacy for Victory: FDR and Unconditional Surrender* (1971), and *Force and Diplomacy: Essays Military and Diplomatic* (1972), as well as several articles in historical journals.

FRANK E. VANDIVER holds the John H. and Sara H. Lindsey Endowed Chair in Liberal Arts at Texas A&M University and is director of the Mosher Institute for Defense Studies. For many years he was professor of history at Rice University. He also held teaching posts at Washington University (St. Louis, Missouri) and the U.S. Military Academy and was Harmsworth Professor of American History at Oxford University. He has served on historical advisory councils for the Department of the Army and the Secretary of the Navy, as well as on numerous other historical committees, commissions, panels, and editorial boards. His books include *Ploughshares into Swords: Josiah Gorgas and Confederate Ordnance* (1952), *Rebel Brass: The Confederate Command System* (1956), *Mighty Stonewall* (1957), *Jubal's Raid: General Early's Famous Attack on Washington in 1864* (1960), *Their Tattered Flags: The Epic of the Confederacy* (1970), and *Black Jack: The Life and Times of John J. Pershing* (2 vols., 1977). In addition, he edited the war memoirs of Confederate generals Josiah Gorgas, Joseph E. Johnston, and Jubal Early, as well as other books on the Civil War period. He has written many chapters, reviews, and articles published in historical journals, encyclopedias, edited books, magazines, and newspapers.

INDEX

219

INDEX